PRAYERS THAT AVAIL MUCH®

Modern Translations

James 5:16

Three Bestselling Volumes
Complete in One Book

By Germaine Copeland

And this is the confidence that we have in him, that, if we ask anything according to his will, he heareth us: and if we know that he hear us, whatsoever we ask, we know that we have the petitions that we desired of him.

1 John 5:14,15

Harrison House LLC
Tulsa, Oklahoma

17 16 15 14 13 12   10 9 8 7 6 5 4 3 2

Prayers That Avail Much Commemorative Edition Modern Translation

ISBN: 978-160683-402-2

Copyright © 2012 by Germaine Copeland

P. O. Box 289

Good Hope, Georgia 30641

Published by Harrison House Publishers

P.O. Box 35035

Tulsa, Oklahoma 74153

www.harrisonhouse.com

Presented to

_____

By

_____

Date

_____

Occasion

_____

Contents

A Word to the Reader   1

How to Pray Prayers That Avail Much   3

What is Prayer?   18

Personal Confessions   32

Part I: Personal Prayers

A. Life in Christ

One with Jesus   39

The Armor of God   41

Beginning Each Day   43

Blessing at the Table   45

Blessing for Food While Traveling   47

Boldness   48

Choosing Godly Friends   49

Forgiveness   51

Fasting   53

Giving Thanks to God   58

Glorify God   62

God–Inside Minded 64

Helping Others 67

Holiness 69

Humility 71

Joy in the Lord 73

Love 76

Praying Effectively 78

Producing Fruit 80

Protection for Travel 82

Protection in the Blood of Jesus 85

Renewing the Mind 87

Safety 89

Spiritual Warfare 91

Submitting All to God 93

Success in Christ 96

Thinking like Christ 99

Tithing 101

Trust in the Lord 102

Walk in the Word 104

Watch What You Say 106

Worry Free 108

B. Healing

Healing from Abuse   113

Breaking the Curse of Abuse   116

Health and Healing   121

Healing from Chronic Fatigue Syndrome   123

Healing for Damaged Emotions   128

Victory Over Depression   131

Healthy Lifestyle   135

Healing from Hypersensitivity   137

Receiving Forgiveness   142

C. Overcoming

Strength to Overcome Cares and Burdens   147

Discouragement   150

Victory Over Fear   154

Overcoming a Feeling of Abandonment   156

Hopelessness   159

Overcoming Intimidation   161

Letting Go of the Past   163

Victory Over Pride   165

Overcoming a Feeling of Rejection   167

Times of Trouble   173

Overcoming Weariness 177

Overcoming Worry 182

D. Wisdom

Confidence in Relationships 187

God's Wisdom and Will 189

For Good Communication 191

To Know God's Will 193

Maintaining Good Relations 195

Prosperity 196

Receiving a Discerning Heart 198

Selling Real Estate 200

Setting of Proper Priorities 202

Success of a Business 205

Part II: Relational Prayers

A. The Father

Adoration: "Your Name Be Honored as Holy" 209

Divine Intervention: "Your Kingdom Come" 213

Submission: "Your Will Be Done" 216

Provision: "Give Us Today Our Daily Bread" 218

Forgiveness: "Forgive Us Our Debts" 220

Guidance and Deliverance: "Do Not Bring Us Into Temptation" 222

Praise: "Yours Is the Kingdom" 224

B. *Children*

Adult Children   229

Children   231

Children at School   234

Children with Special Needs   236

Children's Future   238

To Know Who They Are in Christ   242

Peaceful Sleep   244

Salvation of Grandchildren   246

Strong Willed Child   248

To Understand Their Value   250

To Walk in Faith and Power   252

Wise Choice of Friends   254

C. *Marriage and Family*

Abusive Family Situation   259

Adopting a Child   263

Blessing the Household   265

Broken Marriage Vows   267

Compatibility in Marriage   269

Desiring To Have a Baby   271

Handling Household Finances   273

For My Family Members   280

Godly Order in Pregnancy and Childbirth 281

Harmonious Marriage 284

The Home 286

Husbands: A Prayer of Intercession 288

Husband's Personal Prayer 290

Moving to a New Location 292

New Creation Marriage 294

Prayer of Intercession for a Marriage 297

Parenting with Wisdom 299

Parenting with a Calm Spirit 302

Parenting with Confidence 305

Peace in a Troubled Marriage 307

Pregnancy 309

Training Children in the Way They Should Go 311

Seeking Safety in a Place of Violence 313

The Unborn Child 316

When You Feel Like Giving Up 317

Wife's Personal Prayer 319

D. Single, Divorced and Widowed

Committing to a Life of Purity 325

Complete in Him as a Single 333

Developing Patience   334

Finding a Mate   336

Knowing God's Plan for Marriage   340

Letting Go of Bitterness (in Relationships)   342

Preparing Self for Marriage   345

Single Believer   347

Single Female Trusting God for a Mate   349

Single Male Trusting God for a Mate   350

Part III: Group Prayers

A. God's People, Ministers, and Ministries

The Body of Christ   353

Christian Counselor   355

Church Teachers   357

Ministers   360

Ministry in Need of Finances   362

Ministers to the Incarcerated   365

Ministry in Nursing Homes   368

Ministry Partners   371

Missionaries   374

Office Staff   377

Overcoming Prejudice   379

Personal Prayer of a Pastor for the Congregation 385

Prosperity for Ministering Servants 387

Revival 389

Success of a Meeting 391

Success of a Conference 393

Unity and Harmony 395

Vision for a Church 397

B. Peoples and Nations

American Government 403

Armed Forces 405

Israel 407

Jerusalem 409

Nations and Continents 410

Protection and Deliverance of a City 418

Protection from Terrorism 420

The People of Our Land 422

Salvation of the Lost 424

School Systems and Children 425

C. Special Needs of Others

Those Involved In Abortion 431

An AIDS Patient 434

Comfort for a Person Who Has Lost a Christian Loved One   440

Improving Communication   442

Deliverance from Satan and His Demonic Forces   444

Deliverance from Cults   448

Deliverance from Habits   451

Deliverance from Corrupt Companions   453

Deliverance from Mental Disorder   455

Employment   457

Finding Favor with Others   460

Healing of the Handicapped   462

Overcoming Negative Work Attitudes   466

Hedge of Protection   468

Prison Inmates   470

Renew Fellowship   476

Spirit-Controlled Life   478

To Receive Jesus as Savior and Lord   480

To Receive the Infilling of the Holy Spirit   481

A Word to the Reader

Welcome to the revised edition of *Prayers That Avail Much*, which is three volumes in one. This updated version written in the language of the younger generation is a call for the generations…young and old…to arise and unite in prayer for the will of God to be done in our country and around the world.

The original *Prayers That Avail Much* was a compilation of prayers that I wrote for my marriage and family situations, and included prayers composed by members of a prayer group that I was conducting. The "little yellow book" turned up in unusual places bringing hope, salvation, healing and deliverance to people who were looking for answers. Before long I was receiving letters requesting written Scriptural prayers for situations we had not addressed in the first volume. I am ever grateful to God for giving me the desire to learn to pray the effectual prayer of the righteous. These prayers changed my life, my marriage and opened the heavens for family salvation. My prayer life was built on the legacy of prayer that has come down from generation to generation.

Several books of Scriptural prayers have been written over the years. Today writing and teaching others to pray according to the promises of God is my delight and I offer thanksgiving and give glory to the God of all crea-

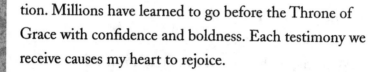
tion. Millions have learned to go before the Throne of
Grace with confidence and boldness. Each testimony we
receive causes my heart to rejoice.

A special thanks to our readers who buy and give
these books to others because the prayers are practical
and workable; they are prayers that avail much! I am
grateful to our publisher and to the churches and
bookstores who continue to believe in the value of
these books, which are proven, effective spiritual tools
for prayer.

This classic book of Scriptural prayers is designed to
enhance your ability to pray effectively for specific needs.
Whether you learned to pray as a child at a family altar
or you are just beginning your prayer journey, always
remember God hears and answers the prayers of His
people. Prayer is the very foundation that enables you to
go from faith to faith and glory to glory.

Sincerely in His Love,

Germaine Copeland
President of Word Ministries, Inc.

Equipping the body of Christ to be effective
Intercessors and fruitful Workers in the Vineyard.

How to Pray Prayers That Avail Much®

Praying Scripture filled with God's promises is a powerful prayer principle. God's Word is His will and by praying what He says in His Word, you are confidently submitting your will to God who knows all things. When you are praying God's will rather than yours, you are obeying the prayer Jesus taught: ...Your will be done on earth as it is in heaven. Isaiah 55:11 confirms God's Word will accomplish its purpose. Through Christ Jesus, every promise in the Bible is available to every child of God. If you can find the promise in God's Word, you can pray it over your life and the lives of others in faith. Since Faith comes by hearing and hearing by the Word of God, and when you pray scriptural prayers consistently, your faith increases. The Word is written on your mind and your heart.

The prayers in this book are written from Scripture promises and although they are not all-inclusive of every promise, they will jump-start your adventure in prayer. The prayers are for you, your personal life, and for others. Praying and meditating on these promises allows the Holy Spirit to make the Word a reality in your heart and you will come to believe that God will do that which He promised. The more you pray these prayers, the more

understanding and insight you will receive. The light
bulb of revelation will be turned on and you will begin
to see your situation from God's perspective. The words
you are praying will transform your mind; you will begin
to think and talk differently. Negative thoughts will
be changed to positive; you will think God-thoughts
and talk God's language. Your desire to know God will
increase and you will find yourself reading and searching
for other promises from His Word, hungering for more
and more of His presence. Seeking God and His way of
doing and being right will become a way of life. The Father rewards everyone who searches for Him (Heb. 11:6).

You can take these prayers a step further by research-
ing the meaning of each Scripture and contemplating the
spiritual significance of each verse listed. Invest in a good
concordance and look for other promises that you can
add; keep a record of your prayer journey. God speaks to
you through the pages of the Bible and as you "practice
the presence of Jesus," you will recognize the voice of the
Good Shepherd speaking to you. Acknowledge the Holy
Spirit who helps you pray concerning your situation.

Prayer is Communication and Relationship with God

Spending time in the Word of God is getting to
know your Heavenly Father. John 1:1 says the Word and

God are one. The prayers in this book are a guide to a more intimate relationship with your Heavenly Father because they are composed from God's Word. The study of the Scriptures transforms your mind and you will learn how to respond to life's problems rather than react. You will receive answers to your prayers, and you will grow more secure in God's love for you. Your desires will begin to change and you will look for ways to please and be a blessing to Him. He joyfully hears that you—His child—are living and walking in the truth (3 John 4). He rejoices over you with singing!

It has been said that words we speak resound throughout time. The Scriptural prayers that we pray are spirit and life. Where do they go? What does heaven do with them? Let us fast forward to Revelation 5:8 where the Apostle John is watching a heavenly performance that concerns this subject of prayer. There in the throne room of Heaven twenty-four elders, each with a harp and a bowl filled with incense mixed with the prayers of God's holy people, release a sweet aroma before the Throne of Grace. Your prayers are forever in the throne room. God honors your prayers and holds them as precious. You are His precious child and the words you speak are just as precious to Him.

Praying in Faith

God already knows your need, but Jesus taught us to ask. "I tell you the truth, my Father will give you whatever you ask in my name.... Ask and you will receive, and your joy will be complete" (John 16:23-24 NIV).

Ask believing...ask in Faith: "This is the confidence we have in approaching God: that if we ask anything according to his will, he hears us. And if we know that he hears us—whatever we ask—we know that we have what we asked of him" (1 John 5:14-15 NIV). Stay in faith by anchoring your soul in what the Scriptures promise: "Do not throw away your confidence; it will be richly rewarded" (Heb. 10:35 NIV).

Praying scriptural prayers will move you into the realm of the spirit. Don't rush out; allow the Holy Spirit to lead your prayers. He may bring another scripture to your remembrance or move you to pray something specific about your situation that may not be included in the prayer you have selected; it may be an aspect that you have never considered. Make sure your words line up with what God's Word says. He doesn't need your counsel or advice on how to manifest His promises...pray according to His will and leave the "how-to" to Him. He has the plan!

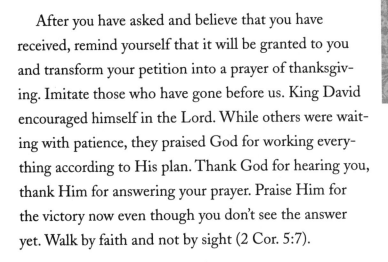

After you have asked and believe that you have received, remind yourself that it will be granted to you and transform your petition into a prayer of thanksgiving. Imitate those who have gone before us. King David encouraged himself in the Lord. While others were waiting with patience, they praised God for working everything according to His plan. Thank God for hearing you, thank Him for answering your prayer. Praise Him for the victory now even though you don't see the answer yet. Walk by faith and not by sight (2 Cor. 5:7).

Don't be moved. Satan may tempt you with fear, pain, or a bad report—resist the temptation to speak negatively and do not allow yourself to be obsessed with how to work it out in your own strength. If you slip up by speaking negatively, ask forgiveness for doubting, and pick up where you left off speaking positively. Never allow Satan to magnify the circumstances. Nothing is too hard for God, and nothing is impossible to the one who believes! James 1:2-4 encourages, "When troubles come your way, consider it an opportunity for great joy. For you know that when your faith is tested, your endurance has a chance to grow. So let it grow, for when your endurance is fully developed, you will be perfect and complete, needing nothing" (NLT).

Use the armor of God. You are to put on the whole armor of God including the belt of truth, the body armor of God's righteousness, and the shoes of the Gospel of peace that prepare you for everything. "Hold up the shield of faith to stop the fiery arrows of the devil. Put on salvation as your helmet, and take the sword of the Spirit, which is the word of God. Pray in the Spirit at all times and on every occasion. Stay alert and be persistent in your prayers for all believers everywhere" (Ephesians 6:16-18 NLT). This is spiritual armor to prepare you for the spiritual and mental battle that attempts to steal your faith. There were times in my life when I had to shout the prayer aloud to drive doubt out of the portals of my mind. Meditating in these scriptures keeps you spiritually strong not only for your prayer time, but for the rest of your day.

The Bible says we *can* overcome the attacks of the enemy. "He (Jesus) canceled the record of the charges against us and took it away by nailing it to the cross. In this way, he disarmed the spiritual rulers and authorities. He shamed them publicly by his victory over them on the cross" (Col. 2:14-15 NLT).

Jesus stripped Satan of his authority and power, and he is a defeated foe. Satan could not keep you from receiving and acknowledging Jesus as your Lord and Savior, but he will attempt to distract and distort the truth. Satan will try to engage you in spiritual warfare

by throwing darts of "what if," or "you aren't worthy."
He would like to convince you that God won't hear
you when you pray, but Satan is a liar. God loves you,
and He longs to hear your voice. You can win by not
giving up: Satan is overcome by the blood of the Lamb
(Jesus Christ) and the word of your testimony—what
you say matters (Rev. 12:11). Speak God's Word boldly
and courageously concerning your situation. Jesus has
conquered the enemy, and you are an enforcer of His
triumphant victory.

- Fight the good fight of faith and resist the temptation to misbelieve. (1 Tim. 6:12.)

- Withstand the attacks in your thoughts and be firm in faith—rooted, established, strong and determined. "Stand firm against him, and be strong in your faith. Remember that your Christian brothers and sisters all over the world are going through the same kind of suffering you are" (1 Pet. 5:9 NLT).

- Run with endurance the race God has set before you by keeping your eyes on Jesus, the Champion who initiates and perfects your faith. (Heb. 12:1-2 NLT.)

- God is always with you and He has given you what

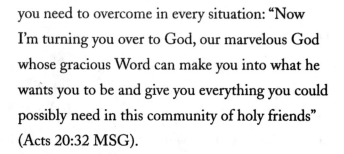

you need to overcome in every situation: "Now I'm turning you over to God, our marvelous God whose gracious Word can make you into what he wants you to be and give you everything you could possibly need in this community of holy friends" (Acts 20:32 MSG).

Prayer offered in the name of Jesus is limitless. Commit yourself to pray about situations right away, and pray the best way—by approaching God with His Word in your mouth, and your heart open to His Spirit. That's what these prayers are all about!

Watch Your Words

James 5:16 says the prayers of a righteous person are powerful and effective. Words are very important—not just in your prayer time, but all the time. Sometimes we look into the mirror of God's Word and see that we can have the petition we desire of Him, and then walk away and forget that we can have the petition we desire of Him. Your everyday conversation is to be in agreement with your prayers. Do not talk negatively or second guess God's promises that you have chosen to pray in faith. I repeat: if you are praying according to God's promises, don't talk the problem; talk the answer. God is working even when you can't see any change. Believe, only

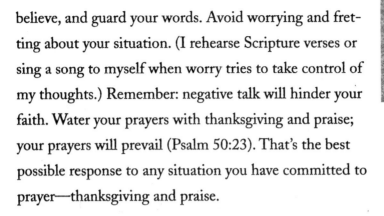

believe, and guard your words. Avoid worrying and fretting about your situation. (I rehearse Scripture verses or sing a song to myself when worry tries to take control of my thoughts.) Remember: negative talk will hinder your faith. Water your prayers with thanksgiving and praise; your prayers will prevail (Psalm 50:23). That's the best possible response to any situation you have committed to prayer—thanksgiving and praise.

The book of James also says to be a doer of the Word and not just a hearer—a hearer who does nothing deceives himself (1:22). Keep your words and your way of life in agreement with your prayers. You release your faith by speaking the good report even before you see the answer. In Matthew 12:37, Jesus says by your words you are justified and by your words you are condemned. You cannot pray effectively for yourself, for someone else, or about something and then talk negatively about the matter and receive the answer that brings glory to the Father. This is being double minded, and a double-minded man receives nothing from God (James 1:6-8).

- Watch the way you talk. Let nothing foul or dirty come out of your mouth. Say only what helps, make each word a gift. Don't grieve God. Don't break His heart. His Holy Spirit, moving and breathing in you, is the most intimate part of your

life, making you fit for Him. Don't take such a gift for granted (Ephesians 4:29-30, MSG).

- Reflect on these words and give them time to keep your perspective in line with God's will. Our Father has much, so very much, to say about that little member, the tongue. Take control of your words: "The tongue also is a fire, a world of evil among the parts of the body. It corrupts the whole body, sets the whole course of his life on fire, and is itself set on fire by hell" (James 3:6 NIV).

- Give the devil no opportunity by getting into worry, unforgiveness, strife, or criticism: "Therefore each of you must put off falsehood and speak truthfully to his neighbor, for we are all members of one body. 'In your anger do not sin': Do not let the sun go down while you are still angry, and do not give the devil a foothold" (Eph. 4:25-27 NIV). Avoid gossip and foolish talking: "Obscene stories, foolish talk, and coarse jokes—these are not for you. Instead, let there be thankfulness to God" (Eph. 5:4 NLT).

- You are to be a blessing to others: "Therefore, whenever we have the opportunity, we should do good to everyone—especially to those in the family of faith" (Gal. 6:10 NLT).

Your attitude about your problem is catching, and many will agree with the confident stand you have taken. Turn a deaf ear to those who try to discourage you. Always have a ready answer by talking the answer, not the problem. The answer is in God's Word. Strive to gain knowledge of that Word—revelation knowledge as mentioned in 1 Corinthians 2:7-16. The Holy Spirit, your Teacher, will reveal the things that have been freely given to you by God—precious promises for your situation. The Holy Spirit wants to help you if you will take the time to listen in your spirit. God sent Him to you for that purpose (John 14:26).

Unite in Prayer

As a believer and an intercessor, unite with others who are of the same faith as you; those who are like-minded. The Word of God is your foundation...never insist on having it your way but God's way. United prayer is a mighty weapon in the prayer arsenal. Matthew 18:19 says, "If two of you agree here on earth concerning anything you ask, my Father in heaven will do it for you" (NLT). What a powerful promise! In Hebrews 10:24-25, the Scriptures encourage believers to meet together: "And let us consider how we may spur one another on toward love and good deeds. Let us not give up meeting together, as some are in the habit of doing, but let us encourage one another" (NIV).

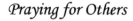

Praying for Others

The prayers in this book that are personal may also be used as intercessory prayers for others simply by praying them in the third person, changing the pronouns "I" or "we" to the name of the person for whom you are interceding and then adjusting the verbs accordingly. Remember that you cannot control another's will, but your prayers prepare the way for the individual to hear and understand truth.

Ministry to Others

As you come into a closer relationship with God and a greater understanding of God's Word through prayer, others may notice a change in your life and come to you requesting prayer or seeking advice. You may not know the exact answer to their need, but as you lead them to the Word of God, you can be confident the Father will minister to them just as He has to you. Caution: never enter into the prayer of agreement casually or superficially. Prayer is serious spiritual business!

Purpose to walk in God's counsel and prize His wisdom (Ps. 1; Prov. 4:7-8). People are looking for something on which they can depend. When someone in need comes to you, share the Scriptures that provide the answer to their problem. Psalm 112 says of the righteous that even in darkness, light dawns for you—you who are gracious and compassionate. Affirm that your heart is secure and steadfast, trusting in the Lord. Blessed are those who trust the Lord and find delight in His Word.

How Often Should I Pray?

An often-asked question is, "How many times should I pray the same prayer?"

The answer is simple: You pray until you know the answer is fixed in your heart. After that, you need to repeat the prayer whenever adverse circumstances or long delays cause you to be tempted to doubt that your prayer has been heard and your request granted.

The Word of God is your weapon against the temptation to lose heart and grow weary in your prayer life. When that Word of promise becomes fixed in your heart, you will find yourself praising, giving glory to God for the answer, even when the only evidence you have of that answer is your own faith. Reaffirming your faith enforces the triumphant victory of our Lord Jesus Christ.

Vain Repetitions

Another question often asked is, "When we repeat prayers more than once, aren't we praying 'vain repetitions'?"

This is referring to the admonition of Jesus when He told His disciples: "And when you pray, do not use vain repetitions as the heathen do. For they think that they will be heard for their many words" (Matt. 6:7 NKJV). Praying the Word of God is not praying the kind of prayer that various religions pray—a kind of formula or chant. It is the living Word of God—alive and full of power (Heb. 4:12). "The world is full of so-called prayer warriors who are prayer-ignorant. They're full of formulas and programs and advice, peddling techniques for getting what you want from God. Don't fall for that nonsense. This is your Father you are dealing with, and He knows better than you what you need" (Matthew 6:7 MSG)

In 1 Kings 18:25-39 is a list of various manners of prayer offered to false gods. Elijah invited the false prophets of the pagan god Baal to call fire down on an altar to prove to the children of Israel that the Lord God was the only true God. The false prophets shouted, danced around their altar, and cut themselves until evening all to no avail. Then Elijah built an altar of stone, put a sacrificial bull on the altar, and covered the sacrifice with water—so much that there was a mote full of water around the altar. After he prayed a short prayer, the Lord sent fire down from heaven and burned up the sacrifice and all the water, even in the mote. The Lord is not impressed by long prayers full of eloquent words; He is impressed with a heart that follows after Him who believes in His Word.

The prayers in this book are written from the Holy Scriptures—they are not vain words. They are spirit and life and mighty through God to pull down the strongholds of the enemy (2 Cor. 10:4-6). You have a God whose eyes are over the righteous and whose ears are open to your prayer; when you pray, He listens (Ps. 34:15).

You were made righteous (or made right with God) in Christ Jesus when you accepted Him as your Lord and your prayers will avail much. They will bring salvation to the sinner, deliverance to the oppressed, healing to the sick, and prosperity to the poor. They will usher in the next move of God on the earth. In addition to affecting outward circumstances and other people, your prayers will also affect you. In the very process of praying, your life will be changed as you go from faith to faith and from glory to glory.

What Is Prayer?

> The earnest (heartfelt, continued) prayer of a right-
> eous man makes tremendous power available [dy-
> namic in its working].
>
> —James 5:16 AMP

Prayer is our communication or conversation with the Father—vital, personal contact with God. As your Heavenly Father and your Friend, He is truly more than enough. For every situation, He has an answer; for every heartache, He has restoration; for every sickness, He has a healing. Determine to stay in constant communion with Him—talk to Him throughout your day, listen for His direction, and do what He leads you to do: "The eyes of the Lord are upon the righteous (those who are upright and in right standing with God) and His ears are attentive to their prayer..."(1 Peter 3:12 AMP).

Prayer is not to be a religious form with no power. Pray with purpose, compose your petition in agreement with God's will. He watches over His Word to perform it (Jeremiah 1:12). An important part of effective prayer is praying God's promises over the situation, understanding that He will watch over His Word to make sure it happens. The Word of God is alive and powerful. It

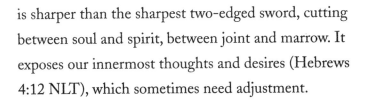

is sharper than the sharpest two-edged sword, cutting between soul and spirit, between joint and marrow. It exposes our innermost thoughts and desires (Hebrews 4:12 NLT), which sometimes need adjustment.

Scriptural prayer is the "living" Word in your mouth. When you pray God's Word, you are speaking faith and it takes faith to please God (Heb 11:6). As you hold His Word up to Him in prayer, He sees Himself in His Word. God's Word is your contact with your Heavenly Father. You put Him in remembrance of His Word (Isa. 43:26), asking Him for what you need in the name of the Lord Jesus. The woman in Mark 5:25-34 placed a demand on the power of God when she said, "If I can but touch the hem of His garment, I will be healed." By faith she touched His clothes and was healed.

If you are in financial need, you "remind" God, with thanksgiving, that He supplies all of your needs according to His glorious riches that have been given to you in Christ Jesus (Phil. 4:19). (An answer to this prayer reminder may require you to seek financial counsel and change your spending habits.) God's Word does not return to Him empty—without producing any results—but it will do all that He pleases and purposes, and it prospers everywhere He sends it (Isa. 55:11). That's good news!

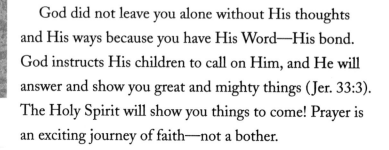
God did not leave you alone without His thoughts
and His ways because you have His Word—His bond.
God instructs His children to call on Him, and He will
answer and show you great and mighty things (Jer. 33:3).
The Holy Spirit will show you things to come! Prayer is
an exciting journey of faith—not a bother.

Prayer Is Crucial

As a Christian, your first priority is to love the Lord
your God with your entire being and your neighbor as
yourself (Mark 12:30-31). Loving God includes getting
to know Him through prayer, reading and meditation
on His Word. All believers are called to pray—it is your
avenue of fellowshipping with your Father. You may or
may not consider yourself an "intercessor" but every believer is to pray. Every one is to pray for one another, for
all saints everywhere and give thanks for all men. When
you intercede (pray) for others, ask for the Father's heart
for them. Just as King David had a heart after God, you
too can find your refuge in your Heavenly Father: "The
one thing I ask of the LORD—the thing I seek most—
is to live in the house of the LORD all the days of my
life, delighting in the LORD's perfections and meditating in his Temple" (Ps. 27:4 NLT).

The importance of knowing God personally is
found throughout the Bible, but one passage in the

New Testament makes it so clear. Jesus speaks of things unbelievers worry about—what to eat, what to wear—and encourages His disciples not to be concerned with those things: "But seek first his kingdom and his righteousness, and all these things will be given to you as well" (Matthew 6:33 NIV).

When you take time to pray in faith believing in God's Word, you are seeking His kingdom and His righteousness and God brings your requests to pass. He says His eyes search the whole earth to show Himself strong in behalf of those who are totally committed to Him (2 Chron. 16:9 MSG). In Christ you are made holy and blameless. You are His very own child (Eph. 1:4-5). He tells you to come boldly to the Throne of Grace and receive mercy and find grace to help in your time of need (Heb. 4:16). You have an open invitation to talk to your Father any time and as much as you want. He wants to hear from you.

The Art of Prayer

The prayers in this book are designed to teach and train you in the art of prayer. There are many different kinds of prayer, such as the prayer of thanksgiving and praise, the prayer of dedication and worship, and the prayer that changes *things* (not God). (It has been my

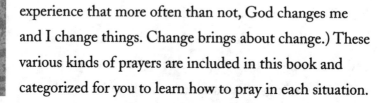
experience that more often than not, God changes me and I change things. Change brings about change.) These various kinds of prayers are included in this book and categorized for you to learn how to pray in each situation.

As you pray scripturally, you will be reinforcing the prayer armor. "Put on the full armor of God, so that you can take your stand against the devil's schemes" (Ephesians 6: 11 NIV). The fabric from which the armor is made is the Word of God: the belt of truth, the breastplate of righteousness, the shoes of readiness that come from the gospel of peace, the shield of faith, the helmet of salvation, and the sword of the Spirit, which is the Word of God (Ephesians 6:14-17). "Pray at all times (on every occasion, in every season) in the Spirit, with all [manner of] prayer and entreaty" (v. 18 AMP). This prayer armor is for every believer to put on and wear at all times.

Second Corinthians 10:4-5 reveals another reference to the battle you face in your walk of faith: "We use God's mighty weapons, not worldly weapons, to knock down the strongholds of human reasoning and to destroy false arguments. We destroy every proud obstacle that keeps people from knowing God. We capture their rebellious thoughts and teach them to obey Christ" (NLT). When you are planning your scriptural prayer strategy, often the mind becomes a battlefield and spiritual warfare ensues. You purpose to do all you know to do to make your stand and having done all, you stand without wavering.

In 1 Timothy 2 we are admonished that, "...requests, prayers, intercession and thanksgiving be made for everyone— for kings and all those in authority, that we may live peaceful and quiet lives in all godliness and holiness. This is good, and pleases God our Savior, who wants all men to be saved and to come to a knowledge of the truth" (1 Tim. 2:1-4 NIV). *Prayer is the responsibility of believers and it is important to our Heavenly Father.*

Prayer must be the foundation of every Christian endeavor. Jesus says you are to live by every word that proceeds from the mouth of God (Luke 4:4). Desire the whole counsel of God because it has the ability to bring positive changes to your life. By receiving His counsel through the Word, you will be "...transformed (changed) by the [entire] renewal of your mind [by its new ideals and its new attitude], so that you may prove [for yourselves] what is the good and acceptable and perfect will of God, even the thing which is good and acceptable and perfect [in His sight for you]" (Rom. 12:2 AMP).

No believer should have to live apart from God's blessings—ignorant of God's Word. God desires for

His people to be successful, to be filled with a full, deep, and clear knowledge of His will (His Word) and to bear fruit in every good work (Col. 1:9-13). Your prayer life is to be effective. God's intent is for you to be victorious in every prayer initiative. You have divine Helpers…Jesus at the right hand of the Father and the Holy Spirit who lives in you! That is how you bring honor and glory to God (John 15:8). He desires for you to know how to pray, for "the prayer of the upright is his delight" (Prov. 15:8).

Using the Word of God in Prayer

Using God's Word on purpose, specifically, in prayer is one kind of prayer, and it is a very effective and accurate method. Jesus says, "The words (truths) that I have been speaking to you are spirit and life" (John 6:63 AMP).

When Jesus faced Satan in the wilderness, He said, "It is written…it is written…it is written." You are to live, be upheld, and be sustained by every word that comes from the mouth of God (Matt. 4:4).

James, by the Spirit, says you do not have because you do not ask. You ask and don't receive because you ask with wrong motives (James 4:2-3 NIV). That's a strong word! Strive to become an expert in prayer—learn to ask God to reveal His will and evaluate your motives. When you spend consistent time in the Word and in prayer, you will be able to correctly explain and handle the Word of Truth (2 Tim. 2:15 NLT). You will gain a greater understanding of how to pray the Word over your situations.

Using the Word in prayer is *not* taking it out of context—God's Word in you is the key to answered prayer—prayer that brings results. When you pray He "...is able to do exceedingly abundantly above all that we ask or think, according to the power that works in us" (Eph. 3:20 NKJV). The power lies within God's Word. It is anointed by the Holy Spirit. The Spirit of God does not lead you apart from the Word; the Word is of the Spirit of God. Apply that Word personally to yourself—not adding or taking from it—in the name of Jesus. Apply the Word to the now—to those things, circumstances, and situations facing you now.

God's Word in prayer is not something you just rush through, uttering once. There is nothing "magical" or "manipulative" about it—no set pattern to follow or device to employ in order to satisfy what you want or think out of your natural mind. Instead, you are holding God's Word before Him. Jesus said for you to ask the Father in His name. Ask and believe, expecting His divine intervention (2 Cor. 4:18). Asking "in the name of Jesus" is not just a byline or magic words you tack on to the end

of your prayers. Asking in the name of Jesus means you are making the same petition as He would make. Always remain in agreement with His word.

The Holy Spirit is Our Helper

The Father has not left you helpless. Not only has He given you His Word, but also He has given you the Holy Spirit to help you in your weakness when you don't know how to pray (Rom. 8:26 NLT). The Holy Spirit is a divine helper, and He will direct your prayer and help you pray when you are struggling. Our Father has provided His people with every possible avenue to ensure their complete and total victory in this life in the name of our Lord Jesus (1 John 5:3-5). Pray to the Father, in the name of Jesus, through the Holy Spirit, according to the Word.

The Prayers of Paul

Paul was very specific and definite in his praying. The first chapters of Ephesians, Philippians, Colossians, and 2 Thessalonians are examples of how Paul prayed for believers. There are numerous others. Search them out. Paul wrote under the inspiration of the Holy Spirit. You can pray these Spirit-given prayers today; they are powerful and effective.

In 2 Corinthians 1:11, 2 Corinthians 9:14, and Philippians 1:4, you see examples of how believers prayed one for another—putting others first in their prayer life with joy. Your faith works by love (Gal. 5:6). You grow spiritually as you reach out to help others—praying for and with them and holding out to them the Word of Life (Phil. 2:16).

The Word of God Changes You

Man is a spirit, he has a soul, and he lives in a body (1 Thess. 5:23). In order to live a successful Christian life, you should take care of each of these three parts. Your body needs food and water for physical strength. The soul, or intellect, needs intellectual stimulation to continue to learn, develop, and stay alert. But it is the spirit—the heart or inward man—that is the real you, the part that has been made brand new in Christ Jesus. It must have spiritual food, which is God's Word, in order to produce and develop faith. As you read, focus, and meditate on God's Word, your mind will become renewed with His Word, and you will have a fresh mental and spiritual attitude (Eph. 4:23-24). You'll begin to think like God thinks which produces life instead of the way the world thinks which produces death: "Letting your sinful nature control your mind leads to death.

But letting the Spirit control your mind leads to life and peace" (Rom. 8:6 NLT).

In the same way you renew your mind, you can also present your body as a living sacrifice: "Give your bodies to God because of all he has done for you. Let them be a living and holy sacrifice—the kind he will find acceptable. This is truly the way to worship him. Don't copy the behavior and customs of this world, but let God transform you into a new person by changing the way you think. Then you will learn to know God's will for you, which is good and pleasing and perfect" (Rom. 12:1-2 NLT).

Refuse to let your physical body or your soul (your natural mind, will, and emotions) dominate your decisions. The very best for your body and soul is to be in subjection to the spirit man where there is life and peace (1 Cor. 9:27). In Proverbs 4:20-22 you find that God's Word is healing and health to our natural man: "Listen carefully to my words. Don't lose sight of them. Let them penetrate deep into your heart, for they bring life to those who find them, and healing to their whole body" (NLT). God's Word affects each part of you—spirit, soul, and body. You become vitally united to the Father, to Jesus, and to the Holy Spirit—one with Them (John 16:13-15; John 17:21; Col. 2:10).

Purpose to hear, accept, and welcome the Word. As you learn to believe the Word, speak the Word, and act on the Word, you'll find it is a creative force. Not only does it change circumstances, but it also changes you. The Word is a double-edged sword, often placing a demand on you to change attitudes and behaviors toward the person for whom you are praying!

Many people agree that the Bible is true but do not do what it says; they are mental assenters. *Real faith is acting on God's Word now.* Sometimes faith is purposing in your heart to believe what you are saying and sometimes it is an action God leads you take. Without practicing the Word you cannot build your faith. To develop an active prayer life, God's Word actually has to be a part of your life. "In the same way, faith by itself, if it is not accompanied by action, is dead" (James 2:17 NIV). The Lord Jesus is in heaven presenting your prayers to the Father—you are to hold tight to *your profession of faith:* "Since we have a great high priest who has gone through the heavens, Jesus the Son of God, let us hold firmly to the faith we profess" (Heb. 4:14 NIV).

Meditation

Prayer does not cause faith to work, but faith causes prayer to work. Any prayer problem is a lack of knowl-

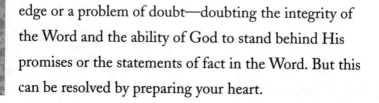
edge or a problem of doubt—doubting the integrity of the Word and the ability of God to stand behind His promises or the statements of fact in the Word. But this can be resolved by preparing your heart.

You can spend fruitless hours in prayer if your heart is not prepared beforehand. Preparation of the heart or the spirit comes from meditation in the Father's Word, meditation on who you are in Christ, and what He is to you. It is the same for you just as God told Joshua (Josh. 1:8), as you meditate on the Word day and night and do according to all that is written, you will make your way prosperous and have good success. Attend to God's Word, submit to His sayings, keep them in the center of your heart, and put away contrary talk (Prov. 4:20-24).

Prayer based upon the Word rises above the senses, contacts the Author of the Word, and sets His spiritual laws into motion. It is not just saying prayers that brings results, but it is spending time with the Father, learning His wisdom, drawing on His strength, being filled with His quietness, and receiving His love.

In this book there is a section of personal confessions (affirmations) that will bring you into agreement with God's will for you. These Scriptures are set aside for you to meditate on and say over your life on a regular basis. When you speak them out, they clear the negative thoughts the enemy brings—thoughts that you are unworthy and powerless. The truth contained in these Scriptures will build your inner being and strengthen your faith to believe and not doubt God's Word. Don't let the lies of the enemy or the cares of this life hold back your prayer life. Discover the person God has made you in Christ Jesus and begin the wonderful, exciting adventure of prayer.

Personal Confessions

LORD, I love You with all my heart, all my soul, and all my mind, and my neighbor as I love myself because You first loved me. (Matthew 22:34-39; 1 John 4:19)

Jesus is Lord over my spirit, my soul, and my body. (Phil. 2:9-11)

I am God's child. He sent Christ Jesus to save me, to make me wise, acceptable to God, and holy. I can do all things through Christ who strengthens me. (1 Cor. 1:30 CEV, Phil. 4:13)

The Lord is my Shepherd. I have all that I need. God supplies all my needs from His glorious riches, given to me in Christ Jesus. (Ps. 23 NLT; Phil. 4:19 NLT)

I do not worry or have anxiety about anything, instead I pray about everything. God cares for me so I turn all my worries over to Him. (Phil. 4:6 NLT; 1 Pet. 5:7 CEV)

I am the Body of Christ. I am redeemed from the curse, because Jesus bore my sickness and carried my diseases in His own body. I was and am healed by His wounds. I forbid any sickness or disease to exist in my body. Every organ, every tissue of my body works in the perfection in which God created it to work. God bought me with a high price and paid for my healing. I honor God and bring glory to Him in my body. (Gal. 3:13; Matt. 8:17; 1 Pet. 2:24 KJV, NLT; 1 Cor. 6:20 NLT)

I have the mind of Christ and hold the thoughts, feelings, and purposes of His heart. I think as Christ thinks. (1 Cor. 2:16 AMP, CEV)

I am a believer and not a doubter. I hold on to my declaration of faith. I decide to walk by faith and practice faith. My faith comes by hearing, and hearing by the Word of God. Jesus is the Author and Developer of my faith. (Heb. 4:14 GW; Heb. 11:6; Rom. 10:17; Heb. 12:2)

God's love has been poured out in my heart by the Holy Spirit who has been given to me. His love abides in me richly. I keep myself in the Kingdom of light, in love, in the Word; God holds me securely and the evil one cannot touch me. (Rom. 5:5; 1 John 4:16; 1 John 5:18 NLT)

God has given me authority to trample on snakes and scorpions and to overcome all the power of the enemy; nothing will harm me. My faith is like a shield and I stop all the flaming arrows of the enemy. God's Spirit in me is greater than the devil who is in the world. (Luke 10:19 NIV; Eph. 6:16 CEV; 1 John 4:4 NCV)

I am delivered from this present evil world. I am seated with Christ in heavenly places. I reside in the Kingdom of God's dear Son. The law of the Spirit of life in Christ Jesus has made me free from the law of sin and death. (Gal. 1:4; Eph. 2:6; Col. 1:13; Rom. 8:2)

I do not fear. God has not given me a spirit of fear and timidity, but a spirit of power, of love, of self-control and a sound mind. God is on my side. (2 Tim. 1:7 NLT, KJV; Rom. 8:31)

I hear the voice of the Good Shepherd. I hear my Father's voice, and the voice of a stranger I will not follow. I roll my works upon the Lord. I commit and trust them wholly to Him. He will cause my thoughts to become agreeable to His will, and so my plans will be established and succeed. (John 10:27; Prov. 16:3)

I am a world overcomer because I am born of God. I represent the Father and Jesus well. I am a useful member in the Body of Christ. I am God's masterpiece, recreated in Christ Jesus to do good works God prepared in advance for me. It is God who works in me to will and to act in order to fulfill His good purpose. (1 John 5:4-5; Eph. 2:10 NLT, KJV, NIV; Phil. 2:13 NIV)

I let the Word of Christ dwell in me richly in all wisdom. He who began a good work in me will continue until the day of Christ. (Col. 3:16, Phil. 1:6)

Throughout this work, you will find listings of various scriptures, which correspond with the prayers that preceed them. As part of your prayer and devotional time, we encourage you to read these verses in their entirety, consulting the various versions listed to increase your knowledge and depth of understanding. For your convenience, we include here a listing of the versions referenced in this work.

AMP - The Amplified Version

ASV - American Standard Version

CEB - Common English Bible

CEV - Contemporary English Version

ERV - Easy-to-Read Version

ESV - English Standard Version

GNT - Good News Translation

GW - God's Word

HCSB - Holeman Christian Standard Bible

KJV - King James Version

MSG - The Message

NASB - New American Standard Bible

NCV - New Century Version

NIRV - New International Readers Version

NIV - New International Version

NKJV - New King James Version

NLV - New Life Version

NLT - New Living Translation

Phillips - J. B. Phillips New Testament

WE - Worldwide English New Testament

PART I:

PERSONAL PRAYERS:
LIFE IN CHRIST

One with Jesus

Lord Jesus, I am sticking with Your Word and living out what You tell me. I desire to be a true disciple of Yours. You will remain in me, and I will remain in You.

Lord, because You are the Vine and I am a branch joined to You, I will produce lots of fruit. Your teachings have become part of me, of who I am. I can ask for anything and it will be granted! My selfish desires have been changed because You are at work in me, energizing and creating in me the power, will and desire to do Your good pleasure.

Producing fruit brings great glory to You. Father, it is by Your grace that I will show and prove myself to be a true follower of Your Son, Jesus who has loved me even as You, Father have loved Him.

Lord, I choose to obey Your commandments, remaining in Your love just as Jesus obeyed your commandments and remained in Your love. You have told me all these things so that I will be filled with joy. Your joy within me overflows! My faith works by love, and I commit to love others in the same way that You have loved me.

Father, thank You for Your Word; the Truth that makes me free. I am one with You, my Lord, and with

Your help I no longer desire to sin because the new life of God is in me. I have become a child of God. Praise You, Father! I treasure Your word above everything else and it keeps me from sin. Christ is in me and I am in Christ. By faith, I will stand firm and be deeply rooted in Your love that is wide and long and high and deep.

I pray that I may know all about Your love, although it is too wonderful to be measured. Then, my life will be filled with all that You are. Your power at work in me can do far more than I dare ask or imagine. Amen.

Scripture References

John 8:31 MSG	1 John 3:9 NCV
John 15:4,5 NLT	Psalm 119:11 CEV
John 15:7-12 CEV&NLT	Ephesians 3:17,18 CEV
John 8:32	Ephesians 3:19-21 CEV
John 17:17	

The Armor of God

In the name of Jesus, I put on all of God's armor so
I am able to stand firm against all strategies of the devil.
I am not fighting against flesh and blood enemies, but
against evil rulers and authorities of the unseen world,
against mighty powers in this dark world, and against
evil spirits in the heavenly places.

Father, I put on every piece of Your armor so I will be
able to resist the enemy in the time of evil. Then after
the battle, I will be standing firm. I stand my ground,
putting on the belt of truth. Lord, Your Word is truth
and it has Your mighty weapons, not worldly weapons,
that I use to knock down the strongholds of human
reasoning and to destroy false arguments.

I put on the body armor of Your righteousness, which
is faith and love. For shoes, I put on the peace that comes
from the Good News so that I will be fully prepared. For
Christ Jesus himself is my peace. I seek peace and pursue
it with others. Father, now You have given me the task of
reconciling others to You.

I hold up the shield of faith to stop all the fiery arrows
of the devil. I put on salvation as my helmet and take the
sword of the Spirit, which is the Word of God. Father,

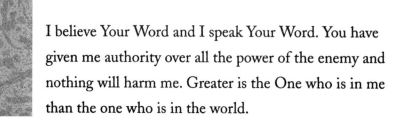

I believe Your Word and I speak Your Word. You have given me authority over all the power of the enemy and nothing will harm me. Greater is the One who is in me than the one who is in the world.

I will pray in the Spirit at all times and on every occasion. I stay alert and I am persistent in my prayers for all believers everywhere. My qualification comes from God. He has enabled me to be a minister of His New Covenant—a Covenant not of written laws but of the Spirit who gives life. Amen.

<u>Scripture References</u>

Ephesians 6:11-14 NLT

John 17:17 NLT

2 Corinthians 10:4 NLT

1 Thessalonians 5:8 NIV

Ephesians 6:15 NLT

Ephesians 2:14 NIV

Psalm 34:14 NIV

2 Corinthians 5:18 NLT

Ephesians 6:16-17 NLT

2 Corinthians 4:13 NCV

Luke 10:19 NIV

1 John 4:4 NIV

Ephesians 6:18 NLT

2 Corinthians 3:5-6 NLT

Beginning Each Day

Father, today belongs to You! I will celebrate and be glad wherever I may be. It is better to obey than to sacrifice so I submit to Your will so that my plans and purposes may be conducted in a manner that will bring honor and glory to You. Thank You for keeping me spiritually and mentally alert in this time of meditation and prayer.

I completely trust You and place myself and those for whom I pray in your keeping knowing You are able to guard everything and everyone that I entrust to You. Thank You for ordering Your angels to protect me, my family and friends. They will hold us up with their hands so that we won't even hurt our feet on a stone. Thank You, Father that Your love never ends and Your mercy never stops. Your loyalty to me is awesome!

Father, I kneel in prayer to You. You are wonderful and glorious. I pray that Your Spirit will make me a strong follower and that Christ will live in my heart because of my faith.

You can do anything, Father – far more than I could ever imagine or guess or request in my wildest dreams by Your Spirit within me. Glory to You forever! Amen.

Scripture References

Psalm 118:24 CEV

1 Samuel 15:22 NCV

2 Timothy 1:12 NLT

Psalm 91:11-12 NLT

Lamentations 3:22-23 NCV

Ephesians 3:14-17 CEV

Ephesians 3:20 MSG

Blessing at the Table

This prayer was written for the head of the household to pray not only to thank and praise God for His blessings, but also to cleanse and consecrate the food received and to sanctify the family members who partake of it. I encourage you to take your place as the head of your household and bless the Father, who gives us our daily bread.

Prayer

Father, thank You for giving us the food that we need today. We receive this food with thanksgiving and praise for everything that You create is good. You bless our bread and water and take sickness from us.

In the name of Jesus, we call this food clean and thank You that it will only act as nourishment to our bodies. Thank You for Your promise in Your Word that even if we drink any deadly thing, it will not hurt us for the Holy Spirit who gives us life in Christ Jesus sets us free from the law of sin and death.

In the name of Jesus, I pray. Amen.

<u>Scripture References</u>

Matthew 6:11 NLT   Mark 16:18

Romans 8:2 CEV   Exodus 23:25

Blessing for Food While Traveling

In the name of Jesus, I worship You, the Lord my God; thank You for blessing our food and drink. And I thank You for taking away sickness from us, just as You promised.

I ask You to give us the wisdom to order that which is healthy and nourishing. I ask in faith and thank You for giving us divine guidance. Thank You for giving us wisdom without rebuke. Should we unknowingly eat or drink anything poisonous, it will not hurt us, for the law of the Spirit of life in Christ Jesus has made us free from the law of sin and death.

Father, everything You created is good, and we should not reject any of it but receive it with thanks. It is made acceptable by the Word of God and prayer.

We receive our food with thanks and will eat the amounts that are sufficient for us, amen.

<u>Scripture References</u>

Exodus 23:25 NIV	Romans 8:2 NKJV
James 1:5-6 NLT	1 Timothy 4:4-5 NLT
1 John 2:16 CEV	Psalm 136:1, 25 NIV
Mark 16:18 NLT	

Boldness

Father, in the name of Jesus, I ask You to give me the courage to speak Your Word with great boldness. When the Holy Spirit came upon me, I received the power to be Your witness. I will tell people about You everywhere. Thank You for giving me this wonderful message of reconciliation that You are no longer counting people's sins agasinst them. I pray for right words to speak so I can make known the mystery of the Gospel for which I am an ambassador of Jesus Christ. God, You make Your appeal through me, and I speak for You when I plead, "Come back to God!"

I take comfort and am encouraged and confidently and boldly say, "The Lord is my Helper; I will not be seized with alarm—I will not fear or dread or be terrified. What can man do to me?" Father God, You made Christ, who never sinned, to be the offering for my sin so that I am made right with You through Christ. I am complete in Him, righteous, and as bold as a lion, in Jesus name, amen.

Scripture References

2 Corinthians 5:19-21 NLT   Hebrews 13:6 AMP

Choosing Godly Friends

Father, help me to show myself friendly and meet new friends. I want to spend time with wise people so that I may become wise by learning from them. I know that You are my source of love, companionship and friendship. Help me to express and receive Your love and friendship with members of the body of Christ.

Just as iron sharpens iron, friends sharpen each other. As we learn from each other, may we share the same love and have one mind and purpose. Help me, Lord to be well-balanced in my friendships so that I will always please You rather than others.

Lord, I ask for divine connections and good friendships and thank You for the courage and grace to let go of detrimental friendships. I ask for Your discernment for developing healthy relationships. Your Word says that two people are better than one because if one person falls, the other can reach out and help.

Father, only You know the hearts of people so help me to discern and not be deceived by outward appearances. Thank You, Lord that every good and perfect gift comes from You and I thank You for quality friends. Help me to be a friend to others and love at all times. When others are happy, I will be happy with them.

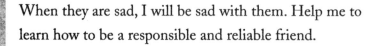

When they are sad, I will be sad with them. Help me to learn how to be a responsible and reliable friend.

Develop in me a fun personality and a good sense of humor. Help me to relax around people and be myself – the person You created me to be. I want to be a faithful and trustworthy friend to the people You are sending into my life. You are my help, Father, in my friendships.

Jesus is my best friend. He is a real friend who is more loyal than a brother. He defined the standard when He said in John 15:13 that there is no greater love than to lay down one's life for his friends.

Thank You, Lord that I can trust You with myself and my need for friends. I praise You that are concerned with everything that concerns me. Hallelujah!

<u>Scripture References</u>

Proverbs 13:20 NIV	1 Corinthians 15:33 CEV
Ephesians 5:20 NIV	James 1:17 NIV
Philippians 2:2,3 NCV	Proverbs 17:17
Proverbs 13:20 NIV	Romans 12:15 CEV
Psalm 84:11 NIV	Proverbs 18:24 NLT
Ecclesiastes 4:9,10 NLT	Psalm 37:4,5 NCV
Proverbs 27:17 CEV	

Walking in Forgiveness

Father, in the name of Jesus I make a fresh commitment to You to live in peace – to get along with everybody – with my brothers and sisters of the Body of Christ, with my friends, associates, neighbors, and family.

Father, I repent of holding on to bad feelings toward others. Today I let go of bitterness, rage, anger, harsh words and slander, and all other types of bad behavior. I ask Your forgiveness for the sin of _____. By faith, I receive Your forgiveness knowing that You cleanse me from all the wrongs that I have done. I ask You to forgive and release all who have wronged and hurt me. In the name of Jesus, I forgive and release them, and will show them kindness and mercy just as You have shown me.

From this moment on, I give up my evil ways, and will be gentle and sensitive to others speaking kind words of encouragement, and I will do what is right. I know that I have right-standing with You, Father and You watch over everyone who obeys You and You listen to my prayers.

Thank You for Your love that has been poured into my heart by the Holy Spirit who is given to me. I believe

that love touches everyone I know. Then all of us will be filled with the fruit of our salvation – which is the righteous character produced in our lives by Christ Jesus. So be it! Amen.

Scripture References

Romans 12:16-18 MSG

Romans 12:10

Philippians 2:2

Ephesians 4:31 NLT

Ephesians 4:27

Philippians 1:9,11 NLT

Mark 11:25

Ephesians 4:32 CEV

1 Peter 3:8,11,12 CEV

Colossians 1:10

Romans 5:5

Fasting

I. Beginning a Fast

Introduction

There are different kinds of fasts: a total fast from foods and liquids for a short interval of time; a liquid fast, in which only water may be drunk; a juice fast, which involves drinking water and a given amount of juices at normal mealtimes; a fast from meats, in which only fruits and vegetables may be eaten.

It is important to understand the effects of fasting on the spirit, soul, and body. Before committing to a fast, I encourage you to study the Word of God and to read books that provide important nutritional and other health information. Understanding will help you avoid harm and injury—both physical and spiritual.

Do not flaunt your fast, but do talk with your family and close associates if necessary to let them know what you are doing. (Personal note: During times of fasting, I continue to prepare meals at home for my family.)

Prayer

Father, I dedicate this fast to You and ask You to give me wisdom and understanding in the areas for which I'm concerned—my faith is in You alone. (Write out your concerns and keep them in front of you. Do not lose sight of the reason for your fast.)

I humble myself before You, Father. In agreement with Daniel 10:2-3, I will eat no _____ for the period of _____.

I honor the words of Jesus by making myself look nice so no one will know I am fasting, except for You, Father. You are always with me and can see what is done in private. It is You who reward me.

I have confidence that if I ask anything according to Your will, You hear me. And if I know that You hear me—whatever I ask—I know I have what I have asked of You.

Father, I delight myself in You, and You give me the desires of my heart. You cause my thoughts to become agreeable to Your will and so my plans are established and succeed.

I determine to fast the way You want: to set free those who are held by chains without any reason, to untie the ropes that hold people as slaves, to set free those who are crushed—to break every evil chain. I will share my food with hungry people, provide homeless people with a place to stay, give naked people clothes to wear, and provide for the needs of my own family. Then the light of Your blessing will shine on me like the rising sun. You will heal me quickly. You will march out ahead of me. And Your glory will follow behind me and guard me.

Father, God of peace, thank You for making me pure, belonging only to You. My motives are weighed by You, Lord, and as I commit this fast to You, You establish my plans—You have the final word.

Father, Your Word lasts forever—it is as permanent as the heavens. Your truth endures through all the ages; You have set the earth in place, and it remains. All things remain to this day because You have ordained it, because they are all Your servants.

In Jesus' name, amen.

Scripture References

James 1:5-6 NLT

Daniel 10:2-3 NLT

Matthew 6:17-18 ERV

Isaiah 58:6-8 NIRV

1 Thessalonians 5:23 NCV

Proverbs 16:2-3 NIV

1 John 5:14-15 NIV

Proverbs 16:1 CEV

Psalm 37:4 NIV

Psalm 119:89-91 MSG

Proverbs 16:3 AMP

II. Ending a Fast

Introduction

It is best to break a fast by eating fruit, broth, or a light salad, gradually adding other foods day-by-day depending on the length of the fast.

Prayer

Lord, You are my Light and my Salvation; whom will I fear? You are the Strength of my life; of whom will I be afraid?

You have given me the desires of my heart. You have answered my prayers—praise You, Lord! May You be glorified! Thank You that I am full of life and strength today. I break this fast as You have directed and thank You for this food because it is made acceptable by Your Word and prayer.

In Jesus' name, amen.

Scripture References

Psalm 27:1 NKJV   Psalm 92:14 NLV

Psalm 37:4 NIV   1 Timothy 4:4-5 NLT

Psalm 34:4 NIV

Giving Thanks to God

Introduction

God saw you before you were born (Ps. 139:13-16). He knew your mother and father and the circumstances of the home where you were to grow up. He knew the schools you would attend and the neighborhood in which you would live.

God gave you the ability to survive and walked with you through good times and bad. He gave you survival techniques and guardian angels to keep and protect you (Ps. 91:11). Even before He made the world, God loved you and chose you in Christ to be holy and without fault in His eyes (Eph. 1:4 NLT).

He cried with you when you cried. He laughed with you when you laughed. He was grieved when you were misunderstood and treated unfairly. He watched and waited, looking forward to the day when you would receive Jesus as your Savior. To as many as received Him, He gave the power, the right, and the authority to become the sons of God (John 1:12 AMP). He longs for your fellowship, desiring for you to know Him more and more intimately.

Your survival techniques were probably different than mine. Whatever they were, and whatever your life may have been like up to this point, the peace of God can change the regrets and the wounds of the past into thanksgiving and praise. You can experience wholeness by earnestly and sincerely praying this prayer.

Prayer

Father, I come into Your presence with songs of thanksgiving and praise to Your name. Lord, You are good, Your love is forever, and Your faithfulness goes on and on. It is good to give thanks to You, Lord, and sing praises to You, the Most High.

I shout my praise to You, Lord, with all the earth! I serve You with joy and come before You with singing. I know that You are God. It is You who made me and I belong to You. I am of Your people and the sheep You tend.

Thank you Lord that You will finish the work You started in me. I am the work of Your hands and Your loving-kindness lasts forever. You will never leave me or forsake me.

Thank You for my parents who gave me life—I honor them as You commanded. Thank You that things go well for me and for giving me a long life on the earth.

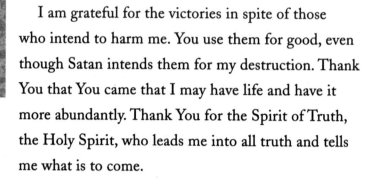

I am grateful for the victories in spite of those who intend to harm me. You use them for good, even though Satan intends them for my destruction. Thank You that You came that I may have life and have it more abundantly. Thank You for the Spirit of Truth, the Holy Spirit, who leads me into all truth and tells me what is to come.

Thank You for Your love and grace, teaching me to believe the best of others, to hope in all circumstances, and to endure everything without weakening. It is You who gives me the desire and power to do what pleases You. I'm grateful to pray and meet with You, and to find You in Your Word. Life is exciting, and I'm thankful I'm alive for such a time as this.

Thank You for making me intelligent and discerning in knowing You personally, that You cause my eyes to be focused and clear so I can see exactly what You are calling me to do. Thank You for helping me to grasp the immensity of this glorious way of life You have for me, the utter extravagance of Your work in me—endless energy, boundless strength! I give thanks to You Lord and praise Your name.

I have victory in life by the blood of the Lamb and the word of my witness. I am Your faithful one, Lord, and will praise You with songs and honor Your holy name.

In the name of Jesus, amen.

Scripture References

Psalm 100:1-5 NCV

Psalm 92:1 NLT

Psalm 138:8 NLT

Hebrews 13:15 NCV

Genesis 50:20 NIV

John 10:10 NKJV

John 16:13 NCV

Ephesians 6:2-3 NLT

1 Corinthians 13:7 AMP

Philippians 2:13 NLT

Esther 4:14 NLT

Ephesians 1:17 MSG

Psalm 100:4 NLT

Philippians 3:1 CEV

Psalm 30:4 CEB

Revelation 12:11 CEV

Glorify God

Because of God's loving kindness to me, I worship Him with my whole being. I let my body be a living and holy gift to Him. He is pleased with this gift of true worship. God is working in me, giving me the desire and the power to do what pleases Him.

Father, since I am right with You, I will live by faith. I refuse to turn back with fear, for that would not please You. My body is the temple of the Holy Spirit who lives in me. I don't belong to myself. Lord, You bought me with a high price and I honor You with my body.

I call on You in times of trouble; You save me, and I honor You. For you have rescued me from the dominion of darkness and brought me into the Kingdom of the Son You love. With all my heart I will praise You, my Lord and my God. I will give glory to Your name forever!

Thank You Lord for the talents You have given me. I want You to say of me, "Well done, good and faithful servant." I will make good use of the gifts given to me by Your grace. I will be a light for other people. I will live so they will see the good things I do give praise to You.

In Jesus' name, I will speak the truth in love, growing in every way more and more like Christ. Everything I say or do, I will do in the name of Jesus, giving thanks to You, God, my Father. In all the work I do, I will do the best I can. I will work as if I were doing it for the Lord and not for people. Amen.

Scripture References

Romans 12:1 NLV

Philippians 2:13 NLT

Hebrews 10:38 NCV

1 Corinthians 6:20 NLT

Psalm 50:15 NCV

Colossians 1:13 NIV

Psalm 86:12 NLT

Matthew 25:21 NKJV

Romans 12:6 NIV

Matthew 5:16 NCV

Ephesians 4:15 NLT

Colossians 3:17 GW

Colossians 3:23 NIV

God-Inside Minded

Father, God of peace, make me pure. Let my whole self—spirit, soul, and body—be safe and kept without fault until the Lord Jesus Christ comes. You are the One who called me and I trust You to do this for me. I may be in the world, but I am not of the world and You have given me Your Word. Thank You for the Spirit of Truth who leads me into all truth and tells me what is to come.

Lord, Your light penetrates my human spirit, exposing every hidden motive. I have received Your Spirit (not the world's spirit) so I can know the wonderful things You have freely given me. I am a child of God, born of the Spirit of God, filled with the Spirit of God, and led by the Spirit of God. I listen for Your voice as I look to the Spirit inside me.

Thank You for teaching me to do what is good and leading me in the way I should go. The peace that You give guides the decisions I make. Plus, You give me a spirit of wisdom and revelation so I can know You better. You want truth deep within my heart and You make me to know wisdom in the hidden part. God's love is made complete in me—perfect love! I'm so glad I have an anointing from the Holy One.

Father, I'm following the Spirit instead of my sinful nature. I allow the Holy Spirit to control me and I think about things that please You. When I let the Spirit of God control my mind, it leads to life and peace.

I trust in You, Lord, with all of my heart and do not depend on my own understanding. I seek Your face and pray that I will obey You in all that I do and You will show me which path to take. Your Word is a lamp to guide my feet and a light for my path. Holy Spirit, You teach me all things and remind me of the things I have learned from God's Word. I continually say what You say in Your Word—thinking about it day and night so I can act on it. Because of this, I prosper and succeed. I don't just listen to God's Word, I do what it says. Amen.

Scripture References

1 Thessalonians 5:23-24 NCV	Ephesians 1:16-17 NCV
John 17:11, 14 NKJV	Psalm 51:6 NLV
John 16:13 NCV	1 John 4:12 MSG
Proverbs 20:27 NLT	1 John 2:20 NIV
1 Corinthians 2:12 NLT	Romans 8:4-6 NLT
Romans 8:14, 16 NIV	Proverbs 3:5-6 NLT
John 3:6-7 NLT	Psalm 119:105 NLT

Ephesians 5:18 NLT

Isaiah 48:17 NCV

Colossians 3:15 GNT

John 14:26 NIV

Joshua 1:8 GW

James 1:22 NLT

Helping Others

Father, in the name of Jesus, I will treat others as I would want to be treated. I want love to be my highest goal! I purpose to make it my aim, my great quest in life.

In the name of Jesus, I will not push my way to the front. I will love others and lend them a helping hand. I purpose to build them up in all ways – spiritually, socially and materially – as I am led by Your Spirit. I desire to imitate you, Father, and encourage others and give them strength.

Father, in the name of Jesus, I will love my enemies and be good to them. I will lend without expecting to get anything back. Then, my reward in heaven will be great! I will be acting as a child of the Most High who is good to people even those who are unthankful and cruel.

Thank You, Father for imprinting Your laws upon my heart and inscribing them on my mind – on my inmost thoughts and understanding. As I would like and desire that men would do to me, I do exactly so to them, in the name of Jesus. Amen.

Scripture References

Luke 6:31 CEV

1 Corinthians 14:1 NLT & AMP

Philippians 2:4 MSG   Ephesians 6:10 NIV

Romans 15:2 NIV & AMP   1 Thessalonians 5:11 NCV

Luke 6:35,36 CEV   Ephesians 5:1,2 AMP

Hebrews 10:16 AMP   Luke 6:31 AMP

Holiness

Thank You Father for making me holy by Your truth; You teach me Your Word, which is truth. Jesus, You gave Yourself as a holy sacrifice for me so I can be made holy by Your truth. Father, in Jesus' name, I confess my sins to You and You are faithful and just to forgive me my sins and to cleanse me from all wickedness.

You live in me and walk with me—You are my God and I am Your child. So I leave the corruption and compromise; I leave it for good. You are my Father, and I will not link up with those who would pollute me, because You want me all for Yourself. I make myself pure—free from anything that makes body or soul unclean. I will try to become holy in the way I live because I respect God.

I throw off my old sinful nature and former way of life. I let the Spirit renew my thoughts and attitudes. I put on my new nature, created to be like God—truly righteous and holy. Lord, You made the way so I can have new life through Christ Jesus. Christ is my wisdom. Christ made me right with You. Now I am set apart for You and made holy. Christ bought me with His blood and made me free from sin.

I turn from evil and learn to do good, to seek justice, and help the oppressed. All who make themselves clean

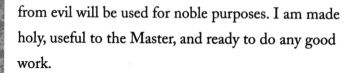

from evil will be used for noble purposes. I am made holy, useful to the Master, and ready to do any good work.

Thank you, Lord, that I eat the best from the land, because You have given me a willing and obedient heart. Amen.

Scripture References

John 17:17, 19 NLT	Ephesians 4:22-24 NLT
1 John 1:9 NLT	1 Corinthians 1:30 NLT
2 Corinthians 6:16 NCV	Isaiah 1:16-17 NLT
2 Corinthians 6:17 MSG	2 Timothy 2:21 NIV
2 Corinthians 7:1 NCV	Isaiah 1:19 GW

Humility

Father, help me to serve others in humility. You oppose the proud but favor the humble and so I humble myself under Your mighty power. At the right time, You will lift me up in honor.

In the name of Jesus, I give all my worries and cares to You, Father, for You care for me. I'm not impressed with my own wisdom; instead, I fear the Lord and turn away from evil. This brings healing for my body and strength for my bones.

Father, I humble myself and submit to Your Word that is living and powerful and is a discerner of the thoughts and intents of my heart. I judge my own actions and I do not compare myself with others. I'm responsible for myself.

I listen carefully to wisdom and set my mind on understanding. True humility and fear of the Lord lead to riches, honor, and life.

Father, I hide Your Word in my heart that I might not sin against You. As one of Your people—loved and chosen by You to be Your own—I clothe myself with compassion, kindness, humility, gentleness, and patience.

I am tolerant with others and forgive others just as
You have forgiven me. To all these qualities I add love,
which binds all things together in perfect unity. I let
the peace that Christ gives guide me in the decisions
I make; for it is to this peace that You have called me,
and I am thankful.

Father, may Your will be done on earth in my life as it
is in heaven, amen.

Scripture References

1 Peter 5:5-7 NLT

Proverbs 3:7-8 NLT

Hebrews 4:12 NKJV

Galatians 6:4-5 NCV

Proverbs 2:2 NCV

Proverbs 22:4 NLT

Psalm 119:11 NLT

Colossians 3:12-15 GNT

Matthew 6:10 NIV

Joy in the Lord

This is the day the Lord has made. I am full of joy and I will be glad because I belong to the Lord. I am happy because You are the Lord, my God!

Father, You win victory after victory and are always with me. You celebrate and sing because of me. You refresh my life with Your love. Thank You for giving me happiness that will last forever! I have joy and gladness and all sadness and sorrow is gone far away. Where the Spirit of the Lord is, there is freedom and I live in that freedom.

Father, I study Your perfect law—Your Word—that makes people free. I do what it says and it makes me truly happy. You satisfy me and I praise You with songs of joy! I am filled with the Holy Spirit, singing psalms, hymns, and spiritual songs, making music in my heart to You, Lord. My happy heart is a good medicine and my cheerful mind works healing. The light in my eyes rejoices the hearts of others. I have a good report and it brings health. My countenance radiates the joy of the Lord.

Father, I remain in You and Your words remain in me. When I ask what I wish, I receive and bear fruit for Your

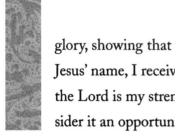

glory, showing that I am Your disciple. When I ask in Jesus' name, I receive and my joy is complete. The joy of the Lord is my strength. If trouble comes my way, I consider it an opportunity for great joy, knowing that when my faith is tested, my endurance has a chance to grow.

I am strong in the Lord and in His great power. I keep Your commandments; they are not burdensome. As Your child, I defeat this evil world and achieve victory through my faith. Satan is under the authority of Jesus Christ, who is in me. Jesus was made sin for me so I am made the righteousness of God in Him. I am part of the Kingdom of God—a Kingdom of righteousness, peace, and joy in the Holy Spirit! Amen.

Scripture References

Psalm 118:24 NLV	Proverbs 15:30 NKJV
Philippians 4:4 NLV	Proverbs 15:13 NKJV
Philippians 3:1 NCV	John 15:7-8 NIV
Psalm 144:15 NCV	John 16:23-24 NIV
Zephaniah 3:17 CEV	Nehemiah 8:10 NIV
Isaiah 51:11 NCV	James 1:2 NLT
2 Corinthians 3:17 NIV	Ephesians 6:10 NCV
James 1:25 NCV	1 John 5:3-4 NLT
Psalm 63:5 NLT	Ephesians 1:22 NLT
Ephesians 5:18,19 NLT	2 Corinthians 5:21 NIV
Proverbs 17:22 AMP	Romans 14:17 NIV

Love

Father, in Jesus name, I thank You that You fill my heart with love by the Holy Spirit which has been given to me. I keep and treasure Your Word. Your love and my love for You has truly reached its goal in me; and that true love chases all my worries away.

Father, I am Your child and I commit to walk in the God-kind of love. I will never give up. I care more for others than myself. I don't strut. I don't want what I don't have. I don't force myself on others or think about me first. I don't fly off the handle. I don't keep score of others' sins. I don't revel when others grovel but I take pleasure in the flowering of truth. I put up with any-thing. I trust God always. I always look for the best, never looking back; I keep going until the end. The love of God in me never dies.

Father, I bless and pray for those who would harm me. I wish them well and do not curse them. Because of this, my love will overflow more and more in knowledge and understanding. I will live a pure and blameless life until the day of Christ's return. I am filled with the fruits of righteousness – the righteous character produced in my life by Christ Jesus.

Everywhere I go, I commit to plant seeds of love. I thank You, Father for preparing hearts ahead of time to receive this love. I know that these seeds will produce Your love in the hearts of those to whom they are given.

Father, I thank You that as I walk in Your love and wisdom, people are being blessed by my life and ministry. Father, You make me to find favor, respect and affection with others (name them).

My life is strong and built on love. I know that You are on my side and nothing is able to separate me from Your love, Father which is in Christ Jesus my Lord. Thank You, Father, in Jesus' precious name. Amen.

Scripture References

Romans 5:5

1 John 2:5 NCV

1 John 4:18 CEV

1 Corinthians 3:6

Romans 12:14 NCV

Matthew 5:44

Philippians 1:9-11 NLT

John 13:34

1 Corinthians 13:4-8 MSG

Daniel 1:9 NLT

Ephesians 3:17 NCV

Romans 8:31,39

Praying Effectively

Father, in the name of Jesus, I thank You for calling me to be a fellow worker in Your field. I will always pray and never lose hope.

Jesus, You are the Son of God and I will never stop trusting You. You help me in my weaknesses. There are times that I do not know how to pray as I should. But Your Spirit prays for me with deep feelings that words cannot explain. You see what is in my heart and Your Spirit prays for me in harmony with Your own will. This is why I can be so sure that every detail in my life is worked into something good.

I will not worry about anything but will pray and ask You for everything that I need, always giving thanks. I believe that I have received the things that I ask for in prayer because You will give them to me.

Father God, You made Jesus who had no sin to be sin for me, so that in Him I might become righteous. Thank You that I have right standing with You, Father. When I pray, You hear and answer prayer so that You are glorified. I will produce much fruit and show that I am Your follower and this will bring glory to You. Amen.

Scripture References

1 Corinthians 3:9 NLT   Mark 11:24 NCV

Luke 18:1 NCV   2 Corinthians 5:21 NIV

Romans 8:26,27 CEV& NLT

James 5:16b NCV   Romans 8:28 MSG

John 15:7,8 NCV   Philippians 4:6 NCV

Producing Fruit

Lord Jesus, You are the True Vine and the Father is the Gardener. He prunes every branch that produces fruit so that it will produce even more fruit. I produce much fruit and show that I am Your follower, which brings glory to the Father.

You promised if I remain in You and follow Your teachings, that I can ask anything I want and it will be given to me. Thank You, for choosing me and appointing me to go and produce lasting fruit. I honor Your command to love others as You have loved me.

The apostle Paul said to always be filled with the fruit of my salvation—the righteous character produced in my life by Jesus Christ—for this will bring much glory and praise to You, my Father God. He was also eager for the fruit that increases to my credit [the harvest of blessing that is accumulating to my account]. So I commit myself to the Holy Spirit who produces this kind of fruit in my life: love, joy, peace, patience, kindness, goodness, faithfulness, gentleness and self-control. Since I belong to Christ Jesus, I have nailed the passions and desires of my sinful nature to His cross and crucified them there.

A seed doesn't produce anything unless it is planted in the ground and dies. My old self has been crucified with Christ. It is no longer I who live, but Christ lives in me. So I live in this earthly body by trusting the Son of God who loved me and gave Himself for me.

Thank You, Father, that my heart is good soil—I truly hear and understand Your Word , and I'm producing a harvest of thirty, sixty, or even a hundred times as much as has been planted! I am like a tree planted by streams of water, which yields its fruit in season and whose leaf does not wither—whatever I do prospers.

Father, in Jesus' name, thank You for giving me complete knowledge of Your will and spiritual wisdom and understanding that the way I live will always honor and please You. My life produces every kind of good fruit and I grow as I learn to know God better and better. Amen.

Scripture References

John 15:1-2 NCV

John 12:24 GW

John 15:7-8 NCV

Galatians 2:20 NLT

John 15:16-17 NLT

Matthew 13:23 NLT

Philippians 1:11 NLT

Psalm 1:3 NIV

Philippians 4:17 AMP

Colossians 1:9-10 NLT

Galatians 5:22-24 NLT

Protection for Travel

Father, today, in Jesus' name, I speak Your words over my travel plans knowing that Your words do not return empty, but they make things happen that You want to happen and they succeed in doing what You send them to do. Thank You for watching to make sure Your words come true.

As I prepare to travel, I remember it is You alone, Lord, who keeps me safe. I live under the protection of God Most High. If I face any problems or trouble, You are a mighty tower that I can run to for safety. My trust is in the Lord and I am safe. Believing in the written Word of God, I speak peace, safety, and success over my travel plans.

As Your child, my path of travel is guarded by You and my life is protected. You order Your angels to protect me wherever I go. I will proceed with my travel plans without fear of accidents, problems, or any type of frustrations—You have given me a calm, well-balanced mind. I have Your peace and it guards my heart and mind as I live in Christ Jesus. Thank You, Father, that in every situation, You are there to protect me. No matter in what means of transportation I choose to travel, You will protect me. You are my Heavenly Father and I am Yours. Through my faith in You, I have the power to trample on snakes and scorpions and to overcome all the power of the enemy—nothing will harm me. Even if I were to contact something poisonous, it will not hurt me. In fact, I'm able to place my hands on the sick and they will be healed.

Whatever I forbid on earth will be forbidden in heaven and whatever I permit on earth will be permitted in heaven. I can ask for anything in the name of Jesus and He will do it, so that the Son can bring glory to the Father. (Asking in the name of Jesus indicates I am asking in agreement with His will.)

Father, I honor You and Your mercy is upon me and my family, and our travels will be safe. Thank You for Your guidance and safety—You are worthy of all praise, amen.

Scripture References

Isaiah 55:11 NCV	2 Timothy 4:18 NIV
Jeremiah 1:12 NCV	Isaiah 43:1-3 NCV
Psalm 4:8 NLT	Luke 10:19 NIV
Psalm 91:1 CEV	Psalm 91:13 CEV
Proverbs 18:10 CEV	Mark 16:18 NLT

Proverbs 29:25 GW

Mark 11:23-24 NIV

Proverbs 2:8 NLT

Psalm 91:11-12 NLT

2 Timothy 1:7 AMP

Philippians 4:7 NLT

Matthew 18:18 NLT

John 14:13 NLT

Daniel 9:18 NIV

Luke 1:50 GNT

Luke 21:18 NIV

Protection in the Blood of Jesus

I. Morning Prayer [1]

Father, I declare the blood of Jesus over my life and all that belongs to me.

The blood of Jesus covers my mind, my emotions, my will, and my body (the temple of the Holy Spirit). I am protected by the blood of the Lamb which gives me access to the Most Holy Place—Your presence.

I declare the blood over the places where my children, my grandchildren and their children dwell, and on all those whom You have given me in this life.

Lord, You have said that the life of the body is in the blood. I'm so thankful for the blood of Jesus that has cleansed me from sin and has begun the eternal agreement with your people, the New Covenant, of which I am a part. Amen.

---

[1] Based on a prayer written by Joyce Meyer in *The Word, the Name and the Blood* (Tulsa: Harrison House, 1995).

II. Evening Prayer[2]

Father, as I lie down to sleep, I declare the blood of Jesus over my life and my family—within us, around us, and between us and all evil.

In Jesus' name, amen.

Scripture References

Exodus 12:7, 13 GW

1 John 1:7 NLT

1 Corinthians 6:19-20 NLT

Hebrews 13:20 AMP

Hebrews 9:6-14 NLT

Hebrews 13:20-21 NCV

Leviticus 17:11 NCV

---

[2]Based on a prayer written by Mrs. C. Nuzum as recorded by Billye Brim in *The Blood and the Glory* (Tulsa: Harrison House, 1995).

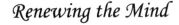

Renewing the Mind

Father, in Jesus' name, thank You that I shall prosper in all things and be in health, just as my soul prospers. You have given me Christ's way of thinking. I trust in You, Lord, with all my heart; I do not depend on my own understanding. I seek Your will in all I do and You show me which path to take.

Today I surrender myself to Your Word, for it exposes and sifts and analyzes and judges the very thoughts and purposes of my heart. Help me to use Your mighty weapons to knock down the strongholds of human reasoning and destroy false arguments—every pretension (intimidation, fears, doubts, unbelief, and failure) that sets itself up against the knowledge of God. I take captive every thought to make it obedient to Christ.

I refuse to be conformed to this age. I am being transformed by the renewing of my mind, so that I may discern what is the good, pleasing, and perfect will of God. I never stop reciting Your words, Lord. I think about them night and day so that I will faithfully do everything written in them. It is then I prosper and succeed.

My thoughts are the thoughts of the diligent, which tend only to plenteousness. So I don't worry about any-

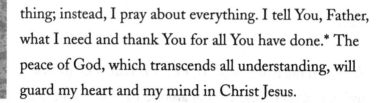

thing; instead, I pray about everything. I tell You, Father, what I need and thank You for all You have done.* The peace of God, which transcends all understanding, will guard my heart and my mind in Christ Jesus.

I fix my thoughts on what is true, and honorable, and right, and pure, and lovely, and admirable. I think about things that are excellent and worthy of praise.

Today I roll my works upon You, Lord—I commit and trust them wholly to You. You cause my thoughts to become agreeable to Your will, and so my plans are established and succeed.

In Jesus' name I pray, amen.

Scripture References

3 John 2 NKJV	Romans 12:2 HCSB
1 Corinthians 2:16 ERV	Joshua 1:8 GW
Proverbs 3:5-6 NLT	Proverbs 21:5 AMP
Hebrews 4:12 AMP	Philippians 4:6-8 NLT
2 Corinthians 10:3-5 NIV	Proverbs 16:3 AMP
2 Corinthians 10:4 NLT	

---

*I encourage you to keep a prayer journal, writing down your petitions (definite requests) in prayer form.

Safety

Father, in the name of Jesus, I lift my family up to You and pray a wall of protection around us – our home and property. Father, You are a wall of fire around us and You have sent Your angels to protect us.

I thank You that we live under the protection of God Most High and we stay in the shadow of God All-Powerful. We will say to You, Lord, that You are our fortress, our place of safety. You are our God and we trust You! You will cover us with Your feathers and hide us under Your wings. We will not fear any danger by night or an arrow during the day. We will watch and see the sinful punished.

You are our fortress and we run to You for safety. Because of this, no terrible disasters will strike us or our home. You will command Your angels to protects us wherever we go. You have said in Your Word that You will save whoever loves You. You will protect those who know You. You will be with us in trouble. You will rescue us and honor us and give us a long, full life and show us Your salvation. Not a hair of our head will perish.

Thank You, Father, for Your watch, care, and protection over my family and me. In Jesus' name. Amen.

Scripture References

Job 1:10 NLT

Zechariah 2:5

Psalm 34:7 CEV

Psalm 91:1,2 CEV

Psalm 91:4,5 NCV

Psalm 91:8 NCV

Psalm 9:9-11 CEV

Psalm 91:14-16 NCV

Luke 21:18 NIV

Spiritual Warfare

Father, though I live in the world, I do not wage war as the world does. The weapons I fight with are not the weapons of the world. On the contrary, they have divine power to demolish strongholds. I demolish arguments and every pretension that sets itself up against the knowledge of You, and I take captive every thought to make it obedient to Christ.

In the name of Jesus, I ask You, Father, to bless those who have mistreated me. Christ himself left me an example: When He was insulted, He remained silent; when He suffered, He did not threaten, but placed His hopes in God to set things right.

When I feel ashamed, help me to remember that I no longer have to be afraid; I will not be put to shame. I do not fear disgrace; I will not be humiliated. I choose to forget the shame of my youth. You created me and formed me. I will not be afraid, for You have saved me. You have called me by my name and I am Yours.

I am being transformed by the renewing of my mind so that I may discern what is the good, pleasing, and perfect will of God. You have good plans for me, to give me a future and a hope. You supply my every need out of Your riches in the glory that is found in Christ Jesus.

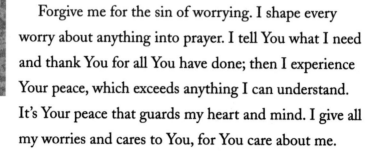

Forgive me for the sin of worrying. I shape every worry about anything into prayer. I tell You what I need and thank You for all You have done; then I experience Your peace, which exceeds anything I can understand. It's Your peace that guards my heart and mind. I give all my worries and cares to You, for You care about me.

You are love, and Your perfect love drives out fear.

In Jesus' name, amen.

<u>Scripture References</u>

2 Corinthians 10:3-5 NIV   Jeremiah 29:11 NLT

Luke 6:28 GNT   Philippians 4:19 CEB

1 Peter 2:21-23 GNT   Philippians 4:6-7 NLT

Isaiah 54:4 GNT   1 Peter 5:7 NLT

Isaiah 43:1 NCV   1 John 4:8,18 NCV

Romans 12:2 HCSB

Submitting All to God

Father, You are the Lord God All-Powerful, who is like You? You are completely trustworthy and I submit myself to You. I live under Your protection, God Most High, and stay in Your shadow, God All-Powerful.

You want everything to be done peacefully and in order. All authority comes from You and those in positions of authority have been placed there by You. I pray for rulers and all who have authority so I can live a quiet and peaceful life full of godliness and dignity.

Father, thank You for pastors and leaders of the Church—those who are submitted to You and are examples to others. I place myself under the authority of the spiritual leaders You have directed me to follow. Help me to serve others with humility, for You oppose the arrogant but favor the humble. Forgive me for times when I have overstepped my bounds.

Lord, Your kingdom come, Your will be done in my life on earth as it is in heaven. I refuse to think of myself more highly than I ought to think. Instead, I will be reasonable since God has measured out a portion of faith to each one of His children.

Father, if I feel that my life is spiraling out of control, I bind my mind to the mind of Christ, and my emotions to the control of the Holy Spirit. I loose obsessive thought patterns that try to confuse me. I give myself completely to You, God; I resist the devil, and he runs from me.

Obedience is far better than sacrifice. Father, You are much more interested in my listening to You than in my offerings of material things. Rebellion is as sinful as witchcraft and stubbornness as bad as worshiping idols. In the name of Jesus, I resist feeling/acting rebellious and stubborn. Thank You, Lord, for taking away my sin. I want Your truth deep within my heart. It is You who makes me know wisdom in the hidden part.

You have rescued me from the kingdom of darkness and transferred me into the Kingdom of Your dear Son, who purchased my freedom and forgave my sins.

Lord, I choose to go all the way with You, through thick and thin. My first concern is not to look after myself, because then I will never find myself. But when I forget about myself and look to You, I find both myself and You. In this world I may have trouble, but I take heart because You have overcome the world.

Jesus, even though You are my Lord, You have called me Your friend. As my friend, I ask You to help me walk through the process of surrendering my all to You. When I am blinded by my own desires, open my eyes to see.

Father, I submit to the control and direction of the Spirit of truth—the Holy Spirit—who leads me into all truth and shows me things to come. I surrender all to You and I have the victory by the blood of the Lamb— the Lord Jesus—and the word of my witness.

In Jesus' name I pray, amen.

Scripture References

Psalm 89:8 NCV   1 Samuel 15:22-23 NLT

Psalm 91:1 CEV   Psalm 51:6-7 NLV

1 Corinthians 14:33 CEV   Colossians 1:13-14 NLT

Romans 13:1-2 NLT   Matthew 10:38-39 MSG

1 Timothy 2:2 NCV   John 16:33 NIV

1 Peter 5:5 GW   John 15:15 NCV

Matthew 6:10 NIV   1 John 2:16 NKJV

Romans 12:3 CEB   John 16:13 NCV

Matthew 18:18 NIV   Revelation 12:11 CEB

James 4:7 NCV

Success in Christ

Thank You Father that the teaching of Your Word gives light. The Word You speak (and I speak) is alive and full of power—making it active, operative, energizing, and effective. I receive the spirit of power and of love and of a calm and well-balanced mind and discipline and self-control that You have given to me. My qualification comes from You, and You have enabled me to be a minister of Your New Covenant—not of written laws but of the Spirit, who gives life.

In the name of Jesus, I submit to the destiny You planned for me before the foundation of the world. I give thanks to You, Father, for qualifying me to share in the inheritance of Your holy people in the Kingdom of Light. Father, thank You for showing me that every "failure" is a learning experience and another stepping stone to success.

You rescued me from the dominion of darkness (failure, doubt, and fear) and brought me into the Kingdom of the Son You love. I study and remember Your teachings and it makes me wise and successful. My joy is in Jesus who has come that I may have life and have it more abundantly.

I belong to Christ and I am a new person. The old life is gone and a new life has begun. The past no longer controls my decisions; I forget the things that are behind and look forward to what lies ahead. I have been crucified with Christ and I no longer live, but Christ lives in me. The life I now live in the body, I live by faith in the Son of God, who loved me and gave Himself for me.

Today I listen carefully to God's words. I don't lose sight of them. I let them penetrate deep into my heart, for they bring life to me and healing to my whole body. I guard my heart above all else, for it determines the course of my life.

Today I hold onto kindness and truth. I tie them around my neck and write them upon my heart. So I will find favor and good understanding in the eyes of God and man.

Today my delight is in the teachings of the Lord and I reflect on them day and night. So I am like a tree planted beside streams—a tree that produces fruit in season and whose leaves do not wither. I succeed in everything I do.

Thank You Father for the power Christ has given me. He leads me and makes me win in everything, amen.

Scripture References

Psalm 119:130 NLT	2 Corinthians 5:17 NLT
Hebrews 4:12 AMP	Philippians 3:13 NLT
2 Timothy 1:7 AMP	Galatians 2:20 NIV
2 Corinthians 3:5-6 NLT	Proverbs 4:20-23 NLT
Colossians 1:12-13 NIV	Proverbs 3:3-4 NLV
Joshua 1:8 NCV	Psalm 1:2-3 GW
John 10:10 NKJV	2 Corinthians 2:14 NLV

Thinking like Christ

In the name of Jesus, I take command of my thought life. For though I live in the world, I do not wage war as the world does. The weapons I fight with have divine power to demolish strongholds, arguments, and every pretension that sets itself up against the knowledge of God. I take captive every thought to make it obedient to Christ.

I praise You Lord with all my inmost being. It is You who gives me peace and makes me holy in every way. You keep my whole being—spirit, soul, and body—free from every fault. (Father, expose any thinking that is unlike Christ.) My body is the temple of the Holy Spirit and I honor You with my body.

I take no account of the evil done to me—I pay no attention to a suffered wrong. I am ever ready to believe the best of every person. I think clearly and exercise self-control. I focus on the things that are above—where Christ holds the highest position. I keep my mind on things above, not on worldly things.

I fix my thoughts on what is true, and honorable, and right, and pure, and lovely, and admirable. I think about things that are excellent and worthy of praise, for I have been given Christ's way of thinking.

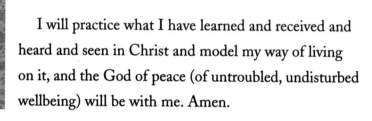

I will practice what I have learned and received and heard and seen in Christ and model my way of living on it, and the God of peace (of untroubled, undisturbed wellbeing) will be with me. Amen.

Scripture References

2 Corinthians 10:3-5 NIV   1 Peter 1:13 NLT

Psalm 103:1 NIV   Colossians 3:1-2 GW

1 Thessalonians 5:23 GNT   Philippians 4:8 NLT

1 Corinthians 6:20 NLT   1 Corinthians 2:16 ERV

1 Corinthians 13:5, 7 AMP   Philippians 4:9 AMP

Tithing

Thank you Father that I have come into the inheritance which You gave me in Christ Jesus. Your mercy is great and You love me very much. Though I was spiritually dead, when I acknowledged Jesus as my Lord, You gave me new life with Christ. I have been saved by Your grace. You rescued me from the kingdom of darkness and transferred me into the Kingdom of Your dear Son.

Jesus, as my Lord and High Priest, I bring the first portion of my income to You and worship the Lord my God with it.

Father, I celebrate because of all the good things that You have given to me and my household. I have obeyed You and done everything You commanded me. Now look down from Your holy dwelling place in heaven and bless me as You said in Your Word. Thank You Father, in Jesus' name. Amen.

<u>Scripture References</u>

Deuteronomy 26:1, 3 AMP   Hebrews 3:1 NCV

Ephesians 2:4-5 NCV

Deuteronomy 26:10-11, 14-15 NLT

Colossians 1:13 NLT

Trust in the Lord

Father, You are my God. I worship You with all my heart; I long for You just as I would long for a stream in a desert. I know that You hear me when I call to You for help. You rescue me from all my troubles. Many are against me, but You keep me safe. You give me the victory! I depend on You and I have chosen to trust You since I first believed. I can be sure that You will protect me from harm. In Christ, I have been made right with God and my prayers have great power and produce wonderful results!

Jesus is the High Priest of my faith. I am completely free to enter the Most Holy Place without fear because of the blood of the Lamb. I can enter through a new and living way that Jesus opened for me. I am confident that You hear me whenever I ask for anything that pleases You. And since I know that You hear me when I make my requests, I also know that You will give me what I ask for.

In the moment that I get tired in the waiting, Holy Spirit, You are right alongside, helping me along. If I don't know how or what to pray, You help me pray, making prayer out of my wordless sighs and my aching groans. You know me far better than I know myself. This is why I can be so sure that every detail in my life is worked into something good.

In the name of Jesus, I will keep on being brave. I know it will bring me great rewards. I will learn to be patient so that I will please You, Lord, and receive what You have promised. I live by faith in the Son of God who loved me and gave Himself to save me. Hallelujah! Praise You Lord!

Scripture References

Psalm 63:1 CEV

Psalm 34:17 NLT

Psalm 55:17,18 NCV

Psalm 71:5 CEV

Proverbs 3:26 CEV

Hebrews 10:35,36 CEV

Galatians 2:20 NIV

Hebrews 3:1 NCV

Hebrews 10:19-25 NCV

1 John 5:14,15 NLT

Romans 8:26-28 MSG

1 Corinthians 1:30 NCV

James 5:16 NLT

Walk in the Word

Father, in the name of Jesus, I commit myself to walk in the Word—to do my best to present myself to You as one approved who correctly handles the Word of Truth. I have the Light of life through Christ, and Your Word living in me produces Your life in this world. Your Word is truth—integrity itself, strong, trustworthy, eternal— and I trust my life to its provisions.

You sent Your Word into my heart and I let the Word live in me in all its wisdom and richness. I think about Your teachings night and day so that I will faithfully do everything written in them, causing me to prosper and succeed. The Imperishable Seed, the Living Word, the Word of Truth, is living in my spirit. That Seed is producing in me every kind of good fruit—Your nature and Your life. It is my counsel, my armor, my protection, my powerful weapon in battle. The Word is a lamp to guide my feet and a light for my path. It makes my way plain before me. I do not stumble, for my steps are directed by the Word.

The Holy Spirit leads me into all the truth. He gives me spiritual wisdom and understanding, for He has rescued me from the kingdom of darkness and transferred me into the Kingdom of God.

I take delight in You and Your Word and You give me the desires of my heart. I commit my way to You, I trust in You. Father, You are working in me, giving me the desire and the power to do what pleases You.

I make the Word the final authority to settle all questions that confront me. I choose to agree with the Word of God; I capture every thought contrary to Your Word, making it obey Christ. My heart is steadfast and secure—trusting in the living Word of God. Amen.

Scripture References

2 Chronicles 34:31 NASB	Psalm 91:4 NLT
2 Timothy 2:15 NIV	Psalm 119:105 NLT
John 8:12 NLV	Psalm 37:23 GW
Hebrews 6:18-20 NLT	John 16:13 NLV
John 6:35 NLT	Colossians 1:9 NLT
Hebrews 4:12 NKJV	Colossians 1:14 NLT
Colossians 3:16 GW	Psalm 37:4-5 NIV
Joshua 1:8 GW	Philippians 2:13 NLT
1 Peter 1:23 NIV	2 Corinthians 10:5 NCV
Colossians 1:10 NLT	Psalm 112:7-8 NIV

Watch What You Say

Father, today I determine with Your help to let everything I say be good and helpful, so that my words will be
an encouragement to those who hear them. I turn from
evil talk and foolish speaking, instead giving thanks to
God. I stay away from useless talk and pointless discus-
sions knowing that those things lead people further away
from You.

Your Word says the tongue is a flame of fire—a whole
world of wickedness, corrupting the entire body. In the
name of Jesus, I make every effort to control my tongue,
which allows me to control myself in every other way. I
use godly wisdom to make knowledge acceptable to others. I have trustworthy things to say and I speak what is
right. I detest lying.

Because I have been made right with God through
Christ, I set the course of my life for obedience, abundance, wisdom, health, and joy. Lord, put a watch over
my mouth, keep watch over the door of my lips. Then I
will tell of Your goodness; I will speak of Your salvation.
I realize that I keep my soul from trouble by watching
over my mouth.

Father, Your words are top priority to me. They are
spirit and life. I let Christ's words with all their wisdom

and richness live in me. I believe Your Word and I speak Your Word—it is alive and powerful in me. My words are words of faith, power, love, and life. They bring good things to my life and to the lives of others as I come to know every blessing I have in Christ Jesus. Amen.

Scripture References

Ephesians 4:29 NCV	John 10:10 NIV
Ephesians 5:4 CEV	Psalm 141:3 NLT
2 Timothy 2:16 CEV	Psalm 71:15 NKJV
James 3:6 NIV	Proverbs 21:23 NKJV
James 3:2 NIV	John 6:63 NIV
Proverbs 15:2 CEV	Colossians 3:16 GW
Proverbs 8:6-7 CEV	Hebrews 4:12 GW
2 Corinthians 5:21 NIV	2 Corinthians 4:13 NIV
Proverbs 4:23 NIV	Philemon 1:6 NCV

Worry Free

Father, thank You that I have been rescued from the dominion of darkness and brought into the Kingdom of the Son You love. I loose the feeling of anxiety from my emotions, and determine to live free from worry in the name of Jesus, for the law of the Spirit of life in Christ Jesus has made me free from the law of sin and death.

I humble myself under Your mighty power and at the right time, You will lift me up in honor. I give all my worries and cares to You, for You care about me. I pile all my troubles on Your shoulders. Thank You for carrying my load and helping me out. You'll never let me fall into ruin. Father, I take delight in You, and You perfect that which concerns me.

I break down every thought and proud thing that puts itself up against the wisdom of God. I take hold of every thought and make it obey Christ. I rid myself of everything that gets in the way and the sin that tries to hold on to me so tightly. I run with determination the race that lies before me, keeping my eyes fixed on Jesus, on whom my faith depends from beginning to end.

I know the One in whom I trust and I am sure that You are able to guard what I have entrusted to You until the day of Your return. I fix my thoughts on what is true, honorable, right, pure, lovely, and admirable. I think about things that are excellent and worthy of praise. I will not let my heart be troubled. I live in You and Your words remain in me and live in my heart. I do not forget what manner of person I am. I look into the perfect law that sets me free; I do what it says; I do not forget what I have heard and God blesses me for doing it.

Thank You, Father. I refuse to worry about anything; instead, I pray about everything and the peace of God which transcends all understanding guards my heart and mind in Christ Jesus. Amen.

Scripture References

Colossians 1:13 NIV	Hebrews 12:1,2 GNT
Romans 8:2 NKJV	2 Timothy 1:12 NLT
1 Peter 5:6-7 NLT	Philippians 4:8 NLT
Psalm 55:22 MSG	John 14:1 NIV
Psalm 37:4 NIV	John 15:7 AMP
Psalm 138:8 NKJV	James 1:22-25 NLT
2 Corinthians 10:5 NLV	Philippians 4:6 NLT

NOTE: Worrying may be one of the most common temptations. It often presents itself in an innocent package. Immediately, upon becoming aware of this insidious, sinful practice, I begin quoting Scripture, which has proven to be a most effective weapon!

PART I:

PERSONAL PRAYERS:
HEALING

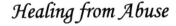

Healing from Abuse

Introduction

This prayer can be applied to any form of abuse—physical, mental, emotional, or sexual. I wrote it after reading T. D. Jakes' book, *Woman, Thou Art Loosed.*[3] By praying it, I personally have experienced victory and freedom—I am no longer a victim but a victor!

Prayer

Thank You, Father, for revealing to me the Person of Jesus. Jesus, You are my great High Priest, and I ask You to loose me from this "infirmity." The abuse I suffered pronounced me guilty and condemned. I was bound in an emotional prison, crippled and could in no way raise myself up. You have called me to Yourself, and I have come.

Thank You for Your anointing to heal broken hearts—the emotional wounds of the past. You are the Truth that reveals the person You created me to be, and I am free from the shame that held me in bondage.

---

[3](Shippensburg, PA: Treasure House, 1993).

Thank You, Lord, for guiding me through the steps to emotional wholeness. You began this good work in me, and You will carry it through to completion on the day of Christ Jesus.

Father, I desire and purpose to live in the Spirit of life in Christ Jesus. This Spirit of life in Christ, like a strong wind, has magnificently cleared the air, freeing me from a fated lifetime of brutal tyranny at the hands of abuse.

With this freedom, I choose to forget the past and look forward to what lies ahead. I press on to reach the end of the race and receive the heavenly prize for which God, through Christ Jesus, is calling me. The past no longer controls my thinking patterns or my behavior.

Because I belong to Christ, I have become a new person. The old life is gone; a new life has begun! Just as Jesus was raised from the dead through the glory of the Father, I too live a new life.

Forgive me, Father, for self-hatred and self-condemnation. Thank You for the blood of Jesus that cleanses me from all sin. You sent Jesus that I may have life and have it more abundantly and I receive this promise.

Your righteousness does not grow from human anger so I throw all spoiled virtue and cancerous evil in the garbage. In simple humility, I submit to You, my Gardener who is landscaping me with the Word, making a salvation-garden of my life.

Father, by Your grace, I forgive my abuser(s) and ask You to help them turn from sin so that they are not lost.

In the name of Jesus I pray, amen.

Scripture References

Hebrews 4:14 NCV

Romans 6:4 NIV

John 14:6 NCV

Philippians 1:6 GW

Romans 8:2 MSG

Philippians 3:13-14 NLT

2 Corinthians 5:17 NLT

Luke 13:11-12 NKJV

1 John 1:7 NLT

John 10:10 NKJV

1 John 3:1-2 NIV

James 1:21 MSG

Matthew 5:44 NIV

2 Peter 3:9 CEV

Breaking the Curse of Abuse

Introduction

Christ redeemed us from the curse of the law by becoming a curse for us, for it is written: "Cursed is everyone who is hung on a tree."

Galatians 3:13 NIV

On a Sunday morning after I had taught a lesson titled "Healing for the Emotionally Wounded," a young man wanted to speak with me. I listened intently as he told me that he had just been released from jail and was now on probation for physically abusing his family. His wife had filed for divorce, and he was living alone. It was not easy for him to confess his sin to me, and I was impressed by his humble attitude.

He said, "I am glad that this message is being given in the church and the abused can receive ministry. Is there anywhere that the abuser can go to receive spiritual help?"

He shared with me that he was attending a support group for abusers. He desired to commit to a church where he could receive forgiveness and acceptance. He knew that any lasting change would have to be from the inside out by the Spirit. I prayed with him, but it would be three years before I could write a prayer for the abuser.

As I read, studied, and sought the Lord, I discovered that the abuser is usually a person who has been abused. Often the problem is a generational curse that has been in the family of the abuser for as far back as anyone can remember. Many times the abuser declares that he will never treat his wife and children as he has been treated, but in spite of his resolve, he finds himself reacting in the same violent manner.

The generational curse can be reversed if the abuser is willing to allow God to remove the character flaws that have held him in bondage.

If you are an abuser, I encourage you to pray this prayer for yourself until it becomes a reality in your life. If you know someone who is an abuser, pray this as a prayer of intercession in the third person.

Prayer

Father, I openly say Jesus Christ is my Lord, and I believe that You raised Him from death. Thank You, Lord, that I am saved and part of Your kingdom. I ask that Your will be done in my life.

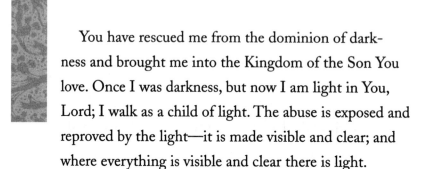

You have rescued me from the dominion of darkness and brought me into the Kingdom of the Son You love. Once I was darkness, but now I am light in You, Lord; I walk as a child of light. The abuse is exposed and reproved by the light—it is made visible and clear; and where everything is visible and clear there is light.

Father, help me to grow in grace (undeserved favor, spiritual strength) and recognition and knowledge and understanding of my Lord and Savior, Jesus Christ, so that I may experience Your love and trust You to be a Father to me.

The history of my earthly family is filled with abusive behavior—hatred, strife, and rage. The painful memory of past abuse (verbal, emotional, physical, and/or sexual) has caused me to be hostile and abusive to others.

I want to do what God's Word says, not just listen to It. I know that nothing good lives in my sinful nature. It seems when I want to do what is right I inevitably do what is wrong. There is another power within me that is at war with my mind—a power that makes me a slave to the sin that is still within me. This pain has caused me to hurt myself and others. Who can free me? Thank God, the answer is in Jesus Christ my Lord. Because I belong to Him, the power of the life-giving Spirit frees me from the power of sin that leads to death.

In Jesus' name, I confess my sin of abuse, resentment, and hostility toward others, and I ask You to forgive me. You are faithful and just to forgive my sin and cleanse me from everything I've done wrong. I renounce the sin of abuse. I refuse to give the devil a way to defeat me by perpetuating the generational curse of anger and abuse.

Jesus Christ rescued me from the curse. When He hung on the cross, He took upon Himself the curse for my wrongdoing. So I stand firm against all strategies of the devil by putting on all of God's armor—truth, righteousness, peace, faith, and salvation. I take the sword of the Spirit, which is the Word of God and stay alert by praying in the Spirit.

Thank You, Father, that the evil power of abuse is broken down. I give myself completely to You. I stand against the devil and he runs from me. The need to hurt others no longer controls me or my family.

In Jesus' name, amen.

Scripture References

Romans 10:9 ERV	1 John 1:9 CEB
Matthew 6:10 NIV	Ephesians 4:26-27 NCV
Colossians 1:13 NIV	Galatians 3:13 NLT

Ephesians 5:8, 13 AMP

2 Peter 3:18 AMP

James 1:22 NLT

Romans 7:18-25 NLT

Romans 7:18-25 NLT

Ephesians 6:11-12 NLT

Ephesians 6:14-18 NLT

2 Corinthians 10:5 NLV

James 4:7 NCV

Health and Healing

Father, Your Word promises healing for Your children and I come before You asking You to remember Your promise in my life. It is written that prayer that comes from faith will heal the sick, for You will restore them to health. And if they have sinned, they will be forgiven. Right now, I let go of all unforgiveness, resentment, anger, and bad feelings toward anyone.

My body is the temple of the Holy Spirit who lives in me and I desire to be in good health. I seek truth that will make me free—both spiritually and naturally (good eating habits, medications if necessary, and appropriate rest and exercise). You bought me with a high price, and I desire to honor You with my body and spirit—they both belong to You.

Thank You, Father, for sending Your Word to heal me and deliver me from all my destructions. Jesus, You are the Word who became human and lived among us. You took on Yourself my troubles (sickness, weakness, and distresses) and carried my sorrows and pains. You were hurt for my wrong-doing. You were crushed for my sins. You were punished so I would have peace. You were beaten so I would be healed and made whole.

Father, I pay attention to what You say and listen carefully to Your words. I will not lose site of them. I let them penetrate deep into my heart, for they bring life and healing to my whole body. You forgive my sins, heal all my diseases, redeem me from death, crown me with love and tender mercies, and fill my life with good things. My youth is renewed like the eagles!

The Spirit of God, who raised Jesus from the dead, lives in me. And just as God raised Christ from the dead, He will give life to my mortal body by this same Spirit living within me. Thank You that I will prosper in all things and be in health, even as my soul prospers.

In the name of Jesus, amen.

Scripture References

James 5:15 CEB	Isaiah 53:4-5 NLV
1 Corinthians 6:19-20 NLT	Proverbs 4:20-22 NLT
John 8:32 NCV	Psalm 103:3-5 NLT
Psalm 107:20 NKJV	Romans 8:11 NLT
John 1:14 NCV	3 John 2 NKJV

Healing from Chronic Fatigue Syndrome

Introduction

All fatigue does not fall into the category of Chronic
Fatigue Syndrome. Most people at one time or another
have feelings of apathy and energy loss—times when
they go to bed tired and get up tired.

There are cases of fatigue that last for weeks, months,
or even years. The medical profession has not determined the causes of Chronic Fatigue Syndrome and does
not know its cure. In most individuals it simply runs its
course.[4] Where there is no way, Jesus is the Way, the
Truth, and the Life. God sent His Word to heal you and
deliver you from all your destructions (Ps. 107:20).

According to those who have shared their experience
with this syndrome, they have flu-like symptoms—they
feel achy with a low-grade fever. One person who suffers
from Chronic Fatigue Syndrome for whom we pray is
considered disabled and cannot work regularly.

You and I are created triune beings—spirit, soul, and
body (1 Thess. 5:23). The apostle John wrote, "Beloved,

---

[4]Editors of Prevention Magazine, *Symptoms, Their Causes &
Cures* (Emmaus, PA: Rodale Press, 1994), pp. 179,181.

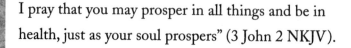

I pray that you may prosper in all things and be in health, just as your soul prospers" (3 John 2 NKJV).

God's Word is medicine to our whole body (Prov. 4:20-22 NLT). If any type of medication is to bring relief and a cure, it is necessary to follow the prescribed dosage. This is true with "spiritual" medicine. It is imperative to take doses of God's Word daily through reading, meditating, and listening to healing Scriptures. The spirit, soul, and body are interrelated; it is the Word of God that brings the entire being into harmony.

God made us and knows us inside and out. He sent His Word to heal us and to deliver us from all our destructions (Ps. 107:20). Prayer prepares us to take action. Jesus said that if we pray in secret, our Heavenly Father will reward us openly (Matt. 6:6). Prayer includes praise, worship, and petition.

Prayer prepares us for change—it equips us for action. It puts us in tune and in harmony with the Spirit of God—He hovered over the waters in the beginning of creation and brings rivers of living waters that flow from within us (Gen. 1:2; John 7:38 NIV). He is waiting for us to speak, to move—to act out our faith. The ministry of the Holy Spirit is revealed in the names ascribed to Him—Comforter, Counselor, Helper, Advocate, Inter-

cessor, Strengthener, Standby (John 16:7 AMP). He is
with us and in us (John 14:17).

Prayer

Father, in the name of Jesus, I come to Your throne
of grace with confidence, so I may receive mercy and
find grace to help in time of need. I praise You, the God
and Father of my Lord Jesus Christ! You have blessed
me with every spiritual blessing that heaven has to offer.
I humble myself under Your mighty hand and cast the
care of this condition onto You. Thank You for giving
me rest.

Today I choose to speak words of life and release my
faith. Father, Chronic Fatigue Syndrome is a curse, not
a blessing. Jesus became a curse and at the same time,
dissolved the curse for our sin. And now, because of that,
the air is cleared and I can see that Abraham's blessing
is present and available for me. I am able to receive Your
life, Your Spirit, just the way Abraham received it.

Christ bought my freedom with His own blood and
the law of the Spirit of life which is in Christ Jesus, the
law of my new being, has freed me from the law of sin
and death.

Christ is in me and the Spirit of God who raised
Jesus from the dead lives in me. And He who raised

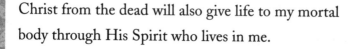
Christ from the dead will also give life to my mortal body through His Spirit who lives in me.

You, Sovereign Lord, have given me Your words of wisdom, bringing comfort to the weary. Morning by morning You waken me and open my understanding to Your will.

I have strength for all things in Christ who empowers me—I am ready for anything and equal to anything through Him who infuses inner strength into me; I am self-sufficient in Christ's sufficiency.

You are my Light and my Salvation—whom will I fear? The strength of the Lord is my life—of whom will I be afraid? Lord, You are a shield around me—my Glory, and the One who holds my head high. When I cry out to You, You answer me. When I lie down and sleep, I wake up in safety, for You are watching over me.

Father, I put on all Your armor so I can stand firm against all the strategies of the devil. I am able to resist the enemy in the time of evil, knowing that You are watching to make sure Your Word will not return to You empty, but will accomplish what You desire and achieve the purpose for which You sent it. You have sent Your Word to heal me!

Christ bore my sins in His body on the cross so I could stop living for sin and start living for what is right. I am healed because of His wounds.

I throw off the spirit of heaviness and exchange it for a garment of praise. Thank You for Christ's great strength that works so powerfully in me.

In the name of Jesus I pray, amen.

Scripture References

Hebrews 4:16 NIV	Psalm 27:1 NKJV
Ephesians 1:3 GW	Psalm 3:3-5 NLT
Galatians 3:13-14 MSG	Ephesians 6:11, 13 NLT
Acts 20:28 NIV	Jeremiah 1:12 NCV
Romans 8:2 AMP	Isaiah 55:11 NIV
Romans 8:10-11 NIV	1 Peter 2:24 NCV
Isaiah 50:4 NLT	Isaiah 61:3 NKJV
Philippians 4:13 AMP	Colossians 1:29 NCV

Healing for Damaged Emotions

Father, in the name of Jesus, I come to You with a feeling of shame and emotional hurt. I acknowledge my sin to You [continually unfolding the past till all is told]. I'm thankful You instantly forgive me from the guilt and iniquity; You are faithful and just to forgive my sins and cleanse me from everything I've done wrong. You are my Hiding Place, and You, Lord, preserve me from trouble. I have chosen life and blessings in You. Your Word says You made all the delicate, inner parts of my body and knit me together in my mother's womb, and that Your workmanship is marvelous! Now I am Your masterpiece, created anew in Christ Jesus.

Father, You did not give me a spirit of fear; I will not be afraid and I will not be put to shame. I will not be humiliated. You gave me beauty for ashes, the oil of joy for mourning, and the garment of praise for the spirit of heaviness that I may be called a tree of righteousness, the planting of the Lord, that You may be glorified. I sing psalms, hymns, and spiritual songs, making music to You, Lord, in my heart. Just as David did in 1 Samuel 30:6, I encourage myself in You.

I stand acceptable to You, Father, because I believe in You, who raised Jesus my Lord from the dead. Jesus was betrayed and put to death because of my misdeeds and was raised to secure my acquittal, absolving me from all guilt before You, Father. You anointed Jesus and sent Him to bind up and heal my broken heart and liberate me from the shame of my youth and the imperfections of my caretakers. Because Jesus is my Lord, I choose to forgive all those who have wronged me in any way. You promised You will not leave me without support as I complete the forgiveness process. I take comfort and am encouraged and confidently say, "The Lord is my Helper; I will not be seized with alarm. What can man do to me?"

Your light penrtrates my spirit, Lord—You are able to see my deepest parts, and the Holy Spirit leads me into all truth. When reality exposes shame and emotional pain, I remember that my present sufferings are not worth comparing with the glory that will be revealed in me! Jesus was punished so I could have peace. He was beaten so I could be healed. As Your child, Father, I have a joyful and confident hope of eternal salvation. This hope will never disappoint, delude, or shame me, for God's love has been poured out in my heart through the Holy Spirit who has been given to me. Amen.

Scripture References

Psalm 32:5-7 AMP

1 John 1:9 CEB

Deuteronomy 30:19 NCV

Psalm 139:13-14 NLT

Ephesians 2:10 NLT

2 Timothy 1:7 NLV

Isaiah 54:4 NIV

Isaiah 61:3 NKJV

Ephesians 5:19 NLV

Romans 4:24-25 AMP

Isaiah 61:1 NKJV

Mark 11:25 NIV

Hebrews 13:5-6 AMP

Proverbs 20:27 NLT

John 16:13 NCV

Romans 8:18 NIV

Isaiah 53:5 NLV

Romans 5:3-5 AMP

Victory Over Depression

It has been stated that an estimated 19 million American adults are living with major depression. Depression was a constant companion of mine for many years, and I know from experience how this medical illness can lead to thoughts of suicide. Several years ago on a gray, dreary day in January, God reached down and lifted me from the deep mud of depression where my feet could not touch the bottom. The Holy Spirit began to teach me how to stand in my deliverance from depression by declaring Scriptures that I posted on my refrigerator and bathroom mirrror. I came to believe that "whom the Son has set free is free indeed" and that I could choose to retain the familiar feelings and negative thoughts -- or -- I could speak God's Word over myself.

It was not easy in the beginning because my feelings had controlled me for many years, but by the grace of God I was persistent and victory is mine in the name of Jesus. Feelings of worthlessness were replaced by "I am accepted in the Beloved;" guilt (self-blame) was replaced with "there is no condemnation to those who are in Christ Jesus." Obsessive thinking was replaced by thinking on good things and/or rewriting past events of failure. I now see every failure, every mistake as a stepping stone to emotional health and spiritual growth.

Prayer

Father, You are my shelter and my refuge in times of trouble, even here in the midst of depression. Regardless of these negative feelings, I choose to lean on and put my trust in You, for You will not abandon me. I put my hope in You and praise You, my Savior and my God. Depression is an enemy and has no place here!

Lord, You lift me up when I am weighed down and protect me when I allow feelings of anxiety. So I purpose to wait on You, Lord, and when I feel weak, the Holy Spirit reminds me to say that I am strong. With Your help, my heart takes courage. You are saving me and helping me establish myself in rightness—in conformity with Your will and order. I resist the feelings of depression and declare I am far from even the thought of oppression or destruction; I am not afraid and terror cannot come near me. I trust in the name of Jesus and I rely on You, Lord.

Father, You have thoughts and plans for my welfare and peace, to give me a future and a hope. When my thoughts are fixed on You, You keep me in perfect peace. Peace of mind and heart I receive from You as a gift so I will not be troubled or afraid.

In the name of Jesus, I loose self-defeating thought patterns from my mind. I tear down strongholds that

have protected bad perceptions about myself. I give myself completely to You, Father, and take my stand against
fear, discouragement, self-pity, and depression. I will not
give the devil a way to defeat me by harboring resentment, holding onto self-hatred, anger toward myself and
others, or feeling guilty. I surround myself with songs
and shouts of deliverance from depression, and I will
continue to gain the victory by the blood of the Jesus and
the word of my witness.

Father, I receive a spirit of power, love, and a calm
and well-balanced mind with discipline and self-control,
which You have given me. I cooperate with the Spirit of
God who is helping me renew my thoughts and attitudes
with Your Word. Thank You for giving me Christ's way
of thinking, so I can now make intelligent decisions
without fear.

You are the Lifter of my head and I walk a straight
path—healed and whole. I arise from the depression and
circumstances that have kept me down. I rise to new life;
I shine with the glory of the Lord.

You have rescued me from this evil world in which
I live and I praise You, for the joy of the Lord is my
strength. Amen.

Scripture References

Psalm 9:9-10 NLT

Psalm 9:10 AMP

Psalm 42:5, 11 GW

Psalm 146:8 NLT

Psalm 31:22-24 CEB

Isaiah 35:3-4 NASB

Isaiah 54:14 AMP

Isaiah 50:10 NKJV

Jeremiah 29:11 AMP

Jeremiah 29:11 NLT

Isaiah 26:3 NLT

John 14:27 NLT

James 4:7 NCV

Ephesians 4:27 NCV

Psalm 32:5-7 AMP

Revelation 12:11 CEB

Luke 4:18-19 GW

2 Timothy 1:7 AMP

1 Corinthians 2:16 ERV

Philippians 2:5 NCV

Ephesians 4:23-24 NLT

Hebrews 12:12-13 CEV

Isaiah 60:1 AMP

Galatians 1:4 NLT

Nehemiah 8:10 NIV

Healthy Lifestyle

Father, I am Your child, belonging only to You. Jesus is Lord over my spirit, soul, and body. Thank you for making me so wonderfully complex. Your workmanship is marvelous—how well I know it.

Lord, thank You for the plans You have for me— plans to prosper me and not to harm me, plans to give me hope and a future. I choose to renew my mind to Your plans for a healthy lifestyle. You have showered your kindness on me, along with all wisdom and understanding. I am sensible and I watch my step. Continue to teach me knowledge and good judgment, for I trust Your commands.

My body is the temple of the Holy Spirit, who lives in me. So here is what I want to do with Your help, Father God. I choose to take my everyday, ordinary life— my sleeping, eating, going-to-work, and walking-around life—and place it before You as an offering. Embracing what You do for me is the best thing I can do for You.

Christ, the Messiah, will be magnified and receive glory and praise in this body of mine and will be boldly exalted in my person.

In Jesus' name, amen.

Scripture References

1 Thessalonians 5:23-24 NCV   Proverbs 14:15 GW

Psalm 139:14 NLT   Psalm 119:66 NIV

Jeremiah 29:11 NIV   1 Corinthians 6:19 NLT

Romans 12:2 NIV   Romans 12:1 MSG

Ephesians 1:8 NLT   Philippians 1:20 AMP

Healing from Hypersensitivity

Introduction

"A new command I give you: Love one another. As I have loved you, so you must love one another. By this all men will know that you are my disciples, if you love one another" (John 13:34-35 NIV).

Hypersensitivity can be an asset, but more often it seems to be a liability. Hypersensitive personalities usually avoid large crowds, and most group activites are energy drains for them. They are most comfortable and energized from being alone. God said it is not good for individuals to be alone. It is difficult to achieve emotional wholeness and spiritual growth alone. The royal law of love is the counteragent for hypersensitivity. Love gives and is developed in community...by fellowship and communion with others.

First Corinthians 13:5 AMP reveals that love "...is not conceited (arrogant and inflated with pride); it is not rude (unmannerly) and does not act unbecomingly. Love (God's love in us) does not insist on its own rights or its own way, for it is not self-seeking; it is not touchy or fretful or resentful; it takes no account of the evil done to it [it pays no attention to a suffered wrong]."

An overly sensitive personality experiences feelings of alienation, irritability, and resentment in relationships. Depression often is a major problem.

The hypersensitive person has usually suffered deep hurt from rejection and needs a great deal of approval and validation from others. This individual is excessively sensitive to remarks that may or may not be intended to be hurtful. It is difficult for a person of this nature to trust others, to accept constructive criticism or advice; and this weakness hinders positive relationships. When presentations or suggestions are rejected, that action is taken as a personal attack.

Hypersensitivity is an enemy that can be overcome by receiving God's unconditional love and renewing the mind. In waging the good warfare, we have God-given weapons to overthrow our adversary—the enemy of the soul. These weapons include, among other things: the anointing that is upon Jesus to bind up and heal the bro-kenhearted (Luke 4:18), the sword of the Spirit, which is the Word of God (Eph. 6:17), the shield of faith (Eph. 6:16), and the help of the Holy Spirit (John 14:16 AMP), which may come through a Christian counselor, a minister, or a friend.

James instructed us, "Confess to one another there-fore your faults (your slips, your false steps, your offenses, your sins); and pray [also] for one another, that you may be healed and restored [to a spiritual tone of mind and heart]. The earnest (heartfelt, continued) prayer of a righteous man makes tremendous power available [dynamic in its working]" (James 5:16 AMP). We are overcomers by the blood of the Lamb and by the word of our testimony! (Rev. 12:11).

Prayer

Father, forgive me for being self-conscious. I have attempted to control situations and demanded others to measure up to my expectations. I realize I have released my anger either by withdrawing or by lashing out inappropriately. I confess this as sin, asking for and receiving Your forgiveness, knowing that You are faithful and just to forgive my sin and cleanse me from everything I've done wrong. I forgive those who have wronged me, and I ask for healing of my anger and unresolved hurts.

I realize that I am responsible for my own behavior, and I am accountable to You for my words and actions. Give me the courage to go to those I have offended and make amends when it is appropriate.

Thank You for the Holy Spirit who leads me into truth—the truth that makes me free. You have sent

Your Word and healed me and delivered me from my destructions.

Father, help me to be strong in You and in Your great power. Your power makes me patient and strong enough to endure anything—hypersensitivity, irritability, and touchiness—and I choose to be truly happy.

I desire to be well-balanced (temperate, sober of mind), vigilant, and cautious at all times; I recognize the enemy—the devil—who roams around like a lion roaring, seeking someone to seize upon and devour. In the name of Jesus, I withstand him, firm in faith [against his onset—rooted, established, strong, immovable, and determined].

I live under the protection of God Most High and stay in the shadow of God Almighty.

I purpose to walk in love toward my family members, my associates, and my neighbors with the help of the Holy Spirit. The Son has set me free and I am absolutely free.

Thank You, Father, for the power Christ has given me. He leads me and makes me to win in everything. I continue to gain the victory in my life by the blood of Jesus and the word of my witness. Amen.

Scripture References

1 John 1:9 CEB

Mark 11:24-25 NIV

Matthew 12:36 CEV

John 16:13 NCV

John 8:32 NCV

Psalm 107:20 NKJV

Ephesians 6:10 NCV

Colossians 1:11 CEV

1 Peter 5:8-9 AMP

Psalm 91:1 CEV

Ephesians 5:2 NKJV

John 8:36 GW

2 Corinthians 2:14 NLV

Revelation 12:11 CEB

Receiving Forgiveness

Father, Your Word says that if I ask for forgiveness, You will forgive me and cleanse me from everything I've done wrong. Help me to believe; help me to receive my forgiveness for past and present sins. Help me to forgive myself. I openly say "Jesus is Lord," believing in my heart that You raised Him from death, therefore I am saved.

Father, Your Son, Jesus said that whatever I ask for in prayer, believe that I have received it, and it will be mine. That if I have faith and really believe, I will receive. Lord, I believe; help me overcome my unbelief.

Father, it is a great blessing when people are forgiven for the wrongs they have done, when their sins are put out of sight. I count myself blessed, how happy I am— I get a fresh start, my slate's wiped clean. You, Father, are holding nothing against me, and You're not holding anything back from me.

When I keep it all inside, my bones turn to powder, and my words become daylong groans. The pressure never lets up; all the juices of my life dry up. I am letting it all out; I am saying once and for all that I am making a clean breast of my failures to You, Lord.

In the face of this feeling of guilt and unworthiness, I receive my forgiveness, and the pressure is gone—my guilt dissolved, my sin disappeared. I am blessed, for You have forgiven my transgressions—You have covered my sins. I am blessed, for You will never count my sins against me.

Father, even before You made the world, You loved me and chose me in Christ to be holy and without fault in Your eyes. You are so rich in kindness and grace that You purchased my freedom with the blood of Your Son and forgave my sins.

Lord, I have received Your Son, Jesus. I believe in His name, and He has given me the right to become Your child. I acknowledge You, Lord, as my Father. Thank You for forgiving me and absolving me of all guilt. I have gained the victory on account of the blood of Jesus and the word of my witness.

In the name of Jesus, amen.

Scripture References

1 John 1:9 CEB	Psalm 32:1-6 MSG
Romans 10:9-10 ERV	Romans 4:7-8 NIV
Mark 11:23-24 NIV	Ephesians 1:4, 7 NLT

Matthew 21:22 AMP

Mark 9:24 NLT

Psalm 32:1 ERV

John 1:12 NIV

Revelation 12:11 CEB

PART I:

PERSONAL PRAYERS:
OVERCOMING

Strength to Overcome Cares and Burdens

Introduction

If you are feeling heavy-hearted and burdened down with problems (family, financial, business, and/or societal changes) of any kind, I encourage you to begin praying this prayer until your burden is lifted. There have been times when I've had to dust off this prayer and read it aloud so I can hear and turn to the One who is my Exceeding Great Joy!

The cares of life have a way of sneaking up on us. Often changes come that we didn't foresee, and we allow pressure to move in. This is an opportunity to rejoice, not because we feel like rejoicing, but because Jesus taught us to be of good cheer. He has overcome the world and deprived it of its power to harm us. Most often it is pride that prevents us from letting go and casting the care over on the Lord. May we be willing to humble ourselves before Him and receive His mercy and grace to help in our time of need.

Prayer

Why am I discouraged? Why is my heart sad? I will put my hope in God! I will praise him again—my Savior and my God!

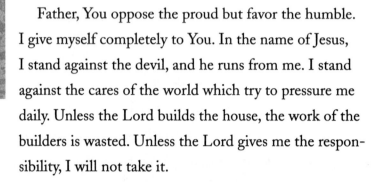

Father, You oppose the proud but favor the humble. I give myself completely to You. In the name of Jesus, I stand against the devil, and he runs from me. I stand against the cares of the world which try to pressure me daily. Unless the Lord builds the house, the work of the builders is wasted. Unless the Lord gives me the responsibility, I will not take it.

Jesus, I am tired and I come to You with my heavy burdens. You promised to give me rest. I accept your teaching and learn from You. You are gentle and humble in spirit and I will be able to rest. The teaching that You ask me to accept is easy and the load You give me to carry is light.

I give my burdens to You, Lord, and You will take care of me. You will not allow me to slip and fall.

In the name of Jesus, I withstand the devil. I am firm in my faith against his onset— rooted, established, strong, immovable, and determined. I enter into God's rest so I can rest from my own works. I try as hard as I can to enter God's rest so that I will not fail to obey Him.

Father, thank You that Your presence goes with me and that You give me rest. I am still and rest in You, Lord; I wait for You and patiently lean upon You. I will not fret, for You left me a gift—peace of mind and heart—so I will not be troubled or afraid. I will put my hope in You, God. I will praise You again my Savior and my God! Amen.

Scripture References

Psalm 42:11NLT

James 4:6-7 NCV

Psalm 127:1 NLT

Matthew 11:28-30 ERV

Psalm 55:22 NLT

1 Peter 5:9 AMP

Hebrews 4:10-11 NCV

Exodus 33:14 NIV

Psalm 37:7 AMP

John 14:27 NLT

Psalm 42:11 NLT

Discouragement

Introduction

Moses returned to the Lord and said, "O Lord, why have you brought trouble upon this people? Is this why you sent me? Ever since I went to Pharaoh to speak in your name, he has brought trouble upon this people, and you have not rescued your people at all" (Exodus 5:22-23 NIV).

Here in this passage, we find Moses discouraged, complaining to God.

It is important that we approach God with integrity and in an attitude of humility. But because we fear saying something negative, we sometimes cross the line of honesty into the line of denial and delusion.

Let's be honest. God already knows what we are feeling. He can handle our anger, complaints, and disappointments. He understands us. He is aware of our human frailties (Ps. 103:14) and can be touched with the feelings of our infirmities (Heb. 4:15).

Whether your "trouble" is a business failure, abandonment, depression, a mental disorder, a chemical imbalance, oppression, a marriage problem, a child who is in

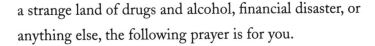

a strange land of drugs and alcohol, financial disaster, or anything else, the following prayer is for you.

Sometimes when you are in the midst of discouragement, it is difficult to remember that you have ever known any Scripture. I admonish you to read this prayer aloud until you recognize the reality of God's Word in your spirit, soul, and body. Remember, God is watching over His Word to perform it (Jer. 1:12 AMP). He will finish the work He started in you (Ps. 138:8 NLT).

Prayer

Lord, I do not understand why this trouble has come. I have exhausted all my possibilities for changing my situation; in my own strength, I am powerless. I believe in You; help me overcome my unbelief. Your Word says what is impossible with men is possible with God. I humble myself under Your mighty power, knowing You will lift me up.

I have a great High Priest who has gone through the heavens: Jesus, Your Son. I hold firmly to the faith I profess. My High Priest is able to empathize with my weaknesses. He was tempted in every way, just as I am— yet He did not sin. I approach Your throne of grace with confidence, so that I may receive mercy and find grace to help in my time of need.

In the face of discouragement, disappointment, and anger, I choose to believe that Your word to Moses is Your word to me. You are delivering me. With Your mighty hand, You have defeated the forces set against me. You are the Lord, God Almighty. You appeared to Abraham, to Isaac, and to Jacob and established Your covenant with them.

Father, I believe that You have heard me. I live to see Your promises of deliverance and rest fulfilled in my life. You have not failed in even one word of Your good promises.

It is You who is bringing me out of bondage with great power and strength. You have freed me from being a slave to _____. You have taken me as Your own and paid for me with a high price—You are my God, a father to me. You have rescued me from the past that held me in bondage and brought me into the Kingdom of the Son You love. I no longer settle for the pain of the past. Where sin increased, God's grace increased much more!

Father, what You have promised, I take hold of in the name of Jesus. I am willing to fight the good fight of faith. I rid myself now, in the name of Jesus, of everything that gets in the way and the sin that so easily trips me up, and I am running with determination the race that lies before me. I am established in rightness, in conformity with Your will and order. I am far from even the thought of oppression or destruction, for I will not fear. Terror will not come near me. In all these things I have complete victory through Him who loves me. Amen.

Scripture References

(This prayer is based on Exodus 5:22-6:11 and includes other verses where applicable.)

Mark 9:24 NLT	1 Corinthians 6:19-21 NIV
Luke 18:27 AMP	Colossians 1:13 NIV
1 Peter 5:6 NLT	Romans 5:20 GNT
Hebrews 4:14-16 NIV	1 Timothy 6:12 NIV
Exodus 6:3-4 AMP	Hebrews 12:1 GNT
Genesis 49:22-26 CEV	Isaiah 54:14-16 AMP
1 Kings 8:56 NIV	Romans 8:37 GNT
Deuteronomy 26:8 NCV	

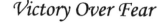
Victory Over Fear

Father, when I am afraid, I will trust in You. I praise You for Your Word. I trust you, God, so I resist fear and renounce fear of man. What can human beings do to me?

Thank You for giving me a spirit of power and of love and of a sound mind. Because of this, I am not ashamed of the testimony of my Lord. I have not received a spirit that makes me a fearful slave. I acknowledge Your Spirit that I received when You adopted me as Your own child. Now, I can call you, "Abba Father."

Jesus, You rescued me by Your death. Because You embraced death and took it upon Yourself, You destroyed the devil's hold on death and freed me from cowering in life, being scared to death of death. I receive the gift that You gave me – peace! You give me Your own peace. This is not like when the people of the world say "peace" to me. You say it differently. You tell me not to fear and not to let anything trouble my heart. I receive this gift because I believe in You, God.

Lord, You are my light and the One who saves me. Why should I fear anyone? You protect my life from danger so why should I tremble? Evil people may try to destroy me. My enemies and those who hate me attack me, but they are defeated. Even if an army surrounds me, I will not be afraid. If I am attacked, I will trust in You, Lord.

Thank You, Holy Spirit, for bringing these things to my remembrance when I am tempted to be afraid. I will trust in my God. In the name of Jesus I pray, amen.

Scripture References

Psalm 56:3 NCV

2 Timothy 1:7,8 NKJV

Romans 8:15 NLT

Hebrews 2:15 MSG

John 14:1,27 NLT

Psalm 27:1-3 NCV

Overcoming a Feeling of Abandonment

Introduction

"Even if my father and mother abandon me, the Lord will hold me close" (Psalm 27:10 NLT).

This prayer was prompted by a letter I received from a man who was in prison. According to his letter, he grew up in a family of fighters and felt abandoned by his family and so-called friends. His pugnacious attitude controlled him, and eventually his aggressive temperament caused him to almost kill someone.

In prison he was ridiculed and harassed by inmates who encouraged him to fight. His wife divorced him, and again he was left alone. Thoughts that "no one likes me" continually tormented him, but he desired to know how to change his thinking.

A messenger of hope introduced him to Jesus and my book, *Prayers That Avail Much, Volume 1*. He still had trouble controlling his temper, even with those who might have been his friends. His letter was filled with the pain of loneliness and abandonment. The following is a revised and expanded version of the original prayer I wrote, encouraging him to pray for himself.

Prayer

Father, I have confessed Jesus as my Lord and believe in my heart that You raised Him from the dead. I need and ask You, Holy Spirit, to help me overcome the resentment I feel toward those who abused and abandoned me.

Now I am Your child. When other people leave me and I feel unloved, I am thankful that You have promised that You will never, ever fail me or abandon me.

Jesus, You gave Your life for me and called me a friend. You live in my heart and I am on my way to heaven. I have so much to be thankful for and I will do as Your Word says and be thankful in all circumstances. So, when I am lonely or discouraged, I will think of things that are true and honest and right.

Heavenly Father, I ask You to make me strong and to help me while in the presence of dangers surrounding me. You have ordered Your angels to guard me wherever I go. I am not alone. Your Word says that nothing can ever separate me from Your love- not even my fears for today or worries about tomorrow. I will come to the top of every circumstance or trial through God's love.

Lord, You are concerned with the smallest detail of my life. You will work out Your plans for my life and I

can trust You because You are ready to help when I need You. Lord, I need You at all times!

Lord, I ask You for true friends. Teach me how to trust others and be a friend who sticks by them like God-fearing family. Help me to walk in Your love and show myself friendly.

Scripture References

Romans 19:9,10 NIV

Hebrews 13:5 NLT

John 15:13-15 NIV

1 Thessalonians 5:18 NLT

Philippians 4:8 NLT

Isaiah 41:10 NCV

Psalm 91:11 MSG

Romans 8:35,39 NLT

Psalm 138:8 NLT

Psalm 46:1 MSG

Proverbs 18:24 MSG

Hopelessness

Father, I come asking You to hear my prayer. Listen, O God, and do not ignore my cry for help! Please listen and answer me, for I am overwhelmed by my troubles. I am scared and shaking and terror grips me.

I wish I had wings like a dove! Then I would fly away and rest. How quickly I would escape, far away from the wind and storm.

I call out to You God, and I know You will rescue me. You redeem my life in peace from this battle of hopelessness that has come against me. I pile my troubles on Your shoulders and thank You for carrying my load and helping me out. Hopelessness lies in wait to swallow me up or trample me all day long. Whenever I am afraid, I choose to have confidence and put my trust and reliance in You. By Your help, God, I praise Your Word. On You I lean, put my trust; I do not entertain fear.

You keep track of all my sorrows. You have collected all my tears in Your bottle. You have recorded each one in Your book. Now I'm thanking You with all my heart. You pulled me from the brink of death, my feet from the cliff edge of doom. Now I stroll at leisure with You in the sunlit fields of life.

I am confident I will see Your goodness while I am here in the land of the living. I wait patiently for You, Lord. I am brave and courageous. Yes, I am waiting patiently.

Father, I give You all my worries and cares, for You care about me. I am well-balanced and cautious—alert, watching out for attacks from Satan, my great enemy. I am standing firm and strong in faith remembering that other Christians all around the world are going through the same kind of sufferings.

In the name of Jesus, I gain the victory by the blood of the Lamb and by the word of my witness. Amen.

Scripture References

Hebrews 4:16 NIV	Psalm 56:8 NLT
Psalm 55:1 MSG	Psalm 56:13 MSG
Psalm 55:1-2 NLT	Psalm 27:13-14 NLT
Psalm 55:5-8 NCV	1 Peter 5:7 NLT
Psalm 55:16 CEB	1 Peter 5:8 AMP
Psalm 55:18 AMP	1 Peter 5:8-9 NLT
Psalm 55:22 MSG	Revelation 12:11 CEB
Psalm 56:2-4 AMP	

Overcoming Intimidation

Father, forgive me when I allow others to intimidate me and make me afraid to do Your will. Forgive me when I give in to the coercion, whether real or imagined. You created me for Your good pleasure and ordained good works that you have anointed me to fulfill.

Father, I come to You in the name of Jesus, asking You to forgive me for allowing intimidation to cause me to stumble. I receive Your forgiveness for thinking of myself as inferior, for I am created in Your image and I am Your masterpiece. Jesus, You said that the Kingdom of God is in me. Because of that, the same mighty power that raised You from the dead and seated You in the place of honor at the Father's right hand lives in me and causes me to face life with hope and divine energy.

The Lord is my light and my salvation. So why should I fear anyone? The Lord protects my life. Why should I be afraid? Lord, You said that You would never let me down and never walk off and leave me. Because of that, I can boldly say that You are there, ready to help me. Who or what can get to me? Greater is He who is in me than he who is in the world. If God is for me, then who can be against me? I am free from the fear of man and I am safe because I trust in the Lord.

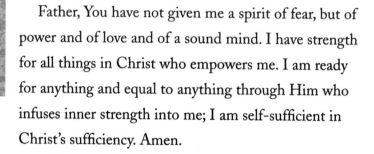

Father, You have not given me a spirit of fear, but of power and of love and of a sound mind. I have strength for all things in Christ who empowers me. I am ready for anything and equal to anything through Him who infuses inner strength into me; I am self-sufficient in Christ's sufficiency. Amen.

Scripture References

1 John 1:9 WE

Luke 17:21 NIV

Colossians 1:29

Hebrews 13:5 MSG

Romans 8:31 NIV

Joshua 1:5

2 Timothy 1:7 NKJV

Ephesians 2:10 NLT

Ephesians 1:19, 20 NLT

Psalm 27:1 NCV

1 John 4:4

Proverbs 29:25 NKJV

Philippians 4:13 AMP

Letting Go of the Past

Father, I realize my helplessness in saving myself, and I honor and praise what Christ Jesus has done for me. I let go of the things I once considered valuable because I'm much better off knowing Jesus Christ my Lord. I throw it all away in order to gain Christ and to have a relationship with Him.

Lord, I have received Your Son, and He has given me the right to become Your child. I unfold my past and put into proper perspective those things that are behind. My old self has been crucified with Christ and I no longer live, but Christ lives in me. I live in this earthly body by faith in the Son of God who loved me and gave Himself for me. I trust in You, Lord, with all my heart and I do not depend on my own understanding. I seek to please You in all I do, and You show me which path to take.

I want to know Christ and experience the power that raised Him from the dead. I want to suffer with Him, even sharing in death so that, one way or another, I will experience the resurrection from the dead! So, whatever it takes, I will be one who lives in the fresh newness of life of those who are alive from the dead.

I don't mean to say that I am perfect. I haven't learned all I should, but I keep working toward that day when I will finally be all that Christ saved me for and wants me to be.

I am bringing all my energies to bear on this one thing: Regardless of my past, I look forward to what lies ahead. I strain to reach the end of the race and receive the prize for which You are calling me up to heaven because of what Christ Jesus did for me.

In Jesus' name I pray, amen.

Scripture References

Proverbs 3:5-6 NLT

Psalm 32:5 AMP

Philippians 3:13 NLT

Philippians 3:12-14 TLB

Philippians 3:7-9 GW

Philippians 3:10-11 NLT

John 1:12 NIV

Romans 6:4 TLB

Galatians 2:20 NIV

Victory Over Pride

Father, in the name of Jesus I resist pride (the spirit that makes me overestimate myself and underestimate others). I remember that You are against the proud but You give grace to the humble. Lord, I repent for having pride in my own resources and humble myself before You. In the name of Jesus, I stand against the devil and he will run from me.

Lord, I will be down to earth and not proud. Because Your strong hand is on me, I will be content with who I am. You will promote me at the right time. I do not think of myself better than I really am. I will measure myself by the amount of faith that You have given to me.

Proverbs 11:2 NLT says, "Pride leads to disgrace, but with humility comes wisdom." Father, I will resist pride when it comes. My desire is that I be a servant because that would bring honor to You.

Father, thank You for living with people who are sad and humble. You give new life to those who are humble and to those whose hearts are broken. Thank You that the reward of true humility leads to riches, honor and long life.

In Jesus name I pray, amen.

Scripture References

Proverbs 6:16, 17 AMP

Proverbs 11:2 NLT

James 4:6,7 NCV

Matthew 23:11 NIV

Proverbs 21:4 NIV

Isaiah 57:15 NCV

1 Peter 5:5,6 MSG

Proverbs 22:4 NLT

Romans 12:3 NCV

Overcoming a Feeling of Rejection

Introduction

Feelings of rejection and fear of rejection seem to cause an identity crisis. When you are thrown into an identity crisis, you have the opportunity to erase old tapes that have played in your mind for a long time and replace those self-defeating thoughts with God-thoughts.

Your Heavenly Father saw you and approved of you even while you were in your mother's womb (Ps. 139:13-16). He gave you survival tools that would bring you to the place where you are today. He is a Father who has been waiting for you to come home to truth – the truth that will set you free (John 8:32). Jesus came to His own people to bring them life; they rejected Him (John 1:11). He was despised and rejected by men; a man of sorrows who understands your feelings. Jesus bore your sorrow and carried your grief…the punishment that brings you peace was upon Him and by His wounds you are healed. (Please read Isaiah 53.)

You were accepted by the Father before the foundation of the world, and there is no higher acceptance than this! When you see yourself as God's workmanship, as

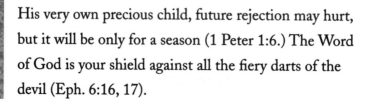
His very own precious child, future rejection may hurt, but it will be only for a season (1 Peter 1:6.) The Word of God is your shield against all the fiery darts of the devil (Eph. 6:16, 17).

For victory over your feeling of rejection, pray the following prayer in faith and joy.

Prayer

Father, I come before You to bask in Your presence where I am accepted, and here I find mercy and grace to help me overcome this fear and feeling of rejection. Forgive me for being self-conscious rather than God-conscious. You chose me and accepted me before the foundation of the world. I am Your child...valuable and precious in Your sight. When I am facing rejection, I will say, "The LORD is my light and my salvation. Why should I be afraid? The LORD is my fortress...so why should I tremble?" (Psalm 27:1 NLT).

Lord, I know right from wrong and hold Your teaching inside me; I won't pay attention to insults or when people mock me. Thank You for the Holy Spirit who helps me through the process of renewing my mind. I accept myself because You accept me just as I am. So, I will choose not to look at the troubles I see now; rather, I will fix my gaze on things that cannot be seen. For the things that I see now will soon be gone, but the things that I cannot see will last forever.

If with my heart and soul I am doing good, then why would I think I can be stopped? Even if I suffer for it, I am still better off. I won't give the opposition a second thought. Through thick and thin, I will keep my heart at attention, in adoration before Christ, my Master. I will be ready to speak up and tell anyone who asks why I am living the way that I am and always with the utmost courtesy. I will keep a clear conscience before God so that when people throw mud at me, none of it will stick. There is wonderful joy ahead, even though the going is rough for a while down here. These trials are only to test my faith, to see whether it is strong and pure. It is being tested as fire tests gold and purifies it – and my faith is far more precious to You, Lord, than mere gold. So if my faith remains strong after being tried in the test tube of fiery trials, it will bring me much praise and glory and honor on the day of Jesus' return.

Even though I have experienced rejection in this life, I will say that everything You say about me in Your Word is true:

I am blessed with all spiritual blessings in heavenly places in Christ (Eph. 1:3).

I am chosen by You, my Father (Eph. 1:4).

I am Your child according to the good pleasure of Your will (Eph. 1:5).

I am accepted in the Beloved (Eph. 1:6).

I am redeemed through the blood of Jesus (Eph. 1:7).

I am a person of wisdom and revelation in the knowledge of Christ (Eph. 1:17).

I am saved by Your grace (Eph. 2:5).

I am seated in heavenly places in Jesus Christ (Eph. 2:6).

I am Your workmanship (Eph. 2:10).

I am near to You by the blood of Christ (Eph. 2:13).

I am a new creation (Eph. 2:15).

I am of Your household (Eph. 2:19).

I am a citizen of heaven (Eph. 2:19).

I am a partaker of Your promises in Christ (2 Pet. 1:4).

I am strengthened with might by Your Spirit (Eph. 3:16).

I allow Christ to dwell in my heart by faith (Eph. 3:17).

I am rooted and grounded in love (Eph. 3:17).

I speak the truth in love (Eph. 4:15).

I am renewed in the spirit of my mind (Eph. 4:23).

I am Your follower (Eph. 5:1).

I walk in love (Eph. 5:2).

I am light in You (Eph. 5:8).

I walk circumspectly (Eph. 5:15).

I am filled with the Spirit (Eph. 5:18).

I am more than a conqueror (Rom. 8:37).

I am an overcomer (Rev. 12:11).

I am Your righteousness in Christ Jesus (1 Cor. 1:30).

I am healed (1 Pet. 2:24).

I am free (John 8:36).

I am salt (Matt. 5:13).

I am consecrated (1 Cor. 6:11 AMP)

I am sanctified (1 Cor. 6:11).

I am victorious (1 John 5:4).

Everything You say about me is true, Lord.

In Your name I pray, amen.

Scripture References

Hebrews 4:14-16 NLT   Isaiah 51:7,8 MSG

Isaiah 53:3-5 NCV   1 Peter 3:12-17 MSG

2 Corinthians 4:18 NLT   1 Peter 1:6,7 TLB

**For further support, I encourage you to read Psalm 27 and the book of Ephesians in their entirety.

Times of Trouble

Introduction

We live in a world where nation is rising against nation, and kingdom against kingdom. There are famines and earthquakes in various places. (Read Matthew 24.) Corruption, oppression, exploitation, conspiracy and injustice are increasing. Many said it could never happen in the United States of America, but terrorism has come to our land and distrust runs rampant. Foreclosures on homes are rising, businesses are failing and many who planned carefully for their retirement are in financial crisis. Christianity and the Bible are being ridiculed. Our world is in a spiritual upheaval! During a time of trouble or calamity, it is sometimes difficult to remember the promises of God. The pressures of the moment may seem overwhelming. At such times, it is often helpful to read, meditate on, and pray the entire chapter of Psalm 91.

It may be that during a stressful time you will find this entire prayer too long. If so, draw from the Scriptures included in the following prayer. You may find yourself praying one paragraph or reading it aloud to yourself or to your family and friends.

I also encourage you to meditate on this prayer during good times. At all times, remember that faith comes by hearing, and hearing by the Word of God (Rom. 10:17).

Prayer

Father, You are a shelter for the oppressed and a refuge in times of trouble. I come to You in the name of Jesus, acknowledging You as my Shelter and Refuge. I give fear no place because You are my God!

In the day of trouble You will keep me safe—in the secret place of Your tent You hide me; You set me high upon a rock. My head is lifted about my enemies around me. I will give gifts to You with a loud voice of joy. I will sing; yes, I will sing praises to You, Lord. Listen to my cry. Show loving-kindness to me and answer me.

I have been made right with You through Christ. When I call to you for help, You hear me and rescue me from all my troubles. You are close to me, for I am bro-kenhearted. You rescue those whose spirits are crushed. Lord, I face many troubles, but You come to my rescue each time.

Thank You for being merciful and gracious to me, O God, for my soul takes refuge and finds shelter and con-fidence in You; yes, in the shadow of Your wings I take

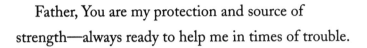

refuge and am confident until calamities and destructive storms are passed. You perform on my behalf and reward me. You bring to pass Your purposes for me, and surely You complete them!

Father, You are my protection and source of strength—always ready to help me in times of trouble.

Lord, You have given a gift—peace of mind and heart—so I won't be troubled or afraid.

By faith, I rejoice when I run into problems or trials for I know that they help me develop endurance. Endurance develops strength of character, and character strengthens my confident hope of salvation. And this hope will not lead to disappointment; such hope never disappoints or deludes or shames me—for I know how dearly God loves me, because He has given me the Holy Spirit to fill my heart with His love.

In Jesus' name, amen.

Scripture References

Psalm 9:9-10 NLT	Psalm 57:1-2 AMP
Psalm 9:9 AMP	Psalm 46:1 ERV
Psalm 27:5-7 NLV	John 14:27 NLT
2 Corinthians 5:21 NLT	Romans 5:3-5 NLT
Psalm 34:17-20 NLT	Romans 5:5 AMP

Overcoming Weariness

Introduction

The original prayer was written for a woman who had asked God for a marriage partner, and she was weary with the wait. This prayer is not limited to the unmarried who are awaiting a life-partner. Many spouses become weary with heartaches that they did not expect to encounter in marriage. Their expected marital bliss has turned into disappointment, additional wounds, and frustration. They are weary with waiting for the healing of the marriage relationship or the deliverance of a spouse, children, or other loved ones from various addictions or negative, destructive behaviors. They long for someone who will heal their wounds without judging them – someone who will love them unconditionally.

Each individual brings baggage into marriage, hoping for a miracle – each partner looking to the other for acceptance and approval.

According to the letters and comments we have received in our ministry, unmarried people experience weariness in matters that married couples may not encounter. Hopefully, we who are married share responsibilities

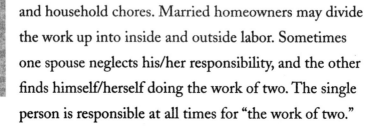

and household chores. Married homeowners may divide the work up into inside and outside labor. Sometimes one spouse neglects his/her responsibility, and the other finds himself/herself doing the work of two. The single person is responsible at all times for "the work of two."

If you have grown weary and are disappointed in your expectations, I encourage you to seek God for His plan for your life. Ask the Holy Spirit to help you trust God and not be afraid.

Prayer

Father, You see my weariness and uneasieness from continually being disappointed. It seems at times that my patience is exhausted and I am discouraged. I am weary of asking and waiting for _____.

My soul melts from heaviness; strengthen me according to Your Word.

Lord, I come to You and You will give me rest. If I do what You tell me and learn what You teach me, then whatever You tell me to do is easy. Whatever You give me to carry is not heavy.

I look to You, Lord, and Your strength; I seek Your face always. You are my Refuge and Strength, a very present and well-proved help in trouble. O my Strength, I will watch for You; You are my Defense, my Fortress and High Tower, the God who shows me mercy and steadfast love. I sing praises to You.

Father, You give power to the weak and strength to the powerless. My trust is in You, my Lord, and I am finding new strength. I am soaring high on wings like eagles. I will run and not grow weary. I will walk and not faint. I am waiting for You, Lord, and I am strong and taking heart, declaring that You are my Strength and my Defense.

Lord , You have become my salvation. You are my God and I will praise and exalt You. In Your mercy, You have led me forth, You have redeemed me. You have guided me in Your strength to Your holy habitation.

You, Sovereign Lord, have given me Your words of wisdom, so that I know how to comfort the weary. Morning by morning, You waken me and open my understanding to Your will.

Lord, You are my light and the One who saves me. So why should I fear anyone? You, Lord, protect my life so why should I be afraid? You are my shield and my God who gives me courage. I pray to You and You will answer me from Your holy mountain.

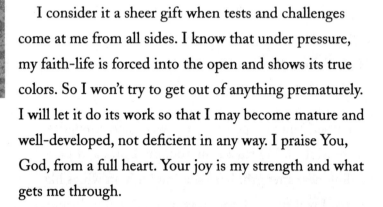

I consider it a sheer gift when tests and challenges come at me from all sides. I know that under pressure, my faith-life is forced into the open and shows its true colors. So I won't try to get out of anything prematurely. I will let it do its work so that I may become mature and well-developed, not deficient in any way. I praise You, God, from a full heart. Your joy is my strength and what gets me through.

I consider Jesus who endured such opposition from sinners so that I will not grow weary and lose heart.

Father, Your grace is all that I need. Your power works best in weakness. I will not get tired of doing what is good. At just the right time, I will reap a harvest of blessing if I don't give up. I am strong in You, Lord, and in Your mighty power.

Scripture References

Psalm 119:28 NKJV	Psalm 27:1 NCV
Matthew 11:28-30 WE	Psalm 3:3,4 NCV
1 Chronicles 16:11 NIV	James 1:2-4 MSG
Psalm 46:1 AMP	Psalm 9:1 MSG
Psalm 59:9, 17 AMP	Nehemiah 8:10
Isaiah 40:29-31 NLT	Hebrews 12:3 NIV
Psalm 27:14 NIV	2 Corinthians 12:9 NLT
Exodus 15:2, 13 NCV	Galatians 6:9 NIV
Isaiah 50:4 NLT	Ephesians 6:10 NIV

For additional strength and guidance, I suggest reading and mediating on the following passages: Psalm 6, Psalm 18, Psalm 27, Psalm 28, Psalm 38, Psalm 71.

Overcoming Worry

Introduction

It was during a time of family crisis that God taught me how to overcome worry. When I couldn't sleep, I walked the floor reading the Scriptures aloud; most often Psalm 91. As I practiced replacing worry with the Scriptures, my faith in God increased. Shaping worries into prayers of petition became a way of life.

Prayer

Father, I will turn away from evil and do good. I search for peace and work to maintain it. When my ways please You, Lord, You make even my enemies be at peace with me.

Lord, You have given me Your peace as a gift. You didn't leave me the way I am used to being left – feeling abandoned. So, for that reason, I won't be upset or distraught because You are leaving me well and whole and full of peace.

I won't worry about anything, but instead I will pray about everything. I will tell You what I need and thank You for all You have done. Then, I will experience Your peace, which exceeds anything that I can understand. Your peace will guard my heart and mind as I live in Christ Jesus.

Thank You, Lord, that You give true peace to those who depend on You. I trust You fully because of this. I let the peace of Christ rule in my heart and I am thankful. Hallelujah!

In Jesus' name, amen.

Scripture References

Philippians 4:6,7 MSG

Colossians 3:15 NIV

Psalm 34:14 NLT

Proverbs 16:7 AMP

Isaiah 26:3 NCV

John 14:27 MSG

PART I:

PERSONAL PRAYERS:
WISDOM

Confidence in Relationships

Lord, You are my hope! I will always praise You.

You alone are the Source of my confidence, faith, hope, love, peace and forgiveness. I thank You for my family, church family and friends who are here to help me develop emotionally and spiritually. I choose as my friends everyone who worships You and obeys Your commandments.

Father, You mean what You say and what You say goes. Your powerful Word is as sharp as a surgeon's scalpel, cutting through everything, whether doubt or defense, laying me open to listen and obey. I submit to You, Lord, and allow Your Word to shape my life so that I may identify and settle unresolved issues that have driven me to form unhealthy relationships in the past. I am focused on one thing: forgetting the past and looking forward to what lies ahead.

Jesus, I thank You that I have a full and true life in You, so I don't need to look to another person to bring me happiness and fulfillment because You make me so happy. I will not take responsibility for the behavior of others, but will assume responsibility for my own actions.

Lord, You are my security and You will keep my foot from being caught in a trap. You have promised to never leave or desert me. I am confident in my relationships because You are my Lord and Master. You have given me everything that I need to live a life that pleases You. All of this was given to me by Your own power. Hallelujah! I am a friend who loves all the time. I will continually think of others and with Your help, I will show them Your unconditional love.

In my relationships, I encourage love and worshipping together. I admit my faults to those with whom I am in fellowship and pray for them so that we both may be healed. When a believing person prays, it is powerful! My relationships are founded on love from a pure heart, a good conscience and a true faith in the name of Jesus. Amen.

Scripture References

Psalm 71:5 NCV	Proverbs 3:26 NLT
Psalm 92:4 MSG	Psalm 119:63 CEV
Hebrews 13:5 CEV	1 Timothy 1:5 NCV
1 Corinthians 2:15,16 MSG	2 Peter 1:3,4 CEV
Hebrews 4:12 MSG	Proverbs 17:17
Philippians 3: 13 NLT	Hebrews 10:24,25
Colossians 2:10 NCV	James 5:16 NCV

God's Wisdom and Will

Lord, You are worthy to receive glory and honor and power. You created all things and by Your will they were created and have their being. You adopted me as Your child through Jesus Christ, in accordance with Your pleasure and will. As I share the faith I have in common with others, I pray that I may come to have a complete knowledge of all the good things I have in Christ.

Father, I ask You to fill me with a knowledge of Your will through all the wisdom and understanding that the Spirit gives so that I will live a life worthy of You, Lord, and please You in every way. Let my life bear fruit in every good work, as I grow in the knowledge of God.

I roll my works upon You, Lord, and You make my thoughts agreeable to Your will, so my plans are established and succeed. You direct my steps and make them sure. I will not act thoughtlessly but will learn what You want me to do. I pray that I will stand firm in all the will of God, mature and fully assured.

Father, You have chosen me and make Your will known to me. Thank You, Holy Spirit, for leading me into all truth and telling me of things to come. God's Spirit and my spirit are in open communion. I am spiritually alive and have access to everything God's Spirit is doing. Christ knows what God is doing and I have His Spirit.

Father, I'm glad to have entered into Your rest and ceased from the weariness and pain of human labors, in Jesus' name, Amen.

<u>Scripture References</u>

Revelation 4:11 NIV   Colossians 4:12 NIV

Ephesians 1:5 NIV   Acts 22:14 WE

Philemon 1:6 GW   John 16:13 NLV

Colossians 1:9-10 NIV   1 Corinthians 2:16 MSG

Proverbs 16:3, 9 AMP   Hebrews 4:10 AMP

Ephesians 5:17 NCV

For Good Communication

Since I am Your child, Father, I am taught by You and You give me great peace. I will not copy the behaviors and customs of this world but I will let You transform me by changing the way that I think. Then, I will know Your will for me which is good and pleasing and perfect.

I will speak the truth in love and grow more like You every day. What I say will be worthwhile and right. I desire to always speak the truth with love and purpose to speak honestly in all situations.

Father, give me an eagerness for Your laws. I do not love the world or anything that comes from the world. Your love, Father, is in me. I am set free from my selfish desires and wanting everything I see. Because of Your love, I know the truth; no lie comes from the truth.

I treasure Your wisdom, Lord, and will speak words of wisdom. I will pay close attention to Your words and will always keep them in mind. For they are the key to life for those who find them; they bring health to my whole body. I will be careful of what I think because my thoughts control my behavior.

I will not be selfish or try to impress others but instead, I will be humble and think of others before myself.

I won't look out for only my interests but I will take an interest in others too.

In my life, I will think and act like You, Jesus. Amen.

Scripture References

Isaiah 54:13 NCV

Romans 12:2 NLT

Ephesians 4:15 NIV

Proverbs 8:6,8 CEV

Psalm 119:36 NLT

1 John 2:15,16,21 CEV

Proverbs 4:8,20-23 NCV

Philippians 2:2-5 NLT

To Know God's Will

Father, in Jesus' name, I thank You for guiding me along the best pathway for my life and advising me and watching over me. I thank You that I am Your child. You sent Jesus to save me and make me pure, acceptable, and holy. Thank You that I do hear Your voice. You are the Good Shepherd and I won't run from You because I know Your voice. You renew my strength and lead me on paths that are right for the good of Your name.

Thank You, Father, that my life is like sunlight at dawn that glows brighter until broad daylight. As I follow You, Lord, I believe that my life shines brighter and becomes clearer each day.

I praise You that I am a follower of Jesus who is my wisdom. You make Your will for me clear and lead me in a plain pathway. I trust in You with all my heart and do not trust in my own judgment. I will always let You lead me and You will show me which path to follow. I believe that as I trust in You completely, You will show me the way of life. Amen.

<u>Scripture References</u>

Psalm 32:8 NLT

John 10:2-5, 11, 14 NLT

Psalm 23:3 NCV

Proverbs 4:18 CEV

1 Corinthians 1:30 CEV

1 Corinthians 14:33

Proverbs 3:5,6 CEV

Psalm 16:11 NLT

Maintaining Good Relations

Father, in the name of Jesus, I will not withhold good from those who deserve it when it is in my power to help them. I will give to everyone what I owe them. I will pay my taxes and government fees to those who collect them and I will give respect and honor to those who are in authority.

I will not become tired of helping others, for I will be rewarded when the time is right if I do not give up. So, right now, every time I get the chance, I will work for the benefit of all, starting with the people closest to me in the community of faith. Help me, Father, to be a blessing to all those around me.

I will not argue just to be arguing, but will do my best to live at peace with everyone around me. Thank You, Father, for Your help in living this way. In the name of Jesus, amen.

Scripture References

Proverbs 3:27 NLT

Proverbs 3:30 CEV

Romans 13:7 NLT

Romans 12:18

Galatians 6:9,10 MSG

—

Prosperity

Father, I come to You in the name of Jesus concerning my financial situation. You are my refuge and strength, always ready to help me in times of trouble. You are more than enough for me, Lord. Your Word says that You will take care of everything that I need. You will use your wonderful riches in Christ Jesus to give me everything that I need.

(If you have not been giving tithes and offerings, include this statement of repentance in your prayer.) Forgive me for robbing You in tithes and offerings. I repent and will change my ways. I will bring my tithe to Your house . Thank You for wise financial counselors and teachers who are teaching me the principles of good stewardship.

Lord, You said, "Test me in this and see if I don't open up heaven itself to you and pour out blessings beyond your wildest dreams. Your crops will be abundant, for I will guard them from insects and disease. Your grapes will not fall from the vine before they are ripe."

Lord, I will remember that it is You who gives me the power to be successful, in order to fulfill the covenant You confirmed to my ancestors with an oath. I will never forget You and will worship only You.

You are the most generous God who gives seed to the farmer that becomes bread for my meals; You are more than extravagant with me. You give me something that I can then give away, which grows into full-formed lives, robust in God, wealthy in every way, so that I can be generous in every way, which produces within me great praise to You! Amen.

Scripture References

Psalm 46:1 NLT   Philippians 4:19 NCV

2 Corinthians 9:8 MSG

Deuteronomy 8:18,19 NLT

Malachi 3:8-12 MSG & NLT

Receiving a Discerning Heart

Father, I thank You for giving me an understanding heart so that I can know the difference between right and wrong.

I pray that my love will keep on growing and that I will grow in knowledge and understanding so that I will still be pure and innocent when Christ returns. May I remain busy until that day doing good things that bring glory and praise to You!

Father, I will trust in You with all my heart and I will not depend on my own understanding. Your commandments give me understanding so no wonder I hate every false way of life. Your Word is a lamp to guide my feet and a light for my path.

Lord, I remember Joseph, in Genesis 41:39-41 NIV, who was described as a discerning and wise man. He was put in charge of the entire land of Egypt! As You were with Joseph, so will You be with me. You will cause me to find favor at my place of employment, at home, or wherever I may be.

I pray that I will have great wisdom and understanding in spiritual things and use common sense in my personal and business decisions so that I will live the kind of life that honors and pleases You in every way. I will produce every kind of good fruit and grow in the knowledge of You. I am learning what You want me to do.

In the name of Jesus I pray, amen.

Scripture References

1 Kings 3:9 NLT	Proverbs 3:1-4
Philippians 1:9-11 CEV	Colossians 1:9,10 NCV
Proverbs 3:5 NLT	Psalm 119:104,105 NLT
Genesis 41:39-41 NIV	Ephesians 5:17 NCV
Joshua 1:5	

Selling Real Estate

Father, I thank You for the wisdom that You give me as I place my house (or other real estate) to be sold. I am preparing my house (property) in the best way so that it may be beautiful and desirable, as though I am preparing it for You to come and live in it. I am asking a fair and competitive market price and will not take advantage of a potential buyer.

Lord, I ask that You prepare and send a ready, willing, and able buyer to purchase my house (property) – a person who has the money available to pay the fair market value, who is pre-qualified and approved by a lending institution and one who has perfect timing of possession that fits my need and theirs.

Thank You for going before me and preparing the way. In Jesus name, I seek peace and ask that only truth prevail in our deliberations. I pray that everyone involved says what is true and says it with love.

Lord, I pray that if anything has been kept hidden in the dark, You will bring it out into the light. I won't ever forget kindness and truth. I wear them like a necklace and write them on my heart. Then, I will be respected as I please You and my potential buyer.

In the name of Jesus, amen.

<u>Scripture References</u>

Proverbs 2:6,9,12,15 NKJV

1 Corinthians 4:5 WE

1 Corinthians 2:9

Proverbs 3:3,4 NCV

Ephesians 4:15 WE

Setting of Proper Priorities

Father, too often I waste my time on useless, mere busywork and I am asking You to help me establish the correct priorities in my work. I confess my weakness of procrastination and lack of organization. I want to use my head and make the most of every chance that I get!

You have given me a seven-day week – six days to work and the seventh day to rest. I want to make the most of every day that You have given me. Help me to plan my time and stay focused on my assignments.

In the name of Jesus, I break down every big idea that tries to stop people from knowing God. I take every thought prisoner to make it obey You, Lord. I want to live a life of obedience to You.

Lord, You are the One who makes my plans succeed. I plan my way, but You direct my steps and make them sure. I trust You to help me organize my efforts, schedule my activities and budget my time.

Jesus, You want me to relax. You will show me how to take a real rest and learn the unforced rhythms of grace. If I keep company with You, I will learn to live freely and lightly.

By the grace given to me, I will not worry about missing out, and my everyday human concerns will be met. I will work first for Your kingdom, do what You call good and then I will have all the other things I need.

Father, through You I have a full and true life. I give all my worries and cares to You because You care about me. At the same time, I will stay alert and watch out for the enemy, the devil.

I cry out for insight and raise my voice for understanding. I make insight my priority!

Father, You sent Jesus that I might live and enjoy life to the full. Help me remember that my relationships with You and with others are more important than anything else. Amen.

Scripture References

Ephesians 5:15-16 MSG	Genesis 2:2 NIV
2 Corinthians 10:5-6 WE	Proverbs 16:3,9 AMP
Matthew 11:29 MSG	Colossians 2:10 NCV
Matthew 6:33 WE	1 Peter 5:7-8 NLT
Proverbs 2:3 AMP	John 10:10 WE

*If you do not know your strengths and weaknesses, ask the Holy Spirit to reveal them to you. The Lord speaks to us: "My grace is sufficient for you, for power is perfected in weakness" (2 Cor. 12:9 NASB).

Success of a Business

Father, Your Word says that since I am Your child
that I will receive blessings from You together with
Christ. You have qualified me to share in the inheritance
of the Kingdom of light! Where Your Word is, there is
light and also understanding. Your Word always produces fruit. It will accomplish all that You want it to and will
prosper everywhere You send it. I will put into action the
generosity that comes from my faith as I understand and
experience all the good things that I have in Christ.

Father, I put You in charge of my work and then what
I have planned will take place. Because You are working
in me, You help me want to do and be able to do what is
pleasing to You. Lord, You have given me wisdom and
understanding and showered Your kindness on me.

I want to obey your Word by doing something useful
with my hands so that I may have something to share with
those in need. By Your grace, I provide for myself and my
own family. Thank You, Father, for generously providing
all that I need. Then I will always have everything that I
need and plenty left over to share with others.

Thank You for the angels that You have assigned to
go forth and bring in customers. Jesus said, "You are the
light of the world." In His name, I will live so that others

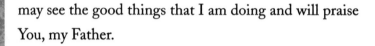
may see the good things that I am doing and will praise You, my Father.

Thank You for Your grace to seek diligence and skill in areas where I am inexperienced. Help me to understand what is right and just and fair in every relationship and dealing that I have. I will listen well to Your words and tune my ears to Your voice. I will keep Your message in plain view at all times. Then, I will really live. My body and soul and business will be bursting with health!

Father, thank You for the success of my business!

In Your name, amen.

Scripture References

Romans 8:17 NCV

Colossians 1:12 NIV

Psalm 119:130

Isaiah 55:11 NLT

Matthew 5:14,16 NLT

Proverbs 22:29

Proverbs 2:9 NIV

Proverbs 4:20-22 MSG

1 Timothy 5:8 NIV

2 Corinthians 9:8 NLT

Hebrews 1:14

Philemon 1:6 NLT

Proverbs 16:3 MSG

Philippians 2:13 NCV

Ephesians 1:7,8 NLT

Ephesians 4:28 NIV

PART II:

RELATIONAL PRAYERS: THE FATHER

Adoration:
"Your Name Be Honored as Holy"

Our Father in heaven, I honor Your name as holy.

Praise the Lord, oh my soul! I call on my entire being to praise Your holy name. You have my adoration and love this day.

I praise Your name, Elohim, the Creator of the heavens and the earth, who was in the beginning. It is You who made me and You have crowned me with glory and honor. You are the God of power and strength. I honor Your name as holy!

I praise Your name, El-Shaddai, the all-powerful One of blessings. You bless me with blessings of the skies above and of the deep springs below. I honor Your name as holy.

I praise Your name, Adonai, my Lord and my Master. You are Jehovah — the Completely Self-Existing One, always present, revealed in Jesus, who is the same yesterday, today, and forever. I honor Your name as holy.

I bless Your name, Jehovah-Jireh, the One who sees my needs and provides for them. I honor Your name as holy.

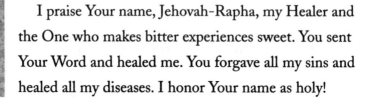

I praise Your name, Jehovah-Rapha, my Healer and the One who makes bitter experiences sweet. You sent Your Word and healed me. You forgave all my sins and healed all my diseases. I honor Your name as holy!

I praise Your name, Jehovah-M'Kaddesh, the Lord who makes me holy. You have set me apart for Yourself. I honor Your name as holy!

Jehovah-Nissi, You are my Victory, my Banner, my Standard. Your banner over me is love. When the enemy—the one who hates me—comes in like a flood, You lift up a standard—a mighty wall—against him. I honor Your name as holy!

Jehovah-Shalom, I praise Your name. You are my Peace—the peace which exceeds anything I can understand. Your peace will guard my heart and mind as I live in Christ Jesus. I honor Your name as holy!

I bless You, Jehovah-Tsidkenu, my Righteousness. You made Christ, who never sinned, to be the offering for my sin, so that I could be made right with God through Christ Jesus. I honor Your name as holy!

Jehovah-Rohi, You are my Shepherd, and I have everything I need. Because I trust in You, I will lack no good thing. I honor Your name as holy!

I praise You, Jehovah-Shammah, the One who will never leave or abandon me. You are always there. I take comfort and am encouraged and confidently and boldly say, the Lord is my Helper; I will not be seized with alarm — I will not fear or dread or be terrified. What can man do to me? I honor Your name as holy!

I worship and adore You, El-Elyon, the Most High God, who is the Possessor and Maker of heaven and earth. You are the Eternal God, the Everlasting Father, the Mighty God, the Merciful God, the Faithful God. You are Truth, Justice, Righteousness, and Perfection. You are El-Elyon—the Highest Sovereign of the heavens and the earth. I honor Your name as holy!

Father, You have made Your name and Your Word greater than anything, and You have magnified Your Word above all Your name. The Word became a human and lived among us—His name is Jesus. I honor Your name as holy! Amen.

Scripture References

Matthew 6:9 HCSB	Judges 6:24 NLT
Psalm 103:1 GNT	Philippians 4:7 NLT
Genesis 1:1-2 NIV	Jeremiah 23:5-6 NLT
Psalm 8:5 NLT	2 Corinthians 5:21 NLT

Genesis 49:24 NCV

Genesis 49:24-25 CEV

Genesis 49:25 NIV

Genesis 15:1-2, 8 ASV

Hebrews 13:8 NIV

Genesis 22:14 NKJV

Psalm 147:3 NLV

Exodus 15:23-26 CEB

Psalm 107:20 NKJV

Deuteronomy 33:27 NLT

Leviticus 20:7-8 NLT

Exodus 17:15 NLT

Song of Solomon 2:4 NCV

Isaiah 59:19 NLV

Psalm 23:1 NCV

Psalm 34:10 NLT

Ezekiel 48:35 NLT

Hebrews 13:5 NCV

Hebrews 13:6 AMP

Genesis 14:19 NLT

Genesis 14:22 AMP

Psalm 91:1 NIV

Psalm 103:3 NIV

Isaiah 9:6-7 NKJV

Deuteronomy 7:9 NKJV

Psalm 91:1 NIV

Psalm 138:2 AMP

John 1:14 NCV

Divine Intervention:

"Your Kingdom Come"

Introduction

Jesus said, "The kingdom of God is within you" (Luke 17:21 NIV). He was speaking of the spiritual kingdom. This kingdom is not a matter of eating and drinking—or physical rules and regulations—but of the righteousness, peace, and joy which the Holy Spirit gives (Rom. 14:17 NIV).

It is easy to get caught up in our present-day circumstances and forget that there is a plan that exceeds our personal goals. In this prayer I have taken the opportunity to focus on our common goal: planning for the time when Jesus returns to establish the visible Kingdom of God here on earth, and the government shall be upon His shoulders (Isa. 9:6). The Kingdom of God is not just a lot of talk; it is living by God's power (1 Cor. 4:20).

Prayer

Father, in Jesus' name, I pray according to Matthew 6:10, "Your Kingdom come." I am looking for the soon coming of our Lord and Savior, Jesus Christ.

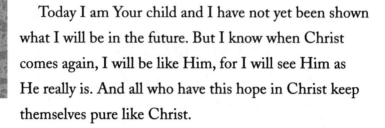

Today I am Your child and I have not yet been shown what I will be in the future. But I know when Christ comes again, I will be like Him, for I will see Him as He really is. And all who have this hope in Christ keep themselves pure like Christ.

God's grace (His unmerited favor and blessing) that can save everyone has come. It teaches me not to live according to ungodliness or worldly passions. Instead that grace teaches me to live in this present age in a self-controlled, upright way—a way that shows I serve God. I live like that while I wait for my great hope and the coming of the glory of my great God and Savior Jesus Christ.

"For the Lord Himself will come down from heaven with a commanding shout, with the voice of the archangel, and with the trumpet call of God. First, the Christians who have died will rise from their graves. Then, together with them, we who are still alive and remain on the earth will be caught up in the clouds to meet the Lord in the air. Then we will be with the Lord forever" (1 Thessalonians 4:16-17 NLT).

I'm excited and looking forward to that day when the Lord my God will come to earth and all the saints and angels with Him. Then the Lord will be King over the whole world. There will be only one Lord and His name alone will be worshipped. The government will be upon His shoulder. Of the increase of His government and peace there will be no end—from that time forward, even forever.

Father, thank You that I will join the loud voices in heaven saying, "The kingdoms of this world have become the kingdoms of our Lord and of His Christ, and He shall reign forever and ever!"

Yours, Lord, is the greatness and the power and the glory and the majesty and the splendor, for everything in heaven and earth is Yours. Yours, Lord, is the Kingdom; You are exalted as Head over all. Your Kingdom come. Amen.

Scripture References

1 John 3:2-3 NCV	Zechariah 14:5, 9 NCV
Titus 2:11 AMP	Isaiah 9:67 NKJV
Titus 2:11-13 NCV	Revelation 11:15 NKJV
1 Chronicles 29:11 NIV	
1 Thessalonians 4:16-17 NLT	

Submission:

"Your Will Be Done"

Father, in the name of Jesus, I pray that the will of God be done in my life as it is in heaven. I am Your masterpiece. You created me anew in Christ Jesus so I can do the good things your planned for me long ago—living the good life You prearranged and made ready for me to live.

Teach me to do Your will, Father, for You are my God. May your gracious Spirit lead me forward on a firm footing. Just as you planned Father, Jesus gave His life for my sins in order to rescue me from this evil world. All glory to God!

In the name of Jesus, I am not conformed to this age, but I am transformed by the renewing of my mind so I may discern the good, pleasing, and perfect will of God. My body is the temple of the Holy Spirit who lives in me and was given to me by God. I do not belong to myself—God bought me with a high price, so I honor God with my body. God wants me to use this body in the right way by keeping it holy and by treating it with dignity instead of abusing it like the people who do not know God.

Father, thank You that even before You made the world, You loved me and chose me in Christ to be holy and without fault in Your eyes. You decided in advance to adopt me into Your own family by bringing me to Yourself through Jesus Christ. This is what You wanted to do and it gave You great pleasure! I want Your will done in my life here on earth as it is planned in heaven, amen.

Scripture References

Matthew 6:9-10 HCSB

Romans 12:2 HCSB

Ephesians 2:10 NLT

Ephesians 2:10 AMP

Psalm 143:10 NLT

Ephesians 1:4-5 NLT

Galatians 1:4 NLT

1 Corinthians 6:19-20 NLT

1 Thessalonians 4:4-5 NLV

Provision:

"Give Us Today Our Daily Bread"

Father, in the name of Jesus, give us today our daily bread. Just as David said in the Psalms, I have never seen the godly abandoned or their children begging for bread. Thank You, Lord, for food, clothing, and shelter.

With Your help, I am learning not to worry about everyday life—whether I have enough food and drink, or clothes to wear. My life is more than food, and my body is more than clothing.

The bread of idleness (gossip, discontent, and self-pity) I will not eat. You, my Father, supply all my needs from Your glorious riches, which have been given to me in Christ Jesus.

I do not live on bread alone, but by everything You say. Father, when Your words came, I listened to every one. I belong to You, Lord God Almighty, and so Your words fill my heart with joy and happiness.

Jesus, You are the Word that became flesh and lived among us. You are the Bread of Life that gives me life, the Living Bread. You came down from heaven and gave Your body for the life of the world. Because I eat of this Bread, I will live forever.

Thank You, Father, for both physical and spiritual provision in Christ Jesus. Amen.

Scripture References

Matthew 6:11 HCSB

Psalm 37:25 NLT

Matthew 6:25 NLT

Proverbs 31:27 AMP

Philippians 4:19 NLT

Matthew 4:4 NCV

Jeremiah 15:16 GNT

John 1:14 NCV

John 6:48-51 AMP

Forgiveness:

"Forgive Us Our Debts"

Father, I forgive everyone who has sinned against me, as You have forgiven me for my sins. I understand that unless I am willing to forgive others, You cannot forgive me. Your Word says if I forgive the sins of anyone, they are forgiven; if I do not forgive them, they are not forgiven. And so Father I choose to forgive, to love my enemies, and to pray for those who persecute me.

In Jesus' name I bring _____ before You. Bless him/her and let their mind be opened to see the light of the Gospel that displays the glory of Christ.

Father, not only will I pray for _____, but I set myself to do good to them and love them in the Lord, even as You love them. My desire is to be like You and I can do everything through Christ because He gives me strength.

Father, thank You for Your great peace in this situation, for I love Your law and refuse to be offended. Great blessings belong to me because I am grafted into the Vine, Christ Jesus.

I roll this work upon You, Father — I commit and trust it wholly to You. You cause my thoughts to become agreeable to Your will, and my plans are established and succeed. Amen.

Scripture References

Matthew 6:12 HCSB, NLT

Matthew 6:14-15 NLT

John 20:23 NIV

Matthew 5:44 NIV

Luke 6:27-30 NLT

2 Corinthians 4:4 NIV

Ephesians 5:1 NCV

Philippians 4:13 NCV

Psalm 119:165 AMP

Luke 7:23 ERV

Proverbs 16:3 AMP

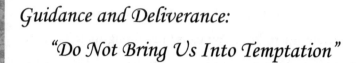

Guidance and Deliverance:
"Do Not Bring Us Into Temptation"

Father, I pray You deliver me from the evil one. The temptations in my life are no different from what others experience. And You are faithful—You will not allow the temptation to be more than I can stand. Thank You Father, that when I am tempted, You show me a way out so I can endure.

When trouble comes my way, I consider it an opportunity for great joy. I know when my faith is tested my endurance has a chance to grow.

When I am tempted, I will not say, "God is tempting me." God is never tempted to do wrong, and He never tempts anyone else.

Thank You, Jesus, for giving Your life for my sins, just as God the Father planned, in order to rescue me from this evil world. All glory to God forever!

God's power working in me can do much more than anything I can ask or imagine. So Father, I will keep watch and pray that I will not give in to temptation, in Jesus' name, amen.

<u>Scripture References</u>

Matthew 6:13 HCSB

James 1:2-3 NLT

James 1:13 NLT

1 Corinthians 10:13 NLT

Galatians 1:4-5 NLT

Ephesians 3:20 NCV

Matthew 26:41 NLT

Praise:

"Yours Is the Kingdom"

Praise the Lord's greatness with me! Let us highly honor His name together!

As for God, His way is perfect. The Word of the Lord has stood the test. You are a shield for all who go to You for refuse.

Let the words of my mouth and meditation of my heart be pleasing in Your eyes, my Lord, my Rock and the One who saves me.

Your Word has given me new life. Your Word, Lord, will last forever. It stands firm in heaven. Your Word is a lamp to guide my feet and a light for my path.

All of Your Word is true, and every one of Your regulations, which are always right, will last forever.

I praise Your name for Your unfailing love and faithfulness; for Your promises are backed by all the honor of Your name.

Accept my prayer like incense placed before You, and my praise like the evening offering. Lord, take control of my tongue; help me be careful about what I say.

I give thanks to You, Lord—a sacrifice that truly honors You. As I keep to Your path, You reveal Your salvation to me.

I am always praising You; all day long I honor You. Because Your love is better than life, I will praise You. I will praise You as long as I live; I will lift up my hands in prayer to Your name.

Your laws are my joy! They give me wise advice. All this in the name of the Lord Jesus I pray, amen.

Scripture References

Matthew 6:13 HCSB

Psalm 138:2 NLT

Psalm 141:2-3 NCV

Psalm 50:23 NLT

Psalm 71:8 NCV

Psalm 63:3-4 NCV

Psalm 119:24 CEB

Psalm 34:3 GW

Psalm 18:30 NLV

Psalm 19:14 NLV

Psalm 119:50 NLV

Psalm 119:89 GNT

Psalm 119:105 GNT

Psalm 119:160 NLV

PART II:

RELATIONAL PRAYERS:
CHILDREN

Adult Children

Father, I bring _____ before You, asking You
to show him/her Your wonderful plan for his/her life;
make it clear to him/her. You have rescued him/her from
the dark power of Satan and brought _____
into the kingdom of Your dear son, Jesus. Father, give
him/her spiritual wisdom and insight so that he/she may
grow in You and so that they will understand the confident hope that You have given to those You called.

_____ made some decisions that could have
destroyed him/her, but You remain faithful even when
we are unfaithful. Thank You that You will rebuild and
restore the wasted years and all the heartaches. You are
the One who saves, forgives and only You will satisfy
_____. As he/she stands now at a crossroads, may
he/she hear and know Your voice. Open his/her eyes that
he/she might see and choose life. Thank you for hearing
and answering my prayer in the name of Jesus.

Scripture References

Jeremiah 29:11

Colossians 1:9, 13 CEV

Ephesians 1:17-19 NLT

2 Timothy 2:13 NLT

Isaiah 58:12 CEV

Jeremiah 30:17

Psalm 103:2-5 NCV

John 10:4-5

John 11:41

Children

Father, in the name of Jesus, I pray and confess Your Word over my children and surround them with my faith- faith in Your Word that You are watching over it to see that it is fulfilled. I believe that all of my children will be Your disciples taught of the Lord, and that they will enjoy great peace because You will fight my enemies and save my children!

Father, You will work out Your plans for my life and theirs. I give all my worries and cares about my children to You, Lord, because I know You care about my children and me. I know You are able to keep safe what I have trusted to You.

I confess that my children obey their parents in the Lord, because this is right. My children _____honor their father and mother; this is the first commandment that has a promise attached to it, "so they will live well and have a long life." I believe that my children will choose life so that they will live. I believe that they will love You and will listen obediently to You and firmly embrace You. Because of this, my children will be the head of things and not the tail. They will be at the top of things and not the bot-

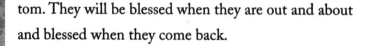
tom. They will be blessed when they are out and about and blessed when they come back.

Thank You for commanding Your angels to protect my children wherever they go. You are their place of safety and protection. You keep their feet grounded and lift their head high.

As parents, we won't come down too hard on them; we won't crush their spirits. We will not irritate or provoke them to anger but we will take them by the hand and lead them in Your way. We will direct them onto the right path and when they are older, they will not leave it.

Lord, our Lord, how majestic is Your name throughout the earth! You have made Your glory higher than heaven! Through the praise of children and infants, You have established a stronghold against Your enemies to silence them. I will be glad and rejoice in You. My children's enemies turn back; they stumble and perish before You. Amen.

Scripture References

Jeremiah 1:12 CEB

Isaiah 54:13 CEB & NLT

Isaiah 49:25 NCV

Psalm 138:8 NLT

Colossians 3:21 MSG

Psalm 91:11 NLT

Psalm 91:2 NCV

Psalm 3:3 MSG

1 Peter 5:7 NLT

1 Timothy 1:12 WE

Children at School

Father, in Jesus' name, I speak Your Word this day over my children as they pursue their education and training at school. You are working in them, giving them the desire and the power to do what pleases You. They will always be on the top and never at the bottom.

You will cause my children to be respected and to be pleasing to both You and to their teachers and class-mates. I ask You to give them wisdom so they can be capable of learning and understanding in all their subjects.

Thank You for giving_____(name your children) an appreciation for education; help them understand that the source of all knowledge is in You. You are creating in them an appetite for education and a desire to learn and know more. You will guide them as they learn, grow and achieve. I pray that they will be diligent in all their ways. I pray for my children, asking that they be made wise and would understand what it means to know You better.

Father, I thank You that my children have protection because they stay in Your shadow. You are their fortress and their place of safety and they can always trust in You. My children will know mercy, grace and truth. They will stand rooted and grounded in Your love, and will not be influenced by every new teaching; they will not fall into the tricks of following the wrong path.

Thank You for the angels that protect my children wherever they go. They don't have to be afraid of anything because evil will not touch them or conquer them. You rescue them from every trap! Thank You that they are confident and fearless and can face their foes triumphantly.

I pray that my children's teachers will be godly men and women of integrity. Give their teachers understanding hearts and wisdom to walk in the ways of virtue. In Jesus' name. Amen.

Scripture References

Philippians 2:13 NLT	Psalm 91:1,2 CEV
Deuteronomy 28:1,2,13 NLT	Ephesians 4:14 NCV
Proverbs 3:4 NCV	Psalm 91:3-11 NLT
1 Kings 4:29	Ephesians 1:17 CEV
Daniel 1:4	Psalm 112:8 NLT

Children with Special Needs

Father, You are the God of miracles and You have performed true miracles throughout history. I pray as Hannah of the Old Testament, asking for Your grace to be manifested in this special child you have entrusted to us.

You formed our child's inward parts; You knitted _____ together in the womb. I praise You, for he/she is fearfully and wonderfully made. Wonderful are Your works. His/Her frame was not hidden from You when he/she was being made in secret, skillfully woven in the depths of the earth. Your eyes saw his/her unformed substance; in your book were written every one of the days that were formed for him/her, when as yet there was none of them. How precious to us are Your thoughts, O God!

I pray for my child who has special needs, asking You for wisdom to teach him/her about You, our Father-God, and Your unconditional love. Flood our hearts with light and help us understand the hope that was given when You gave us this beautiful, precious gift. Thank You for our child who is a blessing to us. I ask You to give peace that passes all understanding to each of us. I pray for _____ to be healthy, for this precious one to be saved and filled with Your Spirit, and for the fruit and gifts of the Spirit to be present in him/her.

I pray that _____ will always put hope in You so that he/she will have no reason to be discouraged or sad. O Lord, You are a shield around _____ and the One who holds his/her head high. Your joy makes him/her strong!

Nothing is too hard or impossible for You. Because we believe and our faith is in You, all things are possible to us. May my prayer be as sweet incense rising- a sweet fragrance to You! Praise the Lord!

In the name of Jesus I pray. Amen

Scripture References

Hebrews 4:16 NIV	Psalm 145:14
Jeremiah 1:12 NCV	Psalm 3:3
Ephesians 1:17,18 CEV	Nehemiah 8:10 NCV
Psalm 119:89	Ephesians 2:10
Luke 1:37	2 Corinthians 1:3
Mark 9:23 NCV	1 Thessalonians 5:23
Psalm 141:2 AMP & MSG	Psalm 42:22 NCV
Psalm 139:13-17 (NKJV)	

Children's Future

Father, Your Word tells me that children are a gift
and reward from You. You promise that they will have
much peace when taught in Your ways. I dedicate
_____to You today, that they may be raised
as You desire and will follow the path that You choose
for them. Father, I speak Your Word this day over them.
I thank You that when we speak Your words out, they
don't return to You without doing everything that You
send them to do.

Heavenly Father, I commit myself as a parent to teach
_____right from wrong, trusting in Your
promise that when they are grown, they will still do
right. I give all my worries of raising my children to You,
my Lord, knowing that You care for them and me. I will
not provoke my children but I will love them and leave
them in Your care. I will do as Your Word tells me to
and teach my children Your commands. I will talk about
them when we are sitting at home, on the road, when we
lie down and when we get up. Thank You for grace to
speak Truth to them. I know that Your power works best
where I am weak.

My children obey and honor both their parents,
which is the first commandment with a promise. They

will have long and happy lives. My children are godly and not ashamed of it, for they know in Whom they trust. They know that You love them and that if they search for You, they will surely find You. I thank You that as they grow, they will come to know You who came to find and restore those who are lost. I thank You that You will see to their salvation and they will walk in obedience to Your ways.

Heavenly Father, I thank You now for sending workers across my children's paths who show them the way of salvation through Your Son, Jesus. I am thankful that we are aware of Satan's schemes and escape from his trap. You have given my children the grace and strength to walk through the gate to life.

I pray that even as Jesus became wise and grew strong, so my children are blessed with the same wisdom and You are pouring out Your favor and blessings on them.

I praise You in advance for my children's future spouses. You desire that my children to be holy and make wise decisions concerning their bodies during their dating years. I speak blessings to the future marriage of each of my children and believe that they will have godly households, letting the love and faith of Christ Jesus be

their pattern. Continue to prepare them to be the men and women of God that You desire them to be.

My children are learning to be diligent and hard-working. You promise great blessings to them and they will always have more than enough. Serving You helps them in every way by bringing blessings in this life and in the future life, too.

Father, thank You for protecting my children and being their place of safety. I trust in You for all of this.

In Jesus' name I pray. Amen.

Scripture References

Psalm 127:3 NLT

Isaiah 54:13 NCV

Isaiah 55:11 CEV

Proverbs 22:6 CEV

1 Peter 5:7 NCV

Ephesians 6:4

Deuteronomy 6:7 NCV

2 Corinthians 12:9 NLT

Ephesians 6:1-3 CEV

2 Timothy 1:12

Matthew 7:14 CEV

Luke 2:52

Hebrews 13:4

1 Thessalonians 4:3 CEV

Ephesians 5:22-25

2 Timothy 1:13 CEV

Proverbs 13:11

Proverbs 20:13 NCV

Romans 12:11

1 Timothy 4:8 NCV

Proverbs 8: 17,32 NLT

Psalm 91:1,11 NLT

Luke 19:10 MSG

Matthew 9:38

2 Corinthians 2:11

2 Timothy 2:26 NLT

Job 22:30

To Know Who They Are in Christ

Father, in the name of Jesus I speak over my children that they have the mind of Christ. Teach them to understand what Christ is thinking! I thank You, Lord, that they are set free by Your blood and they have forgiveness of sins and they know the richness of Your grace.

I ask You to give them wisdom and eyes to see clearly and to understand all You have done for them. Make their way plain so that they will know what pleases You and give them the courage to do Your will.

May they always live in fellowship with You, for they are Your children in Christ Jesus. They can do everything through You because You give them strength.

Open their eyes that they may understand that they have been made the righteousness of God in Christ Jesus and that they are brand new creations in You. The past is forgotten and everything is new. You have chosen them and they are accepted. They are light in a dark world and completely victorious through You.

Thank You, Father, for loving them and giving to them everything that they need in this life.

Scripture References

Ephesians 1

Romans 6:11

1 Corinthians 1:30 NLT

Ephesians 5:8 MSG

1 Corinthians 2:16 CEV

Romans 8:1

Galatians 3:26

2 Corinthians 5:17 CEV

Romans 8:37 NCV

Philippians 4:13 NLT

Peaceful Sleep

Introduction

I know that when your children are young, especially babies, that sleep can be very inconsistent and the nights exhausting. I want to encourage you to pray this prayer over your child. Although their sleep might not become consistent for months and sometimes years, remember that this is just a season and "this too shall pass." Our firstborn slept all night for the first time when he was eighteen months old, but we made it. Our second child slept all night from the time we brought her home from the hospital, for which I was very grateful. The two younger children followed the "norm," sleeping all night after a period of time. Praise God that He made a way for us. Christ Jesus gives you the strength to make it through anything (Philippians 4:13 MSG).

Prayer

Father, thank You for peaceful sleep and for Your angels that protect us. Praise the Lord for angels who are mighty and carry out Your plans. They listen for Your instructions and obey Your voice. You command Your angels to protect us wherever we go.

We capture every thought and make it obey You, Father. I thank You that Your Word says that we can go to bed without fear and we can lie down and sleep soundly. Praise You, Lord for being our guide. Even in the darkest night, we feel Your leading. We will always look to You as You stay close beside us and protect us from fear. With all of our hearts, we rejoice and are glad that we can safely rest. You give sleep to Your children. Thank You, Father, that we can sleep soundly because You keep us safe!

Scripture References

Psalm 34:7 CEV

Psalm 103:20 NCV & NLT

Psalm 91:11 CEV

2 Corinthians 10:5 NCV

Proverbs 3:24 NLT

Psalm 16:7-9 CEV

Psalm 127:2 NCV

Psalm 4:8

Salvation of Grandchildren

Father, I come before You with the names of my children and their children upon my heart as a continual reminder before You. I ask You, Lord, to raise up and send the perfect person to each one to share the gospel message in a way that they will hear and understand. Father, thank You for preparing their hearts and bringing them to repentance by Your kindness and love. My children will not be able to resist the sweet drawing of the Holy Spirit.

Your Spirit is here to show the people of this world the truth about sin and God's justice and the judgment. Father, by Your Spirit You will reveal to them that Jesus is the Son of God, just as You did to Peter in Matthew 16.

Father, I use Your weapons that You have provided for me to knock down the enemy's strongholds that would try to keep my children from hearing and understanding the truth. In the name of Jesus, I break down strongholds and thoughts that would keep them from knowing You.

My children and grandchildren call upon You and they are saved and being saved! They confess that You are Lord and they are turning from darkness to light. By faith, I thank You now for their salvation and redemption. Jesus is Lord over my family!

Scripture References

Exodus 28:29 NCV

Romans 10:9,10

1 John 1:9

2 Corinthians 5:17

John 3:16

John 6:37 NIV

John 10:10

Romans 3:23

2 Corinthians 5:19

John 16:8,9 CEV

Romans 5:8

John 14:6

Romans 10:13

Ephesians 2:1-10 NCV

John 1:12

2 Corinthians 5:21

Strong Willed Child

Father, thank You that I can come to you to vent and bring my frustrations to You. I find it difficult to help _____ with his/her schoolwork and the relationships at school and on the playground. I know sometimes he/she feels so unloved and alone. It hurts my heart when I don't know how to convince them that You have made them in an amazing and wonderful way. Give _____(name of child) revelation of Your unconditional love for him/her. _____ loves Your Word and Your promises.

I know in my heart that You loved _____ from long ago and chose him/her to be a voice of hope to his/her generation. I ask You to help me overcome my feeling of hopelessness as I try to reach him/her. Forgive me for the mistakes that I have made; tell me what to say and show me what to do. I desire to love _____ with the love You have placed in my heart by Your Spirit.

Even though _____ may struggle with perfectionism, help me teach him/her that You are greater than any mistakes he/she makes and that he/she can use his/her perceived failures as stepping stones. You are preparing him/her for the good things that You have planned for them to do. Your kindness and love will always be with _____ each day of his/her life.

I declare that _____ (name of child or names of children) will fulfill his/her divine destiny and win many people for You! Amen.

Scripture References

Psalm 139:14 NCV

Philippians 4:13

Psalm 119:140

Romans 8:28

Jeremiah 31:3

Ephesians 2:10

Ephesians 1:4 CEV

Psalm 23:6

Psalm 25:4 NCV

To Understand Their Value

Father, I come before Your throne where I can receive mercy and grace to help me know how to encourage my children, _____. I receive and welcome these children as gifts from You. They are my reward and I will pray for them and not give up! I will love them unconditionally and build them up, affirming their strengths. Give me wisdom to hear beyond their words and to help them explore how they can overcome their weaknesses. Father, thank You for the Holy Spirit who gives them encouragement and assures them they are wonderfully and fearfully made.

Open their eyes and show them that You are merciful and it is Your wonderful kindness that saves them. You raised them from death to life with Christ and You have given them a place with Him in heaven.

You chose my children before the foundation of the world. You made them who they are and they are Your design. Because You are our God, You will guard them as You would guard Your own eyes. You will hide them in the shadow of Your wings. Hallelujah!

Scripture References

Hebrews 4:16 NCV

Ephesians 2:4-6 CEV

John 15:16

Psalm 17:8 NLT

Psalm 127:3 NLT

Ephesians 1:4

Ephesians 2:10

To Walk in Faith and Power

Father, I thank You that my children have power because the Holy Spirit has come upon them and they will
tell everyone about You all over the world!

In the name of Jesus, I have not stopped giving
thanks to You for _____(names of
children). I always remember them in my prayers asking
that You give them a spirit of wisdom and revelation to
know You better. May they know that Your power is very
great for all of us who believe and that this power is the
same as the great strength God used to raise Christ from
the dead.

Father, thank You for giving to each of my children a
measure of faith. It is by Your grace that they have been
saved through faith and they live by the faith of the Son
of God who has shown them great mercy. You love them
and gave Your life for them. They are strong in You,
Lord, and in Your mighty strength.

I pray that from Your glorious and unlimited resources;
You will empower them with inner strength through
Your Spirit that they may know how wide, how long,
how high and how deep Your love is. May they be made
complete with all the fullness of life and power that
comes from You.

All glory to You, God, who is able through Your mighty power to accomplish infinitely more than we might ask or think. Amen!

Scripture References

Acts 1:8 CEV

Romans 12:3

Galatians 2:20 CEV

Ephesians 3:16-20 NLT

Ephesians 1:16-20 NCV

Ephesians 2:8

Ephesians 6:10 CEV

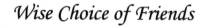

Wise Choice of Friends

Father, I come boldly to Your throne where I will receive Your mercy and find grace to help me when I need it the most! I ask You to help my children meet new friends. I know that You are the source of love and friendship. Every good action and every perfect gift is from You, God. You never deny us any good thing so I am convinced that it is Your will for my children to have godly friendships.

Your Word reveals the purpose and value of healthy friendships. Holy Spirit, I ask You to teach each of my children what he/she needs to know to be a good friend. Help them to be friendly and love at all times. Help them to live in peace with everyone as much as possible.

I pray that when they and their friends come together, they will encourage each other and build each other up instead of bringing each other down. Help them not to play favorites but to honor You by accepting each other just as You accepted them.

Help them to be kind and loving to each other and to forgive each other just as You forgave them in Christ. I pray that they get along with each other and learn to be considerate of one another, cultivating a life in common.

Help them to stand together with one spirit and one purpose to share the Good News with others. May their hearts be joined together in love, that they will truly know You in a personal relationship. May they love each other so much that they would be willing to put their life on the line for each other.

I thank You, Father, for my children's new friends. In Jesus' name I pray, amen.

Scripture References

Hebrews 4:16 NLT

James 1:17 NCV

Psalm 84:11 CEV

Ecclesiastes 4:9,10

Proverbs 13:20

Proverbs 18:24

Proverbs 17:17 NCV

Romans 12:18 NIV

James 2:1 NLT

Romans 15:7 CEV

Ephesians 4:2,32 NCV

1 Corinthians 1:10 MSG

Philippians 1:27 NLT

Philippians 2:2

Colossians 2:2 CEV

John 15:13 MSG

PART II:

RELATIONAL PRAYERS: MARRIAGE AND FAMILY

Abusive Family Situation

Introduction

At the close of a meeting a few years ago, I was approached by an attractive woman who shared about the physical and emotional abuse she had suffered in her marriage. I encouraged her to go to her pastor for counseling, and was astonished by the response of this well educated woman. She had been told by both her husband and her pastor that the beatings were because of her "rebellious nature."

When we turn to the Scriptures, we find that God is much more merciful than religious leaders who devalue women. Jesus is our example, and in one incident He turned around and walked away from the crowd who would have thrown Him off a cliff (Luke 4:28-30). There are times to take action; change brings change. Often we want God to do something when all the time, He is waiting for us to do something: "Trust God from the bottom of your heart; don't try to figure out everything on your own. Listen for God's voice in everything you do, everywhere you go; he's the one who will keep you on track" (Prov. 3:5,6 MSG).

Prayer

In the name of Jesus, I am the redeemed and I plead the blood of Jesus over my family. Abuse is exposed by the light. When the light shines on something , it can be seen and today, the evil power of abuse is broken and cast down out of my family.

Father, You love me and my family so much that You sent Your very own Son, Jesus, to die for our sin so we could live with You forever. Thank You for coming so that we could have a real and eternal life, more and better than we ever dreamed of. I pray that I may become like You, for I am Your child and You love me.

Uncontrollable, irrational anger, rage, and abuse are a curse. Lord, reveal the steps that I should take to break this curse that has been passed down from former generations. Today this behavior is no longer tolerated and shall not be passed down to my children. Jesus redeemed my children and me from the curse by becoming a curse for us. I will use everything that You have given me so that I can stand against the tricks of the devil.

By Your grace, Father, I will live my life in love. Your love in me is not a feeling, but a decision to love with more than my words or speech but with action and truth. I was once full of darkness, but now I have light from the

Lord. So, I will live as a person of light! The light within me produces only what is good and right and true.

Lord, lead me on paths that are right for the good of Your name. I will be very careful how I live. I will not live like those who are not wise, but I will live wisely. I will use every chance I have for doing good, because these are evil times.

Father, I have overcome (conquered) my enemy by the blood of the Lamb and by my testimony. In the name of Jesus, I am committing my life to You – to obey You. Teach me the way of life for me and my family. In Your presence is total joy and at Your right hand I will find eternal pleasures.

Teach me how to guard my heart above all else. I am growing in grace and in the knowledge of You, being changed within by a new way of thinking. I won't worry about anything and I will talk to You about everything. I thank You for what You given me, and ask You for the wisdom and courage to follow where You lead me. In the name of Jesus, amen.

<u>Scripture References</u>

John 3:16 NIV	1 Peter 3:18
John 10:10 MSG	Revelation 12:11 AMP
Ephesians 5:1 Phillips	Psalm 16:11 CEB
1 John 3:18 CEB	Galatians 3:13 CEB
Ephesians 5:8,9 NLT	Ephesians 6:10 WE
Psalm 23:3 NCV	Ephesians 5:13 WE
Ephesians 5:15,16 NCV	Luke 4:18
Ezekiel 22:30 NLT	Psalm 107:20 MSG
John 16:8 MSG	Matthew 5:44
Ezekiel 11:19 NLT	Proverbs 4:23 NLT
Matthew 9:38 NIV	Proverbs 4:23 NLT
Matthew 6:10	Philippians 4:6 WE
Colossians 1:13 Phillips	

Adopting a Child

Father, You alone know my heart and how I longed to conceive and bear my children in my own body. Father, I have blamed You, and ask You to forgve me for railing against You. This has not been an easy cross to bear; I and my family have suffered from the stress of my emotional upheavals. But You, my Lord, by the power of Your Word, have healed me and saved me. Thank You, Lord, for setting me free from my suffering and giving us a child after our own heart. People even say that he/she favors us.

Thank You that by Your power working in us, You can do much more than anything we can ask or imagine. Thank You for giving us the desire to adopt a child and for leading us to this special child that You had planned for us long ago. I ask You to help us train him/her in the right way so that when he/she is older, they will not stray from it.

Prepare our hearts for the day that he/she understands about adoption; give us the right words to say to let him/her know that he/she has always been loved and that this family chose him/her to be a part of us. Help us to show him/her that he/she is a precious member of our family and the one God picked for us!

I ask You to help him/her know that he/she is like a letter written by You and delivered to us. Not a letter written with ink, but written in our hearts by Your Spirit. Father God, thank You for loving _____, we are thankful that Your thoughts are for good and not for disaster, to give him/her a future and a hope. You made _____ in an amazing and wonderful way. You destined that we would be his/her father and mother. We know very well what God has done is wonderful!

Scripture References

Psalm 107:20 CEV

Luke 4:18 CEV

Ephesians 3:20 NCV

Psalm 37:4

Colossians 2:15

Ephesians 2:10 NLT

Proverbs 22:6 NCV

Ephesians 1:4

2 Corinthians 3:3 CEV

Jeremiah 29:11 NLT

Psalm 139:14 NCV

Blessing the Household

Father, as the head of this household, I declare and decree, "Me and my family are going to worship and serve the Lord!"

All praise to You, the Father of our Lord Jesus Christ, who has blessed my family and me with every spiritual blessing in the heavenly realms in Christ. I am led by the Spirit to worship You according to the truth. I know that You seek out those who want to worship You.

Lord, I acknowledge and welcome the presence of Your Holy Spirit here in our home. We thank You, Father, that Your Son, Jesus, is here with us because we have come together in His name and the Holy Spirit is ever present with us.

Lord, Your divine power has given us everything we need to live and to serve You. We have these things because we know You and You called us by Your glory and goodness.

As spiritual leader of this home, I declare on the authority of Your Word that my family will be powerful in the land; my children will be honest people who will be blessed. Their houses will be full of wealth and riches and their goodness will continue forever.

In the name of Jesus I pray. Amen

Scripture References

Revelation 1:6

Joshua 24:15 CEV

Ephesians 1:3 NLT

John 4:23 CEV

Matthew 18:20

2 Peter 1:3 NCV

Psalm 112:2-3 NCV

Broken Marriage Vows

Introduction

This prayer was originally written for a wife whose husband had been unfaithful. If you are a husband who has been betrayed, simply change this prayer to fit your situation.

Prayer

Father, when we became husband and wife, You made us one. My husband has dishonored me, and the rejection and betrayal I'm feeling right now is very painful.

You witnessed the vows we made to each other. Those vows have now been broken, and I am alone. Forgive us for speaking our vows so casually and without understanding.

I ask You to forgive my shortcomings and failures concerning my marriage. Help me to learn from this tragedy and grow spiritually and receive complete emotional wholeness. Give me the grace to forgive my husband of his infidelity.

Only You know my husband's heart and the decisions he will make concerning his future. If

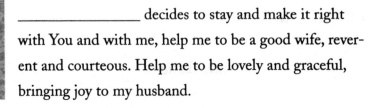

_____ decides to stay and make it right with You and with me, help me to be a good wife, reverent and courteous. Help me to be lovely and graceful, bringing joy to my husband.

If _____ decides to leave, give me the grace to let him go. I know You hate divorce, but will allow it when a spouse has been unfaithful.

Father, I acknowledge You and You direct my path. You promised that You would never abandon me or leave me without support, therefore, I put all my trust in You because You watch over Your Word to perform it.

In Jesus' name I pray. Amen.

Scripture References

Titus 2:4-6 NLT	Ephesians 5:21 MSG
Proverbs 5:15-19 NCV	Jeremiah 1:12 NASB
Hebrews 9:14 NIV	Hebrews 13:5 NIV
1 Corinthians 11:3 NLT	

Compatibility in Marriage

Father, in the name of Jesus, God's love has been poured out in our hearts through the Holy Spirit who has been given to us. Because of this, my spouse and I are learning to never give up and to care more for each other than ourselves. We don't strut or have a swelled head. We don't force ourselves on each other and we aren't always about "me first." We don't fly off the handle and we don't keep score of the sins of each other. We don't revel when one grovels; we take pleasure in the flowering of truth. We put up with anything and trust God always. We always look for the best and never look back but always keep going until the end. Our love never dies.

We are no longer babies. We will not be tossed about like a ship that the waves carry one way and then another, but we will speak the truth in love and grow up in every way into Christ. We are kind and loving to each other and forgive each other just as God forgave us in Christ. We imitate God in everything we do because we are His children.

Thank You, Father, that our marriage grows stronger each day because it is founded on Your Word and on Your kind of love. We give you the praise for it all, Father, in the name of Jesus. Amen.

Scripture References

Romans 5:5 AMP

1 Corinthians 14:1

1 Corinthians 13:4-8 AMP

Ephesians 5:1, 2 AMP

Ephesians 4:14,15,32 NCV

Desiring to Have a Baby

Father, my spouse and I kneel in prayer to You. Our Father, You are wonderful and glorious and all beings in heaven and on earth were created by You. We are strong in You and thank You that You live in our hearts as we trust You. We stand firm in Your love. Your love is too wonderful to be measured, Lord. Because of Your love, our lives will be filled with all that You are.

We praise You, Lord, because You give children to the woman who has none and You make her a happy mother. We thank You because You are the One who is building our family. We receive Your gift of children, for they are a reward from You.

Thank You that we will bear children as a vine bears grapes and our household will be lush as a vineyard. The children around our table will be as fresh and promising as young olive shoots. We stand in awe of You, Lord. Thank You for blessing those who fear You!

In Jesus' name we pray, amen.

Scripture References

Ephesians 3:14-19 CEV   1 John 3:22-23 CEV

Psalm 113:9 NCV   Psalm 128:3-4 MSG

Psalm 127:3 NLT

Handling Household Finances

Introduction

The following prayers may be prayed individually or as a couple. In preparation for marriage, it is great wisdom for the couple to discuss finances. Each party comes with an individual view of how to handle money—spending and/or saving. It is wise to consider setting up a budget that is agreeable to both.

There is a danger in the tendency to assume that the other party has the same opinions and ideas about money or, in case of disagreement, that one's own way is right and the other person's is wrong. Financial differences are one of Satan's greatest weapons for introducing strife and bringing pressure to bear on a marriage. Spending money can quickly evolve into an emotional experience, causing many other problems.

God is El-Shaddai; God Almighty (Ex. 6:3 AMP)— the God who is more than enough—and His intention is that His children enjoy good health and that all may go well with them, even as their souls are getting along well (3 John 2 NIV). Two people coming into agreement with God's financial plan will offset the enemy's schemes to divide and conquer.

If you and your beloved are planning to marry or to establish a financial plan in your existing marriage, listen to one another. Understand what each other is saying. Realize that there are differences in viewpoints about money and allow for those differences. Determine who is more astute in financial matters: balancing the checkbook, paying the bills on time and making wise investments. Set aside time in your schedules to keep each other informed, review goals, and make plans. Wisdom from above is willing to yield to reason; cooperate one with another (James 3:17 AMP).

Prayer

Father, we thank You for giving us the Holy Spirit who leads us into all truth and who is with us as we discuss our financial future together. You began a good work in us and You will perfect it until the day of Christ Jesus. Help us to set up a budget that is pleasing to You and to each of us.

We fix our thoughts on You and we acknowledge You as our High Priest. Therefore, we purpose to give You the first part of our income in tithes and offerings, and worship You with them.

Father, we believe that our union has been ordained by You, and You are Lord of our marriage. We confess Your Word over our life together and our finances. As we do, we believe that Your Word will not come back empty-handed but will complete the assignment You sent it to do. Therefore, we believe in the name of Jesus that You give us everything we need, according to Your wonderful riches in Christ Jesus.

Your Word says that if we give, it will return to us in full—pressed down, shaken together to make room for more, running over, and poured into our lap. For the same amount we give will determine the amount we get back. A stingy planter gets a stingy crop and a lavish planter gets a lavish crop.

Lord, remind us, and we purpose to remember, that we are not rich because of our own power. It is You who gives us the power to become rich, keeping the agreement You promised to our ancestors.

Not only do we give tithes and offerings to You, but we also give to those around us who are in need, because Your Word says that whoever is kind to the poor lends to You and You will reward us. We acknowledge You as we give to benefit the poor.

Thank You, Father, that as You bless us and we bless others, they will praise You and give You thanks and in turn, bless others. It's a never-ending circle of Your love and blessings that will go on into eternity. In the name of Jesus we pray, amen.

<u>Scripture References</u>

John 14:17 NLT   Luke 6:38 NLT

Philippians 1:6 NASB   2 Corinthians 9:6 MSG

Hebrews 3:1 NIV   Proverbs 19:17 NIV

Deuteronomy 8:17,18 NCV   Isaiah 55:11 MSG

Deuteronomy 26:10,11 NCV Proverbs 19:17 NIV

2 Corinthians 9:12-15 NLT Philippians 4:19 NCV

1. Setting Aside the Tithe

Father, Your Word tells us to give You ten percent of our earnings. Therefore, we purpose to set aside the tithe because it belongs to You.

When we bring our tithes to You, You promise to open the widows of heaven and pour out blessings so great that we won't have enough room to take it in! Thank You that the fruit of our ground is abundant because You guard it from being destroyed and it will not fall from the vine before it is ripe.

Father, because we honor Your name, our names are written down in Your book of remembrance. We are Yours and we get special treatment.

Thank You for rescuing us from the dominion of darkness and bringing us into the kingdom of Your Son. In the name of Jesus we pray. Amen.

Scripture References

Malachi 3:10,11 NLT   Colossians 1:13 NIV

Malachi 3:16,17 MSG

II. Giving the Offering

Father, we give offerings by the direction of the Holy Spirit. We are ready and willing to give generous gifts because we remember that those who plant a little will receive a small harvest; but those who plant a lot will receive a big harvest.

We give as we purpose in our hearts and are not sad nor do we feel forced to give, for You love those who give happily. You bless us with more than we need and we have plenty of everything so that we can always be generous and give freely, causing many to give thanks to You.

Your Word says that You will never forsake the righteous or leave our children begging for food. We choose not to worry about our everyday life—whether or not we will have enough food to eat or clothes to wear—because our life is more than food and clothing.

We will not eat the bread of idleness (gossip, discontent, and self-pity), but will stay busy and productive. We thank You that we will remain self-sufficient, requiring no outside aid or support.

Father, You delight in the prosperity of Your servant. Therefore, we declare on the authority of Your Word that our family will be successful everywhere; an entire generation will be blessed and wealthy and their good deeds will last forever. We purpose to be good stewards of Your abundance.

Good things come to us because we are generous and lend freely to the poor. When we don't know what to do, we purpose to boldly ask You for help, because You love to help us and will not find fault in us.

In the name of Jesus, amen.

<u>Scripture References</u>

2 Corinthians 9:5-11 NCV

Psalm 37:25 NIV

Matthew 6:25 NLT

Proverbs 31:27 MSG

Psalm 35:27 NASB

Psalm 112:2,3 NLT

Psalm 37:26 NIV

2 Corinthians 9:9 NCV

James 1:5 MSG

For My Family Members

Thank you, Jesus, that You have poured out Your Spirit from heaven upon my family. Our desert will be like a fertile field and the fertile field like a forest. Justice will be found even in the desert and fairness will be found in the fertile fields. That fairness will bring peace, and it will bring calm and safety forever.

Our family lives in peaceful places and in safe homes and calm places of rest. Because You are our Lord, we have stability even in bad times and You provide a rich store of salvation, wisdom, and knowledge. The fear of and respect for You, Lord, is our treasure.

Lord, be merciful to us for we have waited for You. Be our strong arm each day and our salvation in times of trouble, trials, and tribulations.

Thank You, Father, for being my sure foundation each and every day. I praise You with all of my life! Amen.

Scripture References

Isaiah 32:15-18 NCV   Isaiah 33: 2,6 NLT

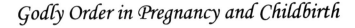

Godly Order in Pregnancy and Childbirth

Father, in Jesus' name, I confess Your Word over my pregnancy and the birth of my child. I ask You to see that Your Word is fulfilled concerning my pregnancy, trusting You that Your Word will not go out from You and return to You empty, but rather it will accomplish what You desire and achieve the purpose for which You sent it. Your Word is alive and active and judges the thoughts and attitudes of my heart.

Right now, I put on Your complete armor so that I can successfully resist all the devil's methods of attack. I know that my fight is not against any physical enemy but against organizations and powers that are spiritual. I am up against the unseen power that controls this dark world. Above all, I will be sure to take faith as my shield, for it can quench every burning missile that the enemy hurls at me. I will stand in faith during this pregnancy and birth and not give room to fear. Your Word promises me in 2 Timothy 1:7 that You have given me power and love and a sound mind.

Heavenly Father, I say that You alone are my refuge and my place of safety. I trust You during this pregnancy and childbirth. I am thankful that You have ordered angels to protect me and my baby. I give all my worries and

cares of this pregnancy over to You, Lord. Your grace is enough for me during this pregnancy. When I am weak, Your power is strong.

Father, Your Word tells me that my baby was created in Your image, wonderfully complex to the praise of You. You have made me a happy mother and my children are my reward from You. I commit this child to You, Lord and pray that he/she will grow up and bless me.

I am not afraid of pregnancy or childbirth because my heart is steady and trusting in You. I believe that my pregnancy and childbirth will free from problems. Thank You, Father, that all decisions regarding my pregnancy and delivery will be godly and that the Holy Spirit will show me what to do. Lord, You are my shelter and I rest in the promise of Your Word that no evil will conquer me and no plague will come near my home. I know that Jesus died on the cross to take away my sickness and pain. Because I have accepted Jesus as my Savior, I confess that my child will be born healthy and whole. Thank You, Father, that Your Spirit gives live in Christ Jesus and that the law of the Spirit has set me free from the law of wrong things and the law of death.

Thank You, Father, for protecting me and my baby and for our good health. Thank You for hearing and answering my prayers. Amen.

Scripture References

Jeremiah 1:12 NIV

Isaiah 55:11 NIV

Hebrews 4:12 NIV

Proverbs 31:28 CEB

Psalm 112:7 CEB

Psalm 91:1,10 NLT

Harmonious Marriage

Father, Your love fills our hearts by the Holy Spirit whom You have given to us. Because You are in us, love will grow more and more. Love is what binds us together so that we can live the kind of life that honors and pleases You.

We will live and conduct ourselves and our marriage with honor, esteeming each other as precious, worthy, and of great price. It is our purpose to honor You by walking in agreement with You and with each other, helping each other fulfill our God-given destinies, individually and together. Father, we believe and say that we are kind and merciful and forgiving of one another and others. We seek peace that will bring calmness and safety forever – the kind of peace that no one can understand but can only come from You.

Our marriage grows stronger day by day because it is deeply rooted in Your love. Father, thank You that You will make every word that You give us come true as together we make a symphony of our marriage in Jesus' name. Amen.

Scripture References

Romans 5:5 NCV

Philippians 1:9 NLT

Colossians 3:14 CEV

Colossians 1:10 NCV

Philippians 2:13

Philippians 2:2 MSG

Ephesians 4:32 CEV

Isaiah 32:17 NCV

Philippians 4:7

1 Peter 3:7

Ephesians 3:17,18 CEV

Jeremiah 1:12 MSG

The Home

Father, I thank You that You have given me every spiritual blessing. I will use wisdom and understanding to establish my home and let knowledge fill the rooms with rare and beautiful treasures. The house of the righteous has great treasure and it stands firm. My house brims with wealth and my generosity never runs dry.

My house is securely built on a solid rock. The floods and rivers may come and try to rush against it, but it will not shake. Jesus is my Cornerstone. Jesus is Lord over my household. My household will work willingly in whatever we do as though we were working for You, Lord, rather than for people. My family loves each other with the love of God and we live in peace. I entrust my home to Your protection and care.

Father, as for me and my family, we will serve the Lord in Jesus' name. Hallelujah!

Scripture References

Ephesians 1:3 NCV

Proverbs 24:3,4 CEV

Proverbs 15:6

Proverbs 12:7

Psalm 112:3 MSG

Luke 6:48 CEV

Acts 4:11

Acts 16:31

Philippians 2:10-11

Colossians 3:23 NLT

Colossians 3:14,15

Acts 20:32

Joshua 24:15 NCV

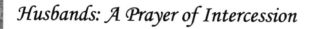

Husbands: A Prayer of Intercession

Father, in the name of Jesus, I take Your Word
and declare this day that _____listens
to You and lives in peace, untroubled by fear of harm.

_____listens carefully to wisdom and sets his
mind on understanding. He applies all of his power to
the quest of it.

He lets kindness and truth always show like a necklace and writes them in his heart. He never walks away
from wisdom, for she guards his life. She will exalt and
promote him and bring honor to him because he has
embraced her. He can be sure that the Lord will protect
him from harm.

When _____walks, the Word and
wisdom will guide him. They will guard him when he
sleeps and speak to him when he is awake. He says only
worthwhile and right things and every word is honest,
not one is misleading or deceptive.

_____will live in a thoughtful way with
_____, his wife. He will treat his wife with honor and
show her respect because God gives her the same blessing that he gives her husband- the grace that gives true
life. He does this so that nothing will stop their prayers.

The fruit of the righteous is a tree of life and the one who is wise saves lives. _____ and _____ and his wife choose to live this way because they love and respect each other.

Thank You, Father that _____ is a man of good report – that he is successful in everything he sets his hand to. He is uncompromisingly righteous. He captures human lives for God as a fisher of men. As he does this he has the confidence that You are the Lord his God who teaches him what is good and leads him along the paths that he should follow. He has Your favor upon Him and Your will is done in his life!

Scripture References

Proverbs 1:33 NLT

Proverbs 2:2 NCV

Proverbs 3:3 CEV

Proverbs 4:8 MSG

Proverbs 3:26 CEV

Proverbs 6:22 NCV

Proverbs 8:6,8 CEV

1 Peter 3:7-9 NCV

Proverbs 11:30 NIV

Isaiah 48:17 NLT

Husband's Personal Prayer

Father, in the beginning Your Word tells us that You provided a helper and companion for man. Now I have found a wife to be my companion and she is my treasure. I have received favor from the Lord. I won't ever forget kindness and truth. I will wear them like a necklace and write them on my heart. Then, I will be respected and please both God and people.

I will say about my wife, "There are many good women, but you are the best!" I will show her respect and praise her in public for all she does for me and our family. I will provide leadership to my wife the way Christ does to His Church, not by being domineering but by cherishing. I will go all out in my love for her, exactly as Christ did for the Church – a love marked by giving, not getting.

In the name of Jesus, I give my wife what is due her, and I share my personal rights with her. Father, I honor my wife and delight in her. In the new life of God's grace, we are equals. I treat my wife as an equal so that our prayers are not hindered.

Lord, I love to worship You and obey Your teachings. My children will have great power in the land because

You bless them. Their houses will be full of wealth and riches and their goodness will continue forever. In the name of Jesus, amen.

Scripture References

Matthew 18:18	Ephesians 5:22,23 MSG
Genesis 2:18 MSG	1 Corinthians 7:3-5 NCV
Proverbs 18:22 NLT	1 Peter 3:7-9 NLT
Proverbs 3:3,4 NCV	Proverbs 31:28-31 CEV
Psalm 112:1-4 CEV, NCV	

Moving to a New Location

Father, Your Word says that You will work out Your plans for my life. Your faithful love endures forever. I bring to You my apprehensions concerning relocation. I ask that You go before me and my family to level the mountains in finding a new home.

Give my spouse and me wisdom to make wise decisions in choosing the movers and packers best suited to handle our possessions. You cause us to find favor and earn a good reputation with You and people – with the utility companies, with the school systems, and with the banks – with everyone involved in this move.

Father, thank You for giving us (my spouse, children and me) new friends that You would want us to have. We are trusting You to lead us to a church where we can worship together with other believers.

Lord, we depend on You for this move, knowing that You are our Provider. We enjoy serving You and know that You will give us what we desire.

I cast all these cares and concerns on You without fretting or worrying. We offer thanksgiving for this sense of God's wholeness, everything coming together for good will come and settle our minds. You are keeping us in perfect peace because our thoughts are fixed on You!

I trust in You, Lord, with all of my heart. I'm not depending on my own understanding. I will remember You in all I do and know that You will give me success.

Thank You, Father, for Your blessing on this move.

Scripture References

Psalm 138:8 NLT

Isaiah 45:2 NIV

James 1:5

Proverbs 3:4 NLT

Hebrews 10:25

Isaiah 26:3 NLT

Psalm 96:1

Psalm 98:1

Psalm 149:1

Psalm 37:4,5 NCV

Philippians 4:6,7 MSG

Proverbs 3:5,6

The New Creation Marriage

The following prayer was given to me by the Holy Spirit for me and my husband.

Husband, you may pray the part for the wife in the third person. Wife, you may pray the part for the husband in the third person.

Find time to pray together if both parties are willing and receptive.

Prayer

The couple prays together:

Father, in the name of Jesus, we come to You as one. We belong to You therefore, we have become new. The old life is gone and a new life has begun! We want to be lights in the midst of a crooked and perverse world.

Open our hearts so that we are willing to receive suggestions from each other and help us to learn to function so that each of us preserves our own personality while fulfilling the desires of the other. We purpose to base our relationship on the analogy of the family of God in Ephesians 5.

We walk in agreement on the authority of Your Word and strive to understand each other, which is more important than being understood. We will be quick to listen, slow to speak, and slow to anger, in the name of Jesus.

The husband prays:

Father, I take responsibility for my family just as Christ does for the Church. I love my wife, just as I love myself, and I provide for my family.

Help me provide leadership to my wife, not by being domineering, but by cherishing her. I will go all out in my love for her – a love of giving, not getting.

I model my love for my wife after the example of Christ's love for the Church—everything He says and does brings the best out of her, dressing her in dazzling white silk, radiant with holiness. I am doing myself a favor since we are "one" in marriage. This is why I left my father and mother—so that we would no longer be two, but one flesh. Your Word says that whatever You have joined together, no man can separate.

Even though I may not understand it all, Father, what is clear is that Christ's love for the Church gives me a good example of how I am to treat my wife, loving myself in loving her.

The wife prays:

Father, in the name of Jesus, I purpose to understand and support my husband as unto You, Lord. I respond to my husband in every aspect of our relationship.

Thank You that I am a good, loyal wife to my husband—he can trust me completely and I trust You to provide for all of his needs. I do him good for as long as I live. I cultivate inner beauty, the gentle, gracious kind that God delights in. I will not become anxious and intimidated. When I speak, I have something worthwhile to say and I say it with kindness.

In Jesus' name, amen.

Scripture References

2 Corinthians 5:17 NLT	2 Corinthians 5:18 MSG
Philippians 2:15 NASB	Ephesians 1:4,6,8 MSG
Ephesians 5:25-30 NIV	Ephesians 5:22,33 NLT
1 Peter 2:6 NASB	1 Corinthians 11:7 NIV
1 Peter 2:23 NCV	Proverbs 31:11,12 NCV
2 Corinthians 3:6 NIV	Matthew 19:5,6 NASB

Excerpts for this prayer were taken from *The Heart of Paul* by Ben Campbell Johnson, published by A Great Love, Inc., Toccoa, GA, 1976.

Prayer of Intercession for a Marriage

Father, in the name of Jesus, _____ and _____ are delivered from this evil world in which they live by Jesus who gave His life for their sins. If the Son of God makes them free, they will be truly free. Because of this, they are delivered from rejection and accepted in the Beloved that they might be made whole and holy by Your love. They forgive each other and those who have wronged them and their hurts from the past are healed because Jesus came to deliver all those who are oppressed, downtrodden, bruised, crushed and broken down.

They are chosen by God. He loves them and has made them holy. So then, they are for each other and are kind and humble. They are patient with each other and forgive each other just as Christ forgave them. They have Your love besides all this, because Your love joins everything together as it should be.

When they were children, they used to speak like children, reason like children, and think like children. But now that they have become man and woman, they have put an end to childish things. Jesus used his own blood as the price to set them free once and for all. It set them free from all the dead-end efforts to make them respectable so that they can live all out for God. They are a son and daughter of the Most High God and Satan's power over them is broken and his strongholds are torn down.

The love of God reigns supreme in their home and the peace of God acts as an umpire in all situations. Jesus is their Lord – spirit, soul and body. Amen.

(NOTE: After you have prayed, do not try to counsel or advise God. He has not called you to perform His Word; He watches over His Word to perform it. Leave your cares and concerns there in the place of prayer.)

Scripture References

Galatians 1:4 NLT	Colossians 3:12-15 WE
John 8:36 NCV	1 Corinthians 13:11 CEB
Ephesians 1:4 MSG	Hebrews 9:14 MSG
Luke 4:18 AMP	Colossians 3:15 AMP

Parenting with Wisdom

Father, I ask You to give me strength and wisdom for the task of raising my children. I do not have the right to claim that I have done anything on my own. You give me what it takes to do all that I do. Hallelujah! In every situation, help me to remember that Your grace is all sufficient; that Jesus is made unto me wisdom. Your power works best in my weakness.

Father, my children are prone to foolishness and fads. I ask You for grace to apply the cure that comes through tough-minded discipline. In the name of Jesus, I will not make my children angry but will raise them with the training and teaching of the Lord.

Thank you, Lord, that You have given me wise words to speak so that I can teach my children to be kind. I will teach them right from wrong so that when they are grown they will still do right because they love You and desire to please You. I will discipline my children with love and resist the temptation to be domineering and demanding.

Father, even when I am tired and worn out, my children need me. I will watch over my children that You have entrusted to me with a willing heart. I won't lord it over my children, but I will lead them by my own good example. I will teach my children Your words over and over again. I will talk about Your commands all the time, both at night and in the morning. Thank You for sending the Holy Spirit who is my Comforter, Strengthener, and Standby.

Real wisdom is Your wisdom. It is gentle and reasonable, overflowing with mercy and blessings, not hot one day and cold the next, not two-faced. I will remember that it is unwise to compare myself with my children or to compete with them. When I was a child, I spoke and thought and reasoned as a child. But when I grew up, I put away childish things. In the name of Jesus, I pull down every controlling, manipulative attitude. Instead, I will guide my children along the right paths for Your name's sake.

In the name of Jesus, I ask You to watch over Your words to make them true in my life. Amen.

Scripture References

Psalm 27:10

2 Corinthians 3:5 CEV

2 Corinthians 12:9 NLT

Proverbs 22:15 MSG

Ephesians 6:4 NCV

Proverbs 31:26 NCV

Proverbs 22:6 CEV

Ephesians 6:1-4

Proverbs 13:24 MSG

1 Peter 5:1-4 NLT

Philippians 2:4 AMP

Deuteronomy 6:7 CEV

John 14:16 AMP

James 3:17 MSG

Colossians 1:13 MSG

James 3

2 Corinthians 10:12

1 Corinthians 13:11 NLT

Psalm 23:3

Jeremiah 1:12 NCV

Parenting with a Calm Spirit

Father, I know that losing my temper is not a fruit of the Spirit and so I repent and ask You to forgive me when I lose my temper. It says in Your Word that negative feelings and actions are selfish desires that my sinful self wants. So today I choose to be guided by Your Spirit so that I won't obey my selfish desires. Your Spirit makes me loving, happy, peaceful, patient, kind, gentle and self-controlled.

You are at work in me and helping me develop self-control. It says in Your Word that You didn't give me a spirit that makes me afraid but a spirit of power and love and self-control. Thank You for that promise!

As You work out Your plan in my life, I will rejoice because You have given me a peaceful heart which leads to a healthy life and body. A miserable heart leads to a miserable life so I choose to have a cheerful heart that fills the day with song.

I will choose to make my decisions calmly and patiently. My soft speech will break down resistance in my children. Thank You, Holy Spirit, for helping me submit to Your control so that I might capture the hearts and minds of my children.

When I am angry, I choose not to sin and I will not go to bed angry. Today, I stop speaking words of anger, wrath and bitterness. I submit to Your Word that exposes unhealed hurts and unresolved anger from my past so I will be healed and ready to give my children a ready answer rather than reacting. I will not yell or be rude. Father, instead I choose to be kind and merciful and forgiving. I will raise my children with the training and teaching of You, Lord. A gentle answer will calm my children but an unkind answer will cause more anger.

Father, You know how I've always screamed when the children are fighting. I don't want to do this anymore! My great aim and quest in life is to live a life filled with love by following Your example. I don't want to discipline by heaping guilt and condemnation on them. Even though I feel like I am screaming louder to be heard, I am doing the very thing I tell them not to do. Help me to develop the fruit of the Spirit so that my life will be a demonstration of Your love.

The Proverbs 31 mother speaks only when she has something worthwhile to say and she says it with kindness. I don't want to just force my children to stop fighting but help me teach them how to resolve conflict. Show me a better way. You are my Teacher and I trust You to give me the wisdom that I need.

Help me to lead a life worthy of my calling because I have been called by You. I will strive to always be humble and gentle and patient with others. You chose me and You can be trusted to help and guide me in this awesome task. Your message works in me because I believe and I know You are working in me to help me want to do and be able to do what pleases You. Amen.

Scripture References

Galatians 5:13-26 CEV	Ephesians 5:2 NLT
Ephesians 4:26	2 Timothy 1:7 NCV
Proverbs 31:26 MSG	Proverbs 14:30 NLT
James 1:5	Ephesians 4:31-32 CEV
Proverbs 15:15 MSG	Ephesians 4:1-3 NLT
1 Thessalonians 2:13 NCV	Ephesians 6:4
Philippians 2:13 NCV	Proverbs 15:1 NCV
1 Thessalonians 5:24 CEV	

Parenting with Confidence

Father, what an incredible job this is, raising these children in the training and instruction of the Lord. They are our future leaders whose lives will be a light for other people. Their lives will show good things and will praise You. Sometimes when we look with our natural eyes, situations in our nation seem hopeless. However, our hope is in the Lord. I will bless You, Lord. You guide me and even at night my heart is confident in You. I am faithful to You and You can trust me. I will sing praises to You, my God.

We will teach our children the right thing to do because we love You and belong to You, Lord. We will choose life and blessings so that our children might live! Lord, You are my hope and I have trusted you since I was young (since I confessed You as my Lord). Thank You, Father, that You have my children's lives all planned out. You plan to take care of them and not to abandon them, and You will give them a hope and a future that will glorify You. Hallelujah!

Scripture References

Ephesians 6:4 NIV

Matthew 5:16 NCV

Psalm 146:5

Zephaniah 3:5

Psalm 16:7 NLT

Psalm 57:7 CEV

Psalm 108:1

Genesis 1:26

Ephesians 6:1-3

Deuteronomy 30:19 NLT

Psalm 71:5 NCV

Jeremiah 29:11 MSG

Peace in a Troubled Marriage

A Prayer of Intercession

Father, in the name of Jesus, we bring this couple that You love and we love before You. We pray and speak Your Word over them, and as we do, we use our faith and are fully confident that Your Word will come to pass according to Your will for them.

We pray that they will make a clean break with all cutting, backbiting, and profane talk. We pray that (names)_____will be gentle and sensitive with others and they will forgive quickly and thoroughly as You forgave them.

_____ and _____will try to be like You, God, because they are Your children whom You love. They will copy You and follow Your example as well-beloved children try to be like their father. _____will live a life of love just as Christ loved them and gave Himself for them as a sweet-smelling offering and sacrifice to God.

Father, we thank You that _____will let the Spirit renew their thoughts and attitudes. They have put on their new nature, created to be like You truly right-

eous and holy. They have woken up and escaped from the trap of the devil. Thank You for creating within them a desire and the power to do Your will, which is loving each other with Your kind of love, united in total peace and harmony and happiness.

Thank You for the answer, Lord. We know it is done now in the name of Jesus. Amen.

Scripture References

Ephesians 4:31,32

Ephesians 4:23,24 NLT

Ephesians 5:1,2 NCV

2 Timothy 2:26 NCV

Matthew 18:18

Pregnancy

Father, You know my heart and know that I have longed to be a mother, and now the miracle has happened! I am so thankful to You and I praise You, knowing that my child's frame is not hidden from You. This baby is being shaped and formed in my womb by You, Lord. You know this baby inside and out. You know every bone in his body. Like an open book, You are watching my baby from conception until birth. All the days of my baby's life were all prepared even before he/she was conceived.

Thank You for this life that is developing within my body. I surround this baby with loving words day and night. You have filled my mouth with laughter and my heart with joy. I treasure every movement of life- the stretching of his/her limbs. I will choose to be full of joy because I know my moods affect this little one. Your praise is always on my lips and I will praise You at all times, even when I don't feel like it.

Lord, You have blessed us and will continue to bless us all the days of our lives and we will live to enjoy our grandchildren. You are so wonderful to include us in Your plan of hope and success for this unborn child.

Scripture References

Psalm 103:14   Psalm 34:1 NCV

Psalm 139:13-16 MSG   Psalm 128:6

Psalm 16:7   Jeremiah 29:11

Philippians 4:4

Train Children in the Way They Should Go

Father, forgive me for looking to my children for fulfillment. They do bring me great joy, but I have been naïve in thinking that they could meet my needs. Forgive me for placing emotional demands on them when You were present to give me everything I need through Your wonderful riches in Christ Jesus. I am so grateful and humbled that You chose me to be the mother of these precious ones. Forgive me for those times when I don't enjoy being a mother or when I blame my children for my ungodly behavior. Help me to make necessary attitude adjustments. Thank You, Holy Spirit, for reminding me to cast down my negative thoughts and thank You for making me Your masterpiece. You created me anew in Jesus so that I can do the good things that You planned for me long ago.

You are my God. I worship You. In my heart I long for You. Help me to quiet the distractions so that I may hear Your voice. You have called me to be a minister to Your precious ones and now You are teaching me to direct them on the right path so that when they are older, they will not leave it. Help me to teach them how to make decisions that are in line with Your plans for them—plans to take care of them, not abandon them and plans to give them a future that they hope for.

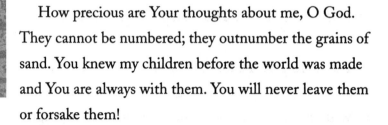

How precious are Your thoughts about me, O God. They cannot be numbered; they outnumber the grains of sand. You knew my children before the world was made and You are always with them. You will never leave them or forsake them!

Father, thank You that You are helping me to teach and train my children in Your Word and teaching them Your ways so that they can live successfully, fulfilling their destinies. Holy Spirit, I ask You to help me mold their thoughts so they will resist the enemy's attempt to lie to them. They will make wise decisions even when I am not with them.

Thank You for giving my children the courage to stand as bright shining lights in a dark and perverse world. I say that my children will be world-changers. Others will see their light shine and give glory to You.

Scripture References

Philippians 4:19 NCV	Psalm 139:17-18 NLT
Ephesians 2:10 NLT	Ephesians 1:4 NCV
Psalm 63:1 CEV	Hebrews 13:5
Proverbs 22:6 NLT	James 4:7
Jeremiah 29:11 MSG	Matthew 5:14, 16

Seeking Safety in a Place of Violence

Father, I am Your child. I have been saved from a useless life. I was bought, not with something that ruins like gold or silver, but with the precious blood of Christ. My sins are forgiven.

As the head of my household, I ask for Divine protection for each of us. Give safety to my children and carry them through each day. Lord, You see the violence that is in the streets and in our schools. Father, I repent on behalf of our nation for taking prayer out of our schools. The drug dealers and the gang members living in our neighborhoods are waiting to snare our children. Lord, I ask You to confuse them and frustrate their plans, for I see the violence and conflict in the city. Its walls are patrolled day and night against invaders but the real danger is wickedness within the city. Everything is falling apart; threats and cheating are rampant in the streets. But I will call on You, Lord, and You will rescue my family and me.

Father, in the name of Jesus, You and You alone are our safety and our protection. My household and I are looking to You, for our strength comes from You – the God who made heaven and earth. You will not let us stumble. You are our Guardian God who will not fall

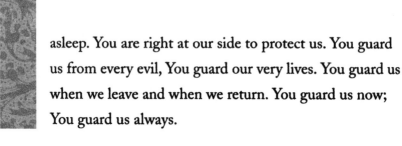

asleep. You are right at our side to protect us. You guard us from every evil, You guard our very lives. You guard us when we leave and when we return. You guard us now; You guard us always.

My household was known and chosen long ago by You, Father, and Your Spirit has made us holy. Because of this, we have obeyed You and have been cleansed by the blood of Jesus. I receive more grace and peace because of what You have provided for me.

Lord, Your Son Jesus became the middle man of a new agreement. The spilling of His blood has more power than Abel's. I proclaim according to Your Word that Jesus is our protection as it says in Exodus 12:13, "...when I see the blood, I will pass over you..." I draw a bloodline around my children and the evil one cannot cross it.

I know that none of the God-begotten make a practice of fatal sin. The God-begotten are also the God-protected. The evil one can't lay a hand on my household. I know that we are held firm by You, Lord.

Father, thank You for Your divine protection. In the name of Jesus I pray, amen.

<u>Scripture References</u>

1 John 3:1   Psalm 121:8 MSG

1 Peter 1:18,19 NCV   1 Peter 1:2 NLT

The Unborn Child

Father, in Jesus' name, I thank You for watching my child as he/she is being formed in utter seclusion in the womb. I treasure this child as a reward from You. Every day of his/her life is recorded in Your book, every moment laid out even before he/she goes through the birthing process. You have known my child since before conception and You know the path that he/she will take with his/her life. I ask Your blessing upon him/her and believe for his/her salvation through Jesus Christ.

Heavenly Father, I thank and praise You for the great things You have done and are continuing to do. I am in awe at the miracle of life You have placed inside of me. Thank You! Amen.

Scripture References

Psalm 139:15-16 NLT

When You Feel Like Giving Up

Father, thank You that I can ask You for help! Being a parent is the most difficult job I have tried to do. Today I am tired of carrying these heavy loads. I come to You, Lord Jesus, to learn Your teachings and find rest for my life. Your burden is easy and your load light. I want to know You and know truth. I desire with all my heart to bring up my children with the discipline and instruction that comes from You, Lord. Nothing will bring me greater happiness than to hear that my children are obeying the truth.

My children were created by You and by Your decision they were created. It overwhelms me when I think about You entrusting them to my care. They could have been born in any time period, but You chose me to conceive and birth them. I may have made my own plans in my mind but You determine my steps, Father.

Thank You for loving me enough to set me on the path that You ordained for me before the beginning of time. Thank You for my wonderful children that You have given to me. I would never have known You as I do today if these precious ones were not a valuable part of my life. Thank You, Father, for being the Keeper and Protector of my children. In the name of Jesus, amen.

Scripture References

Matthew 11:28-30 NCV

Ephesians 6:4 NLT

3 John 1:4 CEV

Revelation 4:11 CEV

Colossians 1:16

Ephesians 2:10 NLT

Daniel 2:21

Proverbs 16:9 NLT

Ephesians 1:4

Romans 8:28

Genesis 14:22

Psalm 91:1-2

Wife's Personal Prayer

In the name of Jesus, I will clothe myself with the beauty that comes from within, the unfading beauty of a gentle and quiet spirit, which is so precious to God. I choose to be a good, loyal wife to my husband and treat him with respect. By God's grace, I will be agreeable, sympathetic, loving, compassionate and humble. I will be a blessing and also receive blessings.

By Your Spirit, I am becoming more and more like You. Your bright glory is shining through me. You are creating a clean heart in me, Lord. I am an honest woman who is a jewel to my husband. I will walk wisely and strengthen my family and not destroy them. Houses and wealth are inherited from parents but a wise wife is a gift from the Lord. Praise You Lord, that You were so rich in kindness and grace that You purchased our freedom with the blood of Your Son and forgave our sins. You have showered Your kindness on us, along with wisdom and understanding.

Holy Spirit, I ask You to help me understand and support my husband in ways that show my support for Christ. Teach me to function so that I preserve my own personality while responding to his desires. We are one

flesh, and I realize that this unity of persons that pre-serves individuality is a mystery, but that is how it is when we are united to Christ. So I will keep on loving my husband and let the miracle keep happening!

Just as my husband gives me all that he owes me, I seek to be fair and will give my husband all that I owe him as his wife.

I am strong and graceful and have no fear of the future. My words are wise and my advice is thoughtful. I take good care of my family and am never lazy. Thank You, Father, that I have the wisdom that comes from You and it is pure, peaceful, gentle and easy to please. This wisdom is always ready to help those who are troubled and to do good for others. It is always fair and honest. Thank You Jesus, for sharing that wonderful wisdom with me to be the best wife that I can possibly be! In Jesus' name, amen.

Scripture References

Matthew 16:19 NKJV

Proverbs 19:14 NCV

Ephesians 1:7,8 NLT

Psalm 51:10 NKJV

Ephesians 5:22-23 MSG

2 Corinthians 3:18 CEV

1 Corinthians 7:2-5 NCV

Proverbs 11:6

Proverbs 31:25-27 CEV

Proverbs 12:4 CEV

James 3:17,18 NCV

Proverbs 14:1 NCV

1 Peter 3:1-5, 8, 9 NLT & MSG

Excerpts taken from *The Heart of Paul* by Ben Campbell Johnson. Copyright © 1976 by A Great Love, Inc., Toccoa, GA. Husbands, I encourage you to pray this prayer in third person for your wife.

PART II:

RELATIONAL PRAYERS: SINGLE, DIVORCED, AND WIDOWED

Committing to a Life of Purity

Father, I come before Your throne of grace in the name of Jesus. In the past I lived the way the world lives, doing all the things my body and mind wanted to do.

But, God—Your mercy is great! Even though I was spiritually dead, You loved me so much that You gave me a new life with Christ. I have been saved by Your grace and raised up with Christ, seated with Him in the heavens.

You are my Father, and I belong to You. Since I am in Christ, I have become a new person. My old life is gone and my new life has begun. Therefore, I rid myself of all malice, deceit, hypocrisy, envy, and slander of every kind. Like a newborn baby, I crave pure spiritual milk, so that I may grow up in Your salvation.

I submit myself to Jesus Christ, who loves me and sacrificed His life for me to make me holy, cleansing me through the baptism of His Word. I am now radiant in Your eyes—free from spot, wrinkle, and any other blemish—I am holy and without guilt.

Thank You for the blood of Christ that cleans me inside and out. Through the Spirit, Christ became an unblemished sacrifice for me, freeing me from all the

dead-end efforts to make myself respectable, so that I can live all out for You! Thank You for giving me the Holy Spirit, who is holy and pure.

I ask for and receive wisdom, which comes from heaven—it is first of all pure; it is also peace loving, gentle at all times, willing to yield to others, full of mercy and good deeds, shows no favoritism, and is always sincere. Change my impure language, Lord, and give me clear and pure speech so that it is pleasing to You.

I purpose not to conform to the ways of this world, but I am transformed by the renewing of my mind, and I take every thought captive to the obedience of Christ. I fix my thoughts on whatever is true, noble, right, pure, lovely, and admirable. I determine to think on things that are excellent or praiseworthy. I am careful what I think on, because thoughts run our lives.

What marvelous love You have extended to me, that I am now called and counted as a child of God! Father, I have no idea where I'll end up, but I do know that when You are openly revealed, I will see You and will become like You.

Because of the blood of the Lamb and the word of my testimony, I will overcome. In Jesus' name I pray, amen.

Scripture References

Ephesians 2:2-6 NCV

2 Corinthians 5:17 NLT

1 Peter 2:1,2 NIV

Philippians 4:8 NIV

Proverbs 4:23 NCV

James 3:17 NLT

2 Corinthians 10:5 NASB

Ephesians 5:25-27 Phillips

1 Thessalonians 4:8 NASB

Proverbs 15:16 NCV

Zephaniah 3:9 NLT

Romans 12:2 NIV

Hebrews 9:14 MSG

1 John 3:1-3 MSG

Revelation 12:11 NASB

Psalm 101:3 AMP

I. A Man of Purity

Father, I pay attention to Your words and listen closely to what You say. I have hidden Your Word in my heart, so that I might not sin against You. It's not wrong to have sexual desires. You made me and I belong to You. I commit myself and my natural affections to You. I give the Holy Spirit control over my life and submit to Your will.

Forgive me for sinning against You, against myself, and against others. Thank You for Your grace that enables me to leave my gift at the altar when I remember a grudge a friend has against me. I go immediately and make things right, then come back and work things out with You, Father.

I flee from sexual immorality because when I commit a sexual sin, I sin against my own body. My body is a temple of the Holy Spirit, who lives in me. I am not my own, but I was bought for a great price. So I will therefore honor You with my body.

When I read Your Word, the truth, it sets me free. My sins have been forgiven and I have overcome the evil one. I am strong in the Word and the Word lives in me. I do not love the world or anything in the world because if I do then I do, not really love You. These worldly things—the craze for sex, ambition to buy anything and everything that appeals to me, and the pride that comes from wealth and importance—are not from You. Those worldly things pass away, but I choose to do the will of God and so I will live forever.

Thank You that You have given me Your Spirit, and I know the truth. I receive the Holy Spirit and He lives within me and He teaches me everything I need to know so that I remain in fellowship with You.

Because I remain in fellowship with You, when You return I will be full of courage and not shrink back from You in shame. I continue to seek first Your Kingdom and Your righteousness and all these thing are given to me. You are my Father, and I model myself after You.

In Jesus' name, amen.

Scripture References

Proverbs 4:20 NCV

1 John 2:12-17 NIV

Psalm 119:11 NLT

1 John 2:20,27-29 NLT

Matthew 5:23,24 MSG

Matthew 6:33 NIV

1 Corinthians 6:18-20 NIV

John 8:32 NASB

Ephesians 5:1 Phillips

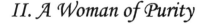

II. A Woman of Purity

Father, I was separated from You, with no hope. But I have acknowledged and confessed with my lips that You are Lord. I believe (adhere to, trust in, and rely on the truth) that You were raised from the dead and I am saved.

I repent of my sins and receive Your forgiveness. I am in You, brought near by the blood of Christ, and my eyes are wide open to Your mercies. I commit my body to You as a living sacrifice. I will not let the world squeeze me into its own mold, but I let You re-mold my mind from within. You have my life all planned out, Lord with plans to take care of me and not abandon me. You give me hope for the future. I belong to You, therefore, I am a new creation. The old things have gone and everything is made new.

I confidently enter the Most Holy Place by the blood of Jesus and I draw near to You, Lord, with a sincere heart and with the full assurance that faith brings, that my heart has been sprinkled and cleansed of a guilty conscience and my body has been washed with pure water. I hold unswervingly to the hope I profess, because He who promised is faithful. I think about how I can spur others toward love and good deeds and I encourage others, and all the more as I see the Day approaching.

In these last days, You pour Your Spirit on me and I will prophesy, telling of future events pertaining to Your Kingdom. I seek Your Kingdom above all else, and I live righteously. You give me everything I need so I do not worry about tomorrow, for tomorrow will bring its own worries. Today's trouble is enough for today. Thank You for showing me Your grace.

Father, I submit to Your will for my life. The way You work surpasses the way I work and the way You think is beyond the way I think. I commit my works to You, Lord, and Your plans will be established. I belong to you—body and soul—so let things happen as You say.

Since others are watching me, I throw off everything that hinders and the sin that so easily entangles. I run with perseverance the race marked out for me, fixing my eyes on Jesus, the pioneer and perfector of faith.

Father, to the pure You show Yourself pure, but to the wicked You show Yourself hostile. You rescue the humble, but Your eyes watch the proud and humiliate them. Lord, You are my lamp, lighting up my darkness. In Your strength I can crush an army and scale any wall. Your way is perfect and Your promises prove true. You are a shield for all who look to You for protection.

O, Father, that I may climb the mountain of the Lord and stand in Your Holy Place. I come with clean hands and a pure heart, refusing to worship idols and never telling lies. I receive Your blessing and have a right relationship with You as my Savior, for You are good to those who are upright and pure in heart.

In Jesus' name I pray, amen.

Scripture References

2 Corinthians 5:17 NCV   Luke 1:28, 30, 37 NCV

Romans 12:1,2 Phillips   Isaiah 55:9 MSG

Jeremiah 29:11 MSG   Proverbs 16:3 NASB

Ephesians 2:12,13 NASB   Luke 1:38 Phillips

Romans 10:9 AMP   Hebrews 12:1,2 NIV

2 Corinthians 5:17 NASB   2 Samuel 22:27-31 NLT

Hebrews 10:19-25 NIV   Psalm 24:3-5 NLT

Acts 2:17 MSG   Psalm 73:1 AMP

Matthew 6:33,34 NLT

Complete in Him as a Single

Father, I thank You that I can steep my life into Your reality and Your provisions. I do not worry about missing out but know that my everyday human concerns will be met. I thank You that I know You love me and I can trust Your Word.

Everything of You, Lord, gets expressed through Jesus so that I can see and hear You clearly. I don't need a telescope, a microscope or a horoscope to realize the fullness of Christ and the emptiness of the universe without Him. When I come to You, that fullness comes together for me too. Your power extends over everything!

So, because of Jesus, I am complete and Jesus is my Lord. I come before You, Father, desiring a born-again Christian mate. I ask that Your will be done in my life. Now, I enter into Your rest by trusting in You, in the name of Jesus. Amen.

<u>Scripture References</u>

Matthew 6:33 MSG   Hebrews 4:10

Colossians 2:9,10 MSG

Developing Patience

Father, I come to You in the name of Jesus. I enjoy serving You, Lord, and I know You want to grant me what I want. Waiting patiently for a marriage partner has become a challenge – a trial, sometimes leading to temptation. I am asking for Your help in developing patience. I depend on You, Lord, and trust You knowing that You will take care of me. I surrender my desire to be married to You.

By Your grace, I surrender my life- all my desires and all that I am and all that I am not—to You. I give control to the Holy Spirit who produces this kind of fruit in me: love, joy, peace, patience, kindness, goodness, truthfulness, gentleness, and the ability to keep my body under control. I belong to Jesus and I strive to live by the Holy Spirit's leading in every part of my life. In exercising self control, I develop patience and in exercising patience, I develop devotion to You.

When trials and temptations crowd into my life, I won't resent them but will realize that they come to test my faith and to produce in me the quality of endurance. I will let the process go on until that endurance is fully developed so that I may become a person of mature character with the right sort of independence.

Father, give me complete knowledge of Your will and spiritual wisdom and understanding. Then, the way that I live will always honor and please You and my life will produce every kind of good fruit. All the while, I will grow as I learn to know You better and better and I will be strengthened with all Your glorious power so that I will have all the endurance and patience I need. I will be filled with joy, always thanking You, Father.

Father, I remove from my life anything that would get in the way and the sin that so easily holds me back and I run the race that is before me and won't ever give up. I look only to Jesus, the One who began my faith and makes it perfect.

With patience, I am able to withstand the difficult times of anxiety and worry and overcome the fear that I may never be married. I have overcome by the blood of the Lamb and by the word of my testimony.

In Jesus' name, amen.

Scripture References

Psalm 37:4,5 NCV

James 1:2-4 Phillips

Colossians 1:9-12 NLT

Galatians 5:22-25 WE

Hebrews 12:1,2 NCV

Revelation 12:11

2 Peter 1:6 NCV & Phillips

Finding a Mate

Introduction

In our ministry we hear from many men and women who desire to be married. If that is your desire, we encourage you to ask the Lord to prepare you for marriage. Submit to God's future plans for your life, and purpose to please Him. Do not make your deliberations without knowing His will, at the expense of your personal spiritual growth and transformation. Going from glory to glory (2 Cor. 3:18) is not dependent on having a spouse.

Very often, each partner brings emotional baggage into the marriage relationship. As you prepare for marriage, remember that the anointing that was upon Jesus (Luke 4:18,19) is within you. This anointing will destroy every yoke of bondage (Isaiah 10:27) as God exposes emotional wounds and heals your brokenness.

Knowing the reality of your completeness in Christ Jesus will enable you to enter into a healthy relationship, one in which both you and your future partner will grow together spiritually and in every other area of life. Seeking first the Kingdom of God and His righteousness (Matthew 6:33) and doing those things that are pleasing in His sight (1 John 3:22) will prepare you to be the person designed by Him to fulfill the role of husband or wife.

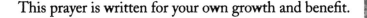

This prayer is written for your own growth and benefit.

Prayer

Father, I come to You in the name of Jesus, asking for Your will to be done in my life as I look to You for a marriage partner.

I ask that You prepare me for marriage by bringing my darkest secrets to light and revealing my motives. I submit to Your Word that exposes wounded emotions, walls of denial, emotional isolation, silence or excessive talking, anger, rigidity, or any wall that separates me from healthy relationships and from Your love and grace. The weapons that You have given me to bring my thoughts into agreement with Your Word are different from those that the world uses. These powerful weapons destroy the enemy's strong places.

I know the One in whom I trust and I am sure that He is able to guard what I have entrusted to Him, whether I remain unmarried or married, until the day of His return.

Because I love You, Lord, and because I know that You are always at work for my good, everything that happens to me fits into a pattern for my good. It's all

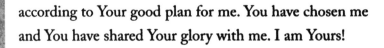
according to Your good plan for me. You have chosen me and You have shared Your glory with me. I am Yours!

I remove anything from my life that would get in the way of the race that is before me. I will never give up. I will always look only to Jesus, the One who began our faith and who makes it perfect. He suffered death on the cross but accepted the shame because of the joy that God put before Him. He is now on God's right side appealing to God for me!

I will run from the temptations that try to capture young people. With Your help, I will always choose to do the right thing. I choose to be faithful, loving, and peaceful. I will enjoy the companionship of people whose hearts are pure. I will stay away from foolish and ignorant arguments that only lead to trouble. I will be kind to everyone, patient and humble.

Father, more than anything else, I put Your work first and what You want. Then, the other things will be mine as well. I won't worry about tomorrow. It will take care of itself.

I know that I can trust You because You loved me first. Even before You made the world, You loved us and chose us in Christ to be holy and without fault in Your eyes. For in Christ, lives all the fullness of God in a human body so I am complete in my union with You.

I come before You, Father, expressing my desire for a Christian mate. I pray that Your will be done in my life. Now, I will enter into Your rest as I trust in You fully. Amen.

Scripture References

Matthew 6:10 NIV

1 Corinthians 4:5 NLT

2 Corinthians 10:4 NCV

2 Timothy 1:12 NLT

Romans 8:28-30 CEV

Hebrews 12:1-3 NCV

Romans 8:34 NCV

2 Timothy 2:22-25 CEV

Matthew 6:33-34 CEV

1 John 4:19

Ephesians 1:4 NLT

Colossians 2:9,10 NLT

Matthew 6:10 NIV

Hebrews 4:10

John 14:1

Knowing God's Plan for Marriage

Lord, I give my life to You. I trust in You, my God! Do not let me be disgraced or let my enemies rejoice in my defeat.

Father, Your Word says, "'I know what I am planning for you. I have good plans for you, not plans to hurt you. I will give you hope and a good future. Then you will call my name. You will call my name. You will come to me and pray to me, and I will listen to you. You will search for me. And when you search for me with all your heart, you will find me! I will let you find me,' says the LORD" (Jeremiah 29:11-14 NCV).

In the name of Jesus, I will always pray and not give up!

Father, I am looking for Your plan, Your answer for my life. It is my desire to be married, but I must be sure that my decision is what You intend for me. Your Word says that marriage may bring extra problems that I may not need to face at this time in my life.

Sometimes I may believe that I am doing right but, You will judge my reasons. So, I depend on You in whatever I do and You will help my plans to succeed.

Lord, You are my Shepherd and I have all that I need.

You let me rest in green pastures and lead me beside the calm streams. You give me new strength. You help me to do what honors You.

Even walking through a dark valley, I will not be afraid, for You are close beside me, guarding and guiding me, making me feel safe all the way.

You provide delicious food for me in front of my enemies. You honor me as Your guest; my blessings overflow!

Your goodness and mercy shall be with me all of my life, and afterward I will live with You forever.

In Jesus name I pray, amen.

Scripture References

Psalm 25:1,2 NLT

Proverbs 16:2,3 NCV

Luke 18:1 NIV

Psalm 23:1 TLB

1 Corinthians 7:1,2 TLB

Letting Go of Bitterness

Introduction

In interviews with divorced men and women, I have
been encouraged to write a prayer on overcoming bitterness.

Often the injustice of the situation in which these
people find themselves creates deep hurts, wounds in the
spirit, and anger that is so near the surface that the individuals involved risk sinking into the trap of bitterness
and revenge. Their thoughts may turn inward as they
consider the unfairness of the situation and dwell on
how badly they have been treated. Also, those who suffer
abandonment by the parent(s) often harbor bitterness.

In a family divorce situation, bitterness sometimes
distorts ideas of what is best for the child/children
involved. One parent (and sometimes both parents) will
use the child/children against the other. Unresolved
anger often moves one marriage partner to hurt the one
he or she holds responsible for the hurt and sense of
betrayal which they feel.

There is healing available. There is a way of escape
for all who will turn to the Healer, obeying Him and
trusting Him.

Prayer

Father, life seems so unjust, so unfair. The pain of rejection is almost more than I can bear. My past relationships have ended in strife, anger, rejection and separation.

Lord, help me to not be bitter or angry or mad. Help me to never shout or say things to hurt others.

You are the One who has come to free those who have been treated unfairly. I receive emotional healing by faith, and I thank You for giving me the grace to stand firm until the process is complete.

Thank You for wise counselors. Thank You for Your Holy Spirit, my Counselor, who comes to show me what is true. Thank You for helping me to work out with fear and trembling what it really means to be saved. You are working in me, creating in my heart the desire and power to do what pleases You.

In the name of Jesus, I forgive those who have wronged me. I choose to live a life of forgiveness because You have forgiven me. With the help of the Holy Spirit, I rid myself of all bitterness, rage, anger, harsh words, and slander. Flood my heart with kindness that I might be tenderhearted and forgiving.

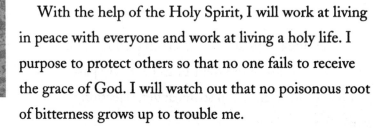

With the help of the Holy Spirit, I will work at living in peace with everyone and work at living a holy life. I purpose to protect others so that no one fails to receive the grace of God. I will watch out that no poisonous root of bitterness grows up to trouble me.

I will watch and pray that I don't enter into temptation or cause others to stumble.

Thank You, Father, that those whom the Son makes free are truly free. I have defeated bitterness and resentment by the blood of the Lamb and Your message.

In Jesus's name, amen.

Scripture References

Ephesians 4:31 NCV	Ephesians 4:31,32 NLT
Luke 4:18 NCV	Hebrews 12:14,15 NLT
Isaiah 10:27	Matthew 26:41
Proverbs 11:14	Romans 14:21
John 15:26 CEV	Jeremiah 1:12 NCV
Philippians 2:12,13 CEV	John 8:36 NCV
Matthew 5:44	Revelation 12:11 CEV

Preparing Self for Marriage

Father, sometimes being single can be so lonely and so painful. Seeing people in pairs, laughing and having fun, makes me feel even more alone and different.

Lord, please comfort me in these times. Help me to deal with my feelings and thoughts in an appropriate way. Help me to remember to work hard on myself so that I will be whole and mature when You bring the right person into my life.

Help me to remember that this is a time of preparation for the day when I will be joined to another human being for life. Show me how to be responsible for myself and how to allow others to be responsible for themselves.

Teach me about boundaries - what they are and how to establish them instead of walls. Teach me about love – Your love and how to say what is true and say it with love.

Father, I don't want to hold my future spouse or myself back. Help me to take a good look at myself and at who I am in Christ Jesus. Lead me to the right people- teachers, preachers, counselors, and to things – books, CD's, seminars – anyone and anything You can use to teach me Your ways of being and doing right.

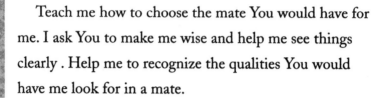
Teach me how to choose the mate You would have for me. I ask You to make me wise and help me see things clearly . Help me to recognize the qualities You would have me look for in a mate.

Father, thank You for revealing to me that the choice of a mate is not to be based only on emotions and feelings, but that You have definite guidelines in Your Word for me to use. I know that when I follow what You tell me to do, I will save myself and others a lot of pain and trouble.

Thank You, Lord, that You know me better than I know myself. You know my situation and You know the qualities that I need in another person to fulfill our destiny, individually and as a couple. I depend on You to protect me from the wrong people, so my plans will succeed.

In Jesus' name I pray, amen.

Scripture References

1 Corinthians 1:3,4 NIV   James 1:5-8 WE

Ephesians 4:15 WE   Proverbs 3:26 AMP

Matthew 6:33 AMP   Proverbs 16:3 AMP

Single Believer

Introduction

Although this prayer was written with the Single Believer in mind, I would encourage anyone who is tempted by leering, seducing flare-ups of your own lust to pray this prayer aloud over yourself!

Today, sex, which is sacred to God, has been perverted and is used to sell almost anything...from cars to hamburgers. One only has to go on the Internet, open a magazine or turn to the news on television to see sexual images. As followers of Jesus, you must constantly keep God's Word before your eyes...write His truth on the tablet of your heart.

Prayer

Jesus is my Lord, and I am a child adopted into Your family. As Your child, I realize that my body is a sacred place, the place of the Holy Spirit. In the name of Jesus, I submit to the control of the Holy Spirit, and will not live however I please, squandering what You paid for with such a high price. This physical part of me is not some piece of property belonging to the spiritual part of me. God, You own the whole works. So I choose to let people see You in and through my body.

I am strong in You, and I choose to shun youthful lusts, flee from them and aim at and pursue righteousness — all that is virtuous and good, right living, conformity to the will of God in thought, word and deed. I aim at and pursue faith, love and peace — which is harmony and concord with others — in fellowship with all Christians who call upon the name of the Lord out of a pure heart.

I am energetic in my life of salvation, reverent and sensitive before You, Father. You are at work in me energizing and creating in me the power and desire to do Your good will. I will bring a breath of fresh air to a polluted society, and carry the light-giving Message into the night.

In Jesus' name, amen.

Scripture References

1 Corinthians 6:17-20 MSG

Philippians 2:12,15,16 MSG

Single Female Trusting God for a Mate

Father, in the name of Jesus, I believe that You are at work in me, energizing and creating in me the power and desire to do Your will for Your good pleasure. You are preparing me to receive my future mate who will provide leadership to me the way You do to Your church, not by being domineering but by cherishing me.

Out of respect for Christ, we will be courteously reverent to one another. Prepare me to understand and support my future husband in ways that show my support for You, the Christ.

Father, I believe because he has been divinely chosen by You, my future mate is full of Your wisdom which is straight-forward, gentle and reasonable, overflowing with mercy and blessings. He speaks the truth in love.

Father, I believe that everything not of You shall be removed from my life. I thank You that every word that You give to me will come true. Father, I praise You for performing Your Word! Amen.

Scripture References

Isaiah 62:5 NCV   Proverbs 8:8 NCV

Ephesians 5:25   Jeremiah 1:12 MSG

James 3:17 MSG

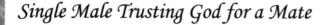

Single Male Trusting God for a Mate

Father, in the name of Jesus, I believe that You are providing a wonderful woman who will understand and support me. I pray that we will walk together with like faith and in agreement. Prepare me to provde leadership to my future wife the way You do to Your church, not by being domineering but by cherishing her.

Father, a wise wife is a gift from the Lord and he who finds a wife finds what is good and receives favor from You.

Father, I have written mercy and truth on the tablets of my heart and bind them about my mind. I will receive favor and good understanding from You and from others.

May Your will be done in my life, even as it is in heaven! Amen!

<u>Scripture References</u>

Ephesians 5:22,23 MSG   Philippians 2:2 MSG

Proverbs 18:22 NIV   Jeremiah 1:12 NLT

Proverbs 19:14

PART III:

GROUP PRAYERS:
GOD'S PEOPLE,
MINISTERS,
AND MINISTRIES

The Body of Christ

Father, I acknowledge and proclaim that Jesus is
Lord of the Church. May we always remember that
all things are under His power, and for the good of the
Church, You have made Him the head of everything.
The Church is the Body of Christ and we are filled with
Christ who completely fills everything.

Father, I pray that we grow up, know the whole truth
and tell it in love – like Christ in everything. We take
our lead from Christ, who is the Source of everything we
do. He keeps us in step with each other. His very breath
and blood flow through us, nourishing us so that we will
grow up healthy in You, robust in love.

You chose us for this new life of love. We will dress
in Your wardrobe which is compassion, kindness, humility, quiet strength, and discipline. Holy Spirit, remind
us that if we have a complaint against another, even as
Christ forgave us, so we must also forgive. Regardless of
what else we put on, we will wear love, which is our ba-
sic, all-purpose garment that we never want to leave off.
Thank You for the peace of Christ that keeps us in tune
with each other and in step with each other.

Full of belief, confident that we're presentable inside
and out, we keep a firm grip on the promises that keep

us going. Father, You always keep Your Word. Now we will see how inventive we can be in encouraging love and helping out, not avoiding worshipping together as some do, but spurring each other on, especially as we see the big Day approaching.

Since we are all called to travel on the same road and in the same direction, we will stay together, both outwardly and inwardly. We have one Master, one faith, one baptism, one God and Father of all, who rules over all, works through all, and is present in all. Everything we are and think and do is permeated with oneness.

Father, we commit to pray for one another, keeping our eyes open and keeping each other's spirits up, so that no one falls behind or drops out. Also, we pray for our spiritual leaders that they will know what to say and have the courage to say it at the right time. We are one in the bond of love, in the name of Jesus.

Scripture References

Ephesians 1:22,23 CEV

Hebrews 10:23-25 MSG

Ephesians 4:15,16 MSG

Ephesians 4:4-6 MSG

Colossians 3:12-15 MSG

Ephesians 6:18,19 MSG

A Christian Counselor

Father, in the name of Jesus, I pray for _____
to encourage and counsel the emotionally wounded. I
ask in faith that Your Spirit will rest upon him/her –
the Spirit of wisdom and understanding, guidance and
power. Give him/her insight and knowledge for understanding his/her counselees' responses to circumstances.

Thank You, Father, that _____is a good lis-
tener to the confessions of his/her counselees. Help him/
her to discern unresolved and unhealed past hurts that
influence reactions to situations around them.

Lord, _____will judge honestly and be fair in his/
her decisions. Goodness and fairness will give him/her
strength like a belt around their waist.

Thank You that _____is full of joy and
promotes peace. Give Your counselor , out of the glorious richness of Your resources, the strength of the
Spirit's power in their inner being, that Christ actually
lives in his/her heart by faith.

You will not leave _____without support as
he/she gives his/her time and concern, helping to complete the forgiveness process. He/she will be confident

about his/her convictions, and will have the knowledge to help Your children in knowing that these are truths that work.

<u>Scripture References</u>

Isaiah 11:2-3 NCV

Isaiah 11:4-5 NCV

Ephesians 3:16 Phillips

Proverbs 22:20,21 MSG

Church Teachers

Father, we come to You in the name of Jesus, asking You for teachers who are called by You for our classes and choirs. We thank You for teachers who are filled with the Spirit of God and have great wisdom, ability and expertise in all kinds of areas to teach the Word of God.

Lord, may these teachers assume great accountability. According to Your Word, they will be judged more strictly than others. Even though we all make mistakes, we thank You that our teachers will not offend people by what they say but pray that they may be able to keep their whole body in check.

Thank You that our teachers are given gifts from You to make them better able to do their work and make the body of Christ become stronger. These gifts are given so that we will all believe the one way and all know the Son of God. The body of Christ must learn and grow in faith so that we will no longer be like children. Sometimes, we are like children when we are pushed this way and that way. Forgive us for changing our minds every time people bring a different teaching. Some teachers teach the lies of men and fool people so that they believe the wrong things. Thank You that our teachers will say what

is true and say it with love. In that way, we will then grow up in all things to be like Christ, who is the head of this body.

Father, thank You that You are at work in our teachers - enabling them to want and to actually live out Your good purposes. It is You who makes them competent administrators and let them deal in the Spirit. The letter of the law ends in death; the Spirit of God alone can give life.

Father, we share the same love and have one mind and purpose with our teachers. We will lift them up and not let selfishness or pride be our guide. Thank You that our teachers are humble and give more honor to others than themselves. They will think and act like Jesus Christ in their lives and they care for Your flock with all the diligence of a shepherd. Not because they have to, but because they want to please You.

Thank You, Lord, that You are watching to see that Your Word is fulfilled. Amen.

<u>Scripture References</u>

Exodus 31:3-4 NLT

Proverbs 8:6

Ephesians 4:12-15 WE

Philippians 2:13 CEB

Philippians 2:2,4,5 NCV

2 Corinthians 3:5,6 Phillips

Romans 12:7

James 3:1,2 NIV

1 Peter 5:2,3 MSG

Jeremiah 1:12 NIV

Ministers

Father, in the name of Jesus, thank You that our pastor/minister is as conscientious and responsible toward those who work with him in this congregation/ministry as he expects them to be toward him. I am so grateful for a minister who does not misuse the authority over the congregation that You have placed in his hands. He is ever mindful that he is responsible to a heavenly Shepherd, who makes no distinction between shepherd and sheep.

As your minister, he realizes that his responsibility is to be just and fair toward those who labor with him in ministry. Thank You for the Holy Spirit who helps him maintain the habit of prayer for them: he is alert and thankful as he prays for each person to find favor with You and with other people. Help him always to give honor where honor is due.

Thank You for giving him Your discernment for those with whom he labors, that he might see their hidden potential and draw it out, helping them to become all that You created them to be. He values those who serve with him as persons called by You for their appointed tasks. I thank You for bringing alongside him personnel

with needed abilities and talents; may he always be sensitive to their spiritual and emotional needs. Although he could be bold and order them to do what they ought to do, help him to always appeal to them on the basis of Your love.

Thank You for Your strength and ability, which enables Your minister to do unto others as he would have them do unto him. Help him to follow Jesus as his example in all that he says and does. May we hold up his hands as together we build your kingdom in joy, faith, and love to Your glory.

In Jesus' name I pray, amen.

<u>Scripture References</u>

Ephesians 6:9 Phillips

Philemon 8-9 NIV

Colossians 4:1-2 Phillips

Matthew 7:12 NIV

Luke 2:52

1 Peter 2:21 NIV

Romans 13:7

A Ministry in Need of Finances

Introduction

This prayer was written in response to an appeal for help from a ministry in a financial crunch. This ministry reaches out to people addicted to drugs, alcohol, and other substances. After we had prayed the following prayer, it was given to our editor and prayer request correspondent. It can be used to pray for the needs of any ministry.

Prayer

Father, in the name of Jesus, I believe that You will take care of everything that _____needs, according to Philippians 4:19 (MSG). I know this ministry gives tithes and offerings to further Your cause to help youth, adults and families come to know You and Your truth. Thank You for the gifts that will be given to them; they will fill their cup, press it down, shake it and let it run over. How much they have given to others is how much God will give back to them.

Father, in the name of Jesus, we ask according to Your Word that those who have planted spiritual seed will also harvest material things, for You have said that those who present the Good News will live by the Good News.

Your ministers who work with _____
ministry want those who give to experience the blessing
that issues from generosity. Their gifts are like a sweet-
smelling sacrifice roasting on the altar, filling the air with
fragrance, pleasing God to no end. They can be sure that
You will take care of everything they need, Your generosity exceeing even theirs in the glory that pours from
Jesus.

Father, we pray for partners who will respond to Your
call to support this ministry both prayerfully and financially.

Lord, we thank You for directing the leader,
_____, who seeks Your ways and lives a quiet
and peaceful life marked by godliness and dignity. Your
anointing, which will end the bondage of Your people,
will abide within him forever. Teach him to pray for the
people and the government of our land. We thank You
for Your Word that is truth and that will set everyone
who hears it free!

Lord, we ask you to strengthen and make
_____what he ought to be, equipping him thor-
oughly for doing Your will. May You produce in him
everything that pleases You through Jesus Christ.

Scripture References

Luke 6:38 WE   Isaiah 10:27 NLT

1 Corinthians 9:11-13 NCV   1 Timothy 2:1-3 NLT

Philippians 4:17-19 MSG   John 8:32

Matthew 9:38 NIV   Hebrews 13:21 Phillips

Ministers to the Incarcerated

Introduction

This prayer was written in response to a letter from an inmate. He had received Jesus, started a Bible study, and wanted to know how to pray for God-called teachers and preachers to come and teach the inmates. He was praying for prisoners who did not know Jesus, believing that revival was coming to the correctional facility where he was housed.

Prayer

Father, everyone who calls on the name of the Lord will be saved. But how can they call on Him to save them unless they believe in Him? And how can they believe in Him if they have never heard about Him? And how can they hear about Him unless someone tells them? We ask You, Lord, to send more workers into the fields of these prisons.

Father, we thank You for ministers who are willing to go and preach deliverance to the prisoners. May You make them very strong in heart by Your Spirit. You have great and wonderful blessings and are able to do this because of the fullness of Your glory.

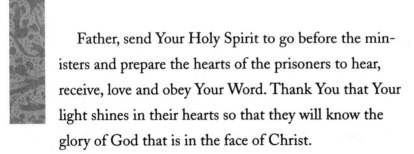

Father, send Your Holy Spirit to go before the ministers and prepare the hearts of the prisoners to hear, receive, love and obey Your Word. Thank You that Your light shines in their hearts so that they will know the glory of God that is in the face of Christ.

Father, thank You for creating a desire within Your ministers to study Your Word with diligence that they will make an effort to present themselves to You as a good worker who doesn't need to be ashamed but one who interprets the Message of Truth correctly. They are living witnesses to those who aren't yet obedient to the Gospel.

Thank You, Father, for pouring Your Spirit out upon the staff and inmates of this facility. We know that people believe because they hear and they hear because people tell them about You. We thank You for the salvation and deliverance for all those who call upon Your name.

In the name of Jesus, we thank You for sending the Holy Spirit who will expose the error of the godless world's view of sin, righteousness and judgment. Reveal who Jesus is to those who seek You, just as You did for Peter in Matthew 16.

We ask You to release Your mercy, Your love, and Your grace to those within these walls that they might be saved through faith.

Thank You, Lord, for hearing our prayer on behalf of the people at this prison/correctional facility.

In Jesus' name, amen.

Scripture References

Romans 10:13, 14 NLT	Romans 15:18
Matthew 9:38 NLT	Acts 2:18
Ephesians 3:16 WE	Romans 10:17 WE
2 Corinthians 4:6 NCV	John 16:8,13 MSG
2 Timothy 2:15 CEB	Ephesians 2:8

Ministry in Nursing Homes

Father, thank You for calling me to minister to Your children in nursing homes. I intend to keep on going by Your power, for You first saved me and then called me to this holy work. I had nothing to do with it. It was Your idea, a gift prepared for me in Jesus long before I knew anything about it.

But I know it now. Since the appearance of our Savior, nothing could be plainer; death defeated, life vindicated in a steady blaze of light – all through the work of Jesus. The One I've trusted in can take care of what He's trusted me to do right to the end.

Thank You for Your Word. The teaching of Your Word gives light so that even the simple can understand. Because You are light, the words that I speak are full of spirit and life. I pray that the light of Your Word will illuminate the minds to these precious people I minister to.

Father, You have given me a gift of understanding so that we all may know what is true. You have touched my hands so that when I lay hands on the sick, they shall be comforted and become well.

Thank You, Lord, for those who welcome me, reaching out for prayer, encouragement and hugs. I pray that the light in my eyes will bring joy to their hearts. Help me to encourage them and teach them to continue in their desire to be useful while fulfilling Your call on their lives.

Father, You have a purpose for them – it is not Your will that they be set aside. You want them to still produce fruit and be healthy and fresh. Help me to convey this to them.

Father, send Your angels of mercy and healing to those who are in fetal positions, not speaking or opening their eyes. Minister Your healing to these souls who will soon meet You face to face. I yield myself to be used as an instrument of righteousness bringing salvation, wholeness, healing, deliverance, and comfort to the sick and elderly.

Father, You take the side of orphans and widows and make short work of the wicked. I take hold of this promise for all those I minister to, knowing that You are watching and will certainly carry out all Your plans.

I do not go in my own strength, but in the divine energy that You provide. It is my purpose to always be obedient to James 1:27 NLT – "Pure and genuine

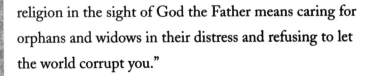

religion in the sight of God the Father means caring for orphans and widows in their distress and refusing to let the world corrupt you."

Thank You, Lord, that I eat good crops from the land because I am willing to obey You. I serve You with a glad heart. Whatever You call me to do, You equip me with all that I need to accomplish it.

In the name of Jesus, amen.

Scripture References

2 Timothy 1:8-10 MSG	Romans 6:13
Deuteronomy 10:18 AMP	Psalm 68:5 AMP
Psalm 119:130 NLT	Psalm 146:9 MSG
John 1:4	Jeremiah 1:12 NLT
John 6:63	Isaiah 39:1
2 Corinthians 4:4 AMP	Genesis 18:14
1 John 2:20,27 WE	James 1:15
Mark 16:18 MSG	2 Timothy 2:21
Psalm 92:14 NCV	Isaiah 1:19
Mark 4:2	

Ministry Partners

I. Prayers for Ministry Partners

Father, we thank You for our financial and prayer partners and for their service and dedication to serve You. Thank You that they bring forth the fruit of the Spirit: love, joy, peace, longsuffering, gentleness, goodness, faith, meekness, and temperance.

Father, thank You that our partners are good ground, that they hear Your Word and understand it, and that the Word bears fruit in their lives. They are like trees planted along the riverbank, bearing fruit each season. Their leaves never wither and they prosper in all they do.

From the first day we heard of our partners, we haven't stopped praying for them, asking You, Father, to give them wise minds and spirits attuned to Your will, that they might acquire a thorough understanding of the ways in which You work. Our partners are merciful as our Father is merciful. They will not judge others so they won't be judged. They do not condemn, and they are not condemned. Our partners forgive others and people forgive them.

They give, and men will give to them – yet their gift will return to them in full – pressed down, shaken together to make room for more, running over, and poured into their lap. The amount they give will determine the amount that they get back.

In Jesus' name we pray, amen.

Scripture References

Colossians 1:9 MSG

Matthew 7:1 NCV

Galatians 5:22,23

Luke 6:37, 38 NLT

Psalm 1:3 NLT

II. *Prayers for Ministry Partners*

Father, I ask You to give our partners wisdom so that good will come to them. Thank You for generous partners who conduct business fairly.

Lord, they do not fear bad news; they confidently trust in You to care for them. They are confident and fearless.

I agree with them and ask that Your plans for them be fulfilled. We thank You for Your great mercies on their behalf.

In the name of Jesus, amen.

<u>Scripture References</u>

Psalm 112:5-8 NLT   Jeremiah 29:11 NIV

Colossians 1:9 NCV

Missionaries

Father, first may we never forget to pray for the
families of martys who are being killed for their faith in
Christ Jesus. Here in this prayer time, we bring before
You those in the Body of Christ who are out in the field
carrying the good news of the Gospel not only in this
country, but also around the world. We lift up those in
the Body of Christ who are suffering persecution – those
who are in prison for their beliefs. Father, we know that
You are watching to make sure that Your words come
true. We know that when Your Word is sent out that
it always produces fruit. It will accomplish all that You
want it to and will prosper everywhere You send it. We
pray here, and others receive the answer there by the
Holy Spirit.

Thank You, Father, for revealing the truth of Your
Word unto Your people so that they can keep their guard
up against the devil. May they be living witnesses to
those who do not know You. Father, You are their light
and the One who saves them. You protect their life.
During danger, You keep them safe in Your shelter. It is
Your will that each one enjoys good health and that all
goes well with them, even as their soul is getting along
well. You set the prisoners free, feed the hungry, execute
justice, rescue and deliver!

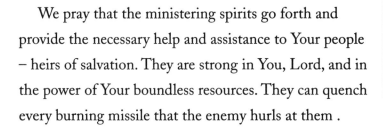

We pray that the ministering spirits go forth and provide the necessary help and assistance to Your people – heirs of salvation. They are strong in You, Lord, and in the power of Your boundless resources. They can quench every burning missile that the enemy hurls at them .

Father, we cover these in the Body of Christ with Your Word. No weapon that is used against them will defeat them and those who speak against them are wrong. Because they are Your children, they will be safe from those that would hurt them and they do not fear those who can kill the body only.

Father, keep them strong until the end – keep them steadfast and give them strength. You are their Warrant against all accusation or indictment. They are not worried about how they will defend themselves, for the Holy Spirit will give them what to say at that time.

Now, we entrust them to Your protection and care. You are so faithful! You strengthen them and set them on a firm foundation and guard them from the Evil One. Our praise will stop and still the avenger. Praise the Lord! Greater is He that is in us than he that is in the world!

In Jesus' name we pray, amen.

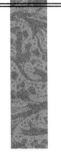
<u>Scripture References</u>

Jeremiah 1:12 NCV	Isaiah 55:11 NLT
Isaiah 54:14, 17 NCV	1 Peter 5:9 MSG
1 Corinthians 1:8 NLT	Psalm 27:1,5 NCV
Luke 12:11,12 NIV	3 John 2 NIV
Ephesians 6:10,16 Phillips	Colossians 4:6
1 John 5:4,5	Acts 20:32
Psalm 146:7	2 Thessalonians 3:3
Psalm 144:7	Psalm 8:2
Matthew 18:18	1 John 4:4
Hebrews 1:14	

Office Staff

Introduction

Our prayer coordinator wrote this prayer for our ministry. It may be used for the members of any ministry or outreach that depends upon the Holy Spirit to go before it and prepare the way for its labor with and for the Lord.

Prayer

Father, today is the day that You have made. I will be glad for this day! I thank You for Your goodness, mercy, and grace toward us as individuals and as a ministry.

Father, I pray for this day with all its decisions, activities, relationships, and creativity. I give it all to You because I know that Jesus is Lord of all. May each staff member bring honor and glory to Your name. We pray for Your will to be done in us individually and as a ministry.

I plead the blood of Jesus over this property, all staff members, every person who enters the doors and the entire ministry network, including all those whom I lift up in prayer to You, Lord. Thank You that You have freed

me from the power of darkness and brought me into the kingdom of Your dear Son.

Father, today I choose life and blessings. Thank You for removing the load that I carry and taking it away. You carry that for me and the power that removes the load resides in me.

Thank You for Your love. The staff and I are Your children so we try to be like You – living a life of love in truth, in light, and in wisdom inside and outside these offices. We are patient, steady and strong.

I ask for Your Spirit and Your rain to be poured out on this ministry. You have called us by grace for such a time as this! Hallelujah!

In the name of Jesus, amen.

Scripture References

Psalm 33:1	1 John 2:27
Psalm 118:24 NKJV	1 Corinthians 6:20
1 Corinthians 12:3 WE	Ephesians 5:1,2 NCV
Matthew 6:10	James 5:7 MSG
Colossians 1:13 NCV	1 Peter 5:10
Deuteronomy 30:19 NLT	Esther 4:14
Isaiah 10:27 NCV	Acts 2:17

Overcoming Prejudice

Introduction

The previous few days in Miami had been exceptionally cool. Jan, my traveling companion, and I did not consider it coat weather, but the Floridians shivered, all bundled up in their winter wear.

The prayer seminar had gone well, and it was now our last service before leaving for home. The preparation for the Sunday morning worship service had been difficult, and I found myself at the mercy of the Holy Spirit. (Not a bad place to be!) During the preliminaries and the praise and worship service, I was crying out inwardly, just for a starting scripture that I could read.

The sanctuary was packed as I stood before the congregation of beautiful skin tones – from almost white to light chocolate to black velvet. Their faces looked back at me. I smiled and began to read a psalm – making comments as I felt prompted by the Holy Spirit.

Where is the flow of the Spirit? I wondered. *God, what is it You want to do in this church today?*

The tension within me was great, and I felt helpless.

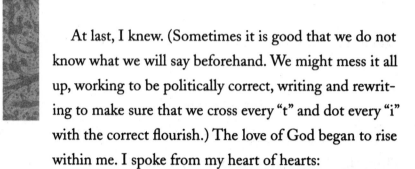

At last, I knew. (Sometimes it is good that we do not know what we will say beforehand. We might mess it all up, working to be politically correct, writing and rewriting to make sure that we cross every "t" and dot every "i" with the correct flourish.) The love of God began to rise within me. I spoke from my heart of hearts:

"You cannot really know me unless I choose to share myself- my thoughts, my ideas, and my feelings. Obviously, I am a Southern white woman. I grew up in cotton mill towns in North Georgia. There, I attended the all-white Pentecostal churches where my dad served as pastor. I attended all-white schools and lived in all-white neighborhoods. The only black people I knew were Smut and Clarabell, tenants on my uncle's farm.

"I don't know if I have any racial prejudice – it has never been tested. I know that at one time I was filled with intellectual prejudice, because God exposed it in a very dramatic way. If I have any racial prejudice, I want the Holy Spirit to uncover it and deliver me. All I know is that I love you, and we are one- one blood. In Christ Jesus there is neither Jew nor Greek, male nor female, black nor white. There is that one new man created in Him."

The barriers came tumbling down. My newly found friends, brothers and sisters in the Lord, no longer hugged from a distance. Many smothered me in bear hugs after the benediction. The unity of the Spirit had prevailed (Eph. 4:3).

Jesus is our peace, and I believe that the Scriptures written by the Apostle Paul in Galatians and Ephesians apply today.

Ethnic groups are assuming responsibility for the sins of the forefathers and asking forgiveness for past wrongs done to one another. We are accountable to God and each other as members of one household, and by the blood of the Lamb and through good communication, we are overcoming the dividing schemes of the devil. God is bringing His people together. Red and yellow, black and white – we are coming together – and we are precious in His sight.

We are no longer strangers or aliens, but fellow citizens with every other Christian – we belong now to God's family (Eph. 2:19 NCV).

Prayer

Father, in the name of Jesus, I come before You, asking Your forgiveness for being intolerant of others because of the color of their skin. Forgive me for tolerating prejudice in the church. Set me free from the influence

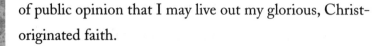

of public opinion that I may live out my glorious, Christ-
originated faith.

Forgive Your church for segregating ourselves by
color, by a measure of wealth or intellect. We are all Your
people, the sheep of Your pasture.

We are one blood. We were bought with blood that
is worth much – the blood of Christ! All of us who have
been baptized into Christ and have taken Him as our
own, there is no longer any difference between us.

I pray for an end to division in Christ's family. All of
us are equal – slave and free, male and female. We are all
in a common relationship with Jesus Christ.

Thank You, Father, for bringing us together in Christ
through His death on the cross. The cross got us to embrace, and that was the end of the hostility.

Lord Jesus, You came and preached peace to us outsiders and peace to us insiders. You treated us as equals
and so made us equals. Through Him we share the same
Spirit and have equal access to You, Father.

The Kingdom of faith is now our home country, and
we are no longer strangers or outsiders. We belong here.

Lord, You are building a home. You are using us

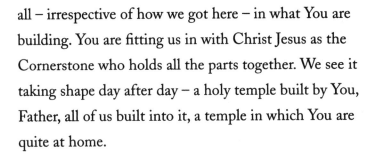

all – irrespective of how we got here – in what You are building. You are fitting us in with Christ Jesus as the Cornerstone who holds all the parts together. We see it taking shape day after day – a holy temple built by You, Father, all of us built into it, a temple in which You are quite at home.

Father, You have called us all to travel on the same road and in the same direction, so we will stay together, both outwardly and inwardly. We have one Master, one faith, one baptism, one God and Father of all who rules over all, works through all, and is present in all. Everything we are and think and do is permeated with oneness.

Father, I make this personal commitment to be like You…to live a life full of love. In the past, I was full of darkness but now I am full of light in You. I am careful how I live. I live wisely and use every chance I have for doing good because these are evil times. I speak to others with psalms, hymns, and spiritual songs, singing and making music in my heart to You, Lord. By love, I will serve others.

Thank You, Father, that prejudice is being rooted out of the Body of Christ, in the name of Jesus. Amen.

Scripture References

James 2:1 MSG

Psalm 100:3 NIV

1 Peter 1:18,19 WE

Galatians 3:27,28 WE

Ephesians 5:15,16,19,20 NCV

Ephesians 2:13-22 MSG

Ephesians 4:3-6 MSG

Ephesians 5:1,2,8 NCV

Galatians 5:13 AMP

Personal Prayer of a Pastor for the Congregation

Father, as the pastor of _____, I come before Your throne of grace on behalf of the membership. I have joy in my heart every time I bring them before You, Lord. I thank You, Lord, for the joy we share in telling Your good news. I am sure that You began to do a good work in all of them and that You will keep on doing it until You have finished it. You will keep on until the day of Jesus Christ.

In the name of Jesus, it is right and appropriate for me to have this confidence and feel this way about them all, because even as they do me, I hold them in my heart as sharers – one and all with me – of grace (God's unmerited favor and spiritual blessing).

Father, You are my witness and know how I long for and pursue them all with love in the tender mercies of Christ Jesus. So this is my prayer: that their love will flourish and that they will not only love much but love well and learn to love appropriately. May they use their heads and test their feeling so that their love is sincere and intelligent, not sentimental gush. I pray that each one will live a lover's life, circumspect and exemplary, a

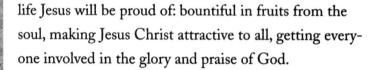

life Jesus will be proud of: bountiful in fruits from the soul, making Jesus Christ attractive to all, getting everyone involved in the glory and praise of God.

I am sure of this, Father: I will stay alive and remain with them to help them grow and experience the joy of their faith and increase their pride in Christ Jesus through my presence. In the name of Jesus, they will live together in a manner worthy of Your gospel.

Thank You, Lord, that they are standing firm, united in one spirit and mind as they remain faithful to the gospel. They are not afraid of anything their enemies do. Their faithfulness and courage are a sign of their enemy's destruction and their salvation, which is from You!

The membership of _____ makes me very, very happy because they live in happiness with one another and have the same lover for each other. They think the same way and agree together about things, all having one purpose in mind.

In Jesus' name, amen.

<u>Scripture References</u>

Philippians 1:4-6 WE

Philippians 1:7 AMP

Philippians 1:8-11 MSG

Philippians 1:25-28 CEB

Philippians 2:2 WE

Prosperity for Ministering Servants

Father, I praise You and thank You for Your Word,
knowing You are watching to see that Your Word is
fulfilled. I am confident that the words You speak and
Your words that I speak, will not return to You empty,
but will accomplish what You desire and achieve the
purpose for which You sent them.

Father, in Jesus' name, I pray and believe that those
in Your body who have sown the seed of spiritual things
will reap material things. The people's gifts, which are
for the spreading of the Gospel, are like a sweet-smelling
offering to You, Father, and it pleases You. You give Your
ministering servants and those who are financial partners
with them everything that they need according to Your
riches in Christ Jesus.

Father, it is Your will that those who learn your
teaching should share all the good things that they have
learned with their teacher. I say that Your people will not
become tired of doing good because they love You and
will receive their harvest of eternal life at the right time
if they do not give up.

God, You will generously provide all that is needed.
I pray that Your ministering servants will always have

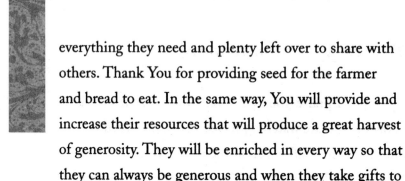

everything they need and plenty left over to share with others. Thank You for providing seed for the farmer and bread to eat. In the same way, You will provide and increase their resources that will produce a great harvest of generosity. They will be enriched in every way so that they can always be generous and when they take gifts to those who need them, they will thank You, Lord.

As it is written in Your Word, "Give and you will receive. Your gift will return to you in full – pressed down, shaken together to make room for more, running over, and poured into your lap" (Luke 6:38 NLT). Praise the Lord!

In Jesus' name, amen.

Scripture References

Jeremiah 1:12 NIV

Galatians 6:6-10 NCV

Isaiah 55:11 NIV

2 Corinthians 9:6-11 NLT

Philippians 4:17-19 WE

Luke 6:38 NLT

1 Corinthians 9:11-14 Phillips

Revival

Father, in the name of Jesus, I ask You to send a revival to Your Church, and let it begin with me. You have given us life again so that Your people will rejoice in You. Thank You for showing us Your love and saving us. Thank You for creating in us a pure heart and making our spirit right again. You have given us back the joy of our salvation and are keeping us strong by giving us a willing spirit. Then we will teach Your ways to those who do wrong and sinners will turn back to You.

Father, forgive us for the times we have rationalized our decisions that were contrary to Truth. We insisted on having our own way rather than obeying Your Word. Energize and create within us the will and desire to stay on the path of purity by living according to Your Word. We seek You with all of our heart so we won't stray from Your commands. We are hiding Your Word in our heart that we might not sin against You. Jesus, thank You for cleansing us through the Word – the teachings which You have given us. We delight ourselves in Your decrees and we won't forget Your Word. Be good to Your servants so that we may live and obey Your Word.

Father, in the name of Jesus, we are doers of the Word and not hearers only, who mislead themselves. Thank

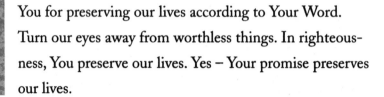

You for preserving our lives according to Your Word.
Turn our eyes away from worthless things. In righteousness, You preserve our lives. Yes – Your promise preserves
our lives.

We have gotten rid of the old way of life and we are
taking on an entirely new way of life – a God-fashioned
life, a life renewed from the inside and working itself
into our conduct as You accurately reproduce Your
character in us. We will not give up! Our bodies may get
weak but our hearts get new strength day after day!
Hallelujah! Amen.

Scripture References

Psalm 85:6,7 NCV   James 1:22 CEB

Psalm 51:10,12,13 NCV   Psalm 119:25 NIV

Psalm 119:9-11 NIV   Psalm 119:37,40,50 NIV

2 Corinthians 7:1 WE   Ephesians 4:22-24 MSG

John 15:3   2 Corinthians 4:16 WE

Psalm 119:16, 17 NLT

Success of a Meeting

Father, in the name of Jesus, we come before your throne of grace boldly and with confidence. When the speaker opens his/her mouth, may the message of the Gospel come across confidently. We ask that those who hear will not be able to resist the wisdom and the Spirit by which this minister speaks.

As Your Word is taught, we ask that people's hearts be flooded with light so that they can understand the confident hope that You have given to them. We pray that their eyes will be opened and that they will turn from darkness to light and from the power of Satan to You so that they may receive forgiveness of their sins.

We commit this meeting to You, Father; we put all these people in Your care and the message of Your grace. Your message is able to give the people strength and blessings. We know that Your Word is alive and working and is sharper than a double-edged sword. Your Word judges the thoughts and feelings of the people's hearts.

We ask You to meet the needs of every person spiritually, physically, mentally and financially.

We thank You, Father, that because we have asked and agreed together, these things will come to pass. May

these words that we have prayed day and night in Your presence give justice to Your people. Then everyone will know that You alone are God and there is no other! Hallelujah! Amen.

Scripture References

Matthew 18:19

Ephesians 6:19 CEB

Acts 6:10 NIV

Ephesians 1:18 NLT

1 Kings 8: 59-60 NLT

Acts 26:18 NIV

Acts 20:32 NCV

Hebrews 4:12 NCV

Philippians 4:19

Success of a Conference

Father, we pray that those who hear the messages at
the _____conference will believe- adhere to
and trust in and rely on Jesus as the Christ, and that all
those You have called to attend the conference will be
there and receive what You have for them.

We clearly state to everyone that it is in the powerful
name of Jesus Christ that this conference is successful
and people experience emotional, mental and physical
healing.

Father, You said that when two of us agree together
on anything at all on earth and make a prayer of it, that
You go into action! In the name of Jesus, we ask that
every person involved –singers, speakers, ushers and
workers – will glorify You in every word and thought.
When people attend this conference, they will know that
they have been with Jesus because of the boldness and
eloquence of the ministers. Everybody will be praising
and glorifying You, Lord, and signs and wonders will be
performed among the people.

Father, in the name of Jesus, we thank You that You
have observed the enemy's threats and You have given
Your ministers the ability to speak Your Word without

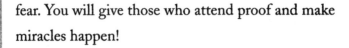
fear. You will give those who attend proof and make miracles happen!

We thank You, Father, that when we pray, the place in which we are meeting will be shaken and we will all be filled with Your Holy Spirit!

We are all meeting together by common consent. People will gather from the north, south, east and west, bringing the sick and the disturbed so that they will be healed.

I pray for each one participating in this conference. May every attitude be an expression of the fruit of the Spirit: love, joy, peace, patience, kindness, goodness, faithfulness, gentleness, and self-control. Lord, I pray that each one will release rivers of living water, which is an outflowing of Your Holy Spirit.

Thank You Father, in the name of Jesus! Amen.

<u>Scripture References</u>

Acts 4:10,13,21 NLT   Acts 5:12,13,16 WE

Matthew 18:18 MSG   Acts 6:3, 10

Acts 5:12 NIV   Galatians 5:22

Acts 4:29-31 NCV

Unity and Harmony

Father, in the name of Jesus, we are sure that You will answer our prayer. If we ask You for anything that You want us to have, You will listen to us. And if we know that You listen to us when we ask for anything, then we know that we have what we asked for.

Holy Spirit, teach us how to live in harmony with each other. Let us be of one mind, united in thought and purpose. If we learn to be of one mind and two of us agree on earth, then You will do whatever we ask.

We pray that as members of the Body of Christ, we will live as humble, gentle, and patient people, accepting each other in love. We are joined together with peace through the Spirit.

We commit, in the name of Jesus and according to His power at work in us, to live like brothers and sisters with true love and sympathy for each other, tenderhearted and humble at all times. We will never pay back a wrong turn with a wrong turn or an insult with another insult, but on the contrary we will pay back with good. For this is our calling – to do good and one day to inherit all the goodness of God.

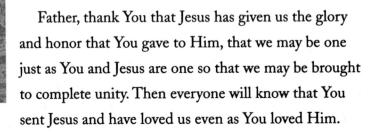
Father, thank You that Jesus has given us the glory and honor that You gave to Him, that we may be one just as You and Jesus are one so that we may be brought to complete unity. Then everyone will know that You sent Jesus and have loved us even as You loved Him.

Father, Your will be done on earth as it is in heaven. Amen, and so be it.

Scripture References

1 John 5:14,15 WE   1 Peter 3:8,9 Phillips

1 Corinthians 1:10 NLT   John 17:22,23 NIV

Ephesians 4:2,3 NCV   Matthew 6:10 NIV

Vision for a Church

Father, in the name of Jesus, we come into Your presence thanking You for _____(name of church). You have called us to be saints in _____(name of city) and around the world. As we lift our voices in one accord , we recognize that You are God and everything was made by and for You. We call into being those things that be not as though they were.

We thank You that we all speak the same thing. There is no division among us, we are perfectly joined together in the same mind. Grant unto us, Your representatives here, a boldness to speak Your Word, which You will confirm with signs following. We thank You that we have workmen in abundance and all manner of cunning people for every manner of work. Each department operates in the excellence of ministry and intercessions. We have in our church the ministry gifts for the edifying of this Body till we all come into the unity of faith and knowledge of the Son of God. None of our people will be children, tossed to and fro and carried about with every wind of doctrine. We speak the truth in love.

We are a growing and witnessing Body of believers becoming _____(number) strong. We have every need met. Therefore, we meet the needs of people who come – spirit, soul, and body. We ask for the wisdom of God in meeting these needs. Father, we thank You for the ministry facilities that will more than meet the needs of the ministry You have called us to. Our church is prospering financially, and we have more than enough to meet every situation. We have everything we need to carry out Your Great Commission and reach the _____(name of city or county) area for Jesus. We are a people of love as love is shed abroad in our hearts by the Holy Spirit. We thank You that the Word of God is living big in all of us and Jesus is Lord!

We are a supernatural church, comprised of supernatural people doing supernatural things, for we are laborers together with God. We thank You for Your presence among us, and we lift our hands and praise Your holy name! Amen.

Scripture References

Acts 4:24	Ephesians 4:11-15
Romans 4:17	Philippians 4:19
1 Corinthians 1:10	Romans 5:5
Acts 4:29	1 Corinthians 3:9
Mark 16:20	Psalm 63:4
Exodus 35:33	

This prayer was written by and used with the permission of
T.R. King, Valley Christian Center, Roanoke, Virginia.

PART III:

GROUP PRAYERS:
PEOPLES AND NATIONS

American Government

Father, in the name of Jesus, I come to You with a
heart of love and concern for America. I intercede for the
President of the United States, his cabinet and administration, for all the men and women who serve in Con-
gress, and for our military leaders in the Pentagon. With
the help of the Holy Spirit, I bring my requests, prayers
and petitions to You and give thanksgiving for all people.
I ask that You pour out Your Spirit upon everyone who is
in authority in our nation and make Your Word known
to them in order that the citizens of this great nation
may live a quiet and peaceful life in complete godliness
and dignity.

In agreement with Your will, I present my petition on
behalf of all who are in authority—our president and all
government officials—that they will accept Your words
and turn their ears toward wisdom, and stretch their
minds toward understanding. When they call out for
insight and cry aloud for understanding, they will understand the fear of the Lord and discover the knowledge of
God. I ask You, Lord, to give our president and his advisors wisdom, knowledge and understanding. I believe
that they will understand righteousness and justice as
well as integrity. The president's heart is like a stream of

water in Your hand, my Lord, and You direct it where You want.

In a multitude of counselors there is safety, and I ask You to give to our president advisors who uphold the ways of righteousness. Give our president and his administration discretion that will guard their hearts; give them understanding that will protect them and wisdom that will rescue them from the evil path, from those who would twist their words.

Blessed is the nation whose God is the Lord. Father, You are our Refuge and Stronghold in times of trouble (high prices, destitution, and desperation). May Your people dwell safely in this land and prosper abundantly.

Thank You for Your Word that continues to grow and increase in the land. We give thanks for this land and the leaders You have given to us, in Jesus' name.

Jesus is Lord over the United States! Amen.

Scripture References

1 Timothy 2:1-3 CEB	Proverbs 1:23 CEB
Deuteronomy 28:10,11	Proverbs 2:10-12,21,22
Romans 8:37 AMP	Psalm 33:12
Proverbs 21:1	Psalm 9:9
Acts 12:24	

Armed Forces

Father, we pray for the safety of the men and women who fearlessly fight to protect our great nation. Nations are rising aganst nations, and there are those who desire to destroy our nation…our form of government. Thank You for the men and women who go into places of danger to defend our freedom.

We plead the blood of Jesus over the troops and their families. We pray that the families of the service men and women will be provided for and protected. Preserve marriages and convince parents to look after their children and children to look up to their mothers and fathers, for Jesus has been made unto these parents wisdom, righteousness, and holiness. Give them comfort and the strength to continue on as their loved ones fight for our freedoms.

We look forward to a day when nations will no longer continue to hurt or destroy each other, when the whole earth will be full of the knowledge of our Lord, just as the sea is full of water. In Jesus' name I pray. Amen.

Scripture References

Ephesians 6:12 NLT

Colossians 2:15 WE

John 10:10 NLT

Ezekiel 22:30 NIV

Acts 2:21 WE

Psalm 98:2 NCV

Malachi 4:6 MSG

1 Corinthians 1:30 NIV

Isaiah 11:9 NCV

Israel

Holy Spirit, I ask You to teach me how to pray effectively for the peace of Jerusalem and that You honor the covenant You made with Jacob, Isaac, and Abraham. You will remember the land and will not turn away from them when they are in the land of their enemies. You will not destroy them or break Your agreement with them because You are their God.

Thank You for the prosperity of all those who love Jerusalem. I pray that hostile outsiders would keep their distance, and no weapon formed against Israel shall succeed. Thank You for bringing peace to the Jews and the Gentiles and for breaking down the wall that divided us so that we can come together as one. I pray for those who have become hardened to Your Word and ask that the eyes of their understanding be opened. Because of their transgressions, salvation has been made for all.

I ask You to give Israel a greater understanding of Your heart so that they may know the hope to which You have called them; that they will know the richness and gloriousness of the blessing You have promised to Your holy people. Because of Your compassion for Israel, You strengthen them and restore them, for You are their

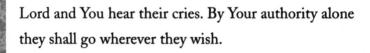

Lord and You hear their cries. By Your authority alone they shall go wherever they wish.

Thank You, Father, for saving Israel and delivering them out of the hands of their enemies. Blessed be the God of Israel! Amen!

Scripture References

Psalm 94:14 NIV	Romans 11:7 WE
Psalm 74:20 NLT	Romans 11:11 NIV
Leviticus 26:42-46 NCV	Ephesians 1:18 NCV
Psalm 122:6-9 MSG	Zechariah 10:6,12 NLT
Ephesians 2:14 WE	Psalm 106:47,48 MSG

Jerusalem

Father, I pray for the peace of Jerusalem. According to Your Word, there are huge numbers of people in the Valley of Decision. I pray that the citizens of Jerusalem will call on the name Yeshua (Messiah) and be saved. Have mercy on Israel, Lord, and protect Your people from their enemies.

You never change Your mind about the people You call and the things You give them. I pray that the leaders and citizens of Israel will obtain Your mercy. Thank You for Your compassion and for Your forgiveness for Your chosen people. Thank You that they are under Your protection and guidance.

I ask You, Holy Spirit, to show me how to pray for the peace of Jerusalem, for Your Word says You will save the people of Israel with eternal salvation and they will never again be humiliated and disgraced. May they prosper who love You. May peace be within the walls of Jerusalem and prosperity within her palaces! Amen.

Scripture References

Joel 3:14 NCV   Romans 11:29 NCV

Job 22:30 NIV   Isaiah 45:17 NLT

Nations and Continents

Father, You are my God, and I proclaim: "The earth is the Lord's and everything in it. The world and all its people belong to Him. For He laid the earth's foundations on the seas and built it on the ocean's depths." I come to You and ask You for the nation (or continent) of

_____.

I pray that the leaders of _____ have godly wisdom and knowledge, and it shall be pleasing to them. Guard them with understanding and keep them from the wicked, those who do not want what is right, but what is evil and dishonest.

We thank You that only the godly and those with integrity shall rule and the wicked shall be removed and uprooted; that those in authority will scatter the wicked from the good like wheat run through a threshing wheel and that these godly leaders are protected by Your unfailing love and faithfulness.

I pray that the hearts of those in authority are controlled by You just as a channel of water is controlled and directed to whatever end You choose. I pray that they will love justice and and righteousness , because their throne is established through righteousness. I thank You that they take pleasure in honesty and they value those who speak what is right, for when a country is led by a leader with understanding and knowledge, it will continue to grow strong. We pray that righteousness will thrive so the people will rejoice.

We thank You that Your Word will be spread throughout _____ by Your army, causing more people to believe on You because we have seen with our own eyes Your salvation. Make the nation of _____ a light to all the nations for Your glory in the name of Jesus.

Scripture References

Psalm 24:1-2 NLT	1 Timothy 2:1,2 NLT
Proverbs 28:2 NCV	Psalm 105:14 MSG
Proverbs 29:2 NIV	Proverbs 2:10-15 NCV
Acts 12:24 WE	Proverbs 2:21,22 NLT
Psalm 68:11 NCV	Proverbs 20:26,28 NLT
Luke 2:30-32 MSG	Proverbs 21:1 MSG
Proverbs 16:10,12,13 NIV	Psalm 2:8 NIV
Psalm 72:11 NIV	

Here is a list of continents and nations to help you as you pray for the world:

Continents

Africa	Europe
Antarctica	North America
Asia	South America
Australia	

Nations

Abkha Republic	Afghanistan
Albania	Algeria
Andorra	Angola
Anguilla	Antigua and Barbuda
Argentina	Armenia
Aruba	Austria
Azerbaijan	Belgium
Beliz	Benin
Bermuda	Bhutan
Bolivia	Bosnia-Herzegovina
Botswana	Brazil

British Antarctic Territory   Brunei

British Indian Ocean Territory

Bulgaria   Bahamas

Burkina Faso   Bahrain

Burma   Bangladesh

Burundi   Barbados

Belarus   Cambodia

Cameroon   Canada

Cape Verde   Cayman Islands

Central African Republic   Chad

Equatorial Guinea   Eritrea

Chile   China

People's Republic Of Colombia

Comoros   Congo

Costa Rica   Cote d'Ivoire

Croatia   Cuba

Cyprus   Czech Republic

Denmark   Djibouti

Dominica   Dominican Republic

East Timor   Eastern Europe

Ecuador   Egypt

El Salvador	Estonia
Ethiopia	Faeroe Islands
Falkland Islands	Fiji
France	Gabon
The Gambia	Georgia
Germany	Ghana
Gibraltar	Great Britain
Greece	Greenland
Grenada	Guadeloupe
Guam	Guatemala
Guinea	Guinea-Bissau
Guyana	Haiti
Honduras	Hong Kong
Hungary	Iceland
India	Indonesia
Iran	Iraq
Ireland	Isle of Man
Israel	Italy
Jamaica	Japan
Jersey	Jordan
Kuwait	Kyrgyzstan

Kazakhstan	Kenya
Kiribati	North Korea
South Korea	Kosovo
Laos	Latvia
Lebanon	Lesotho
Liberia	Libya
Liechtenstein	Lithuania
Luxembourg	Macau
Macedonia	Madagascar
Malawi	Malaysia
Maldives	Mali
Malta	Marshall Islands
Mauritania	Mauritius
Mexico	Micronesia
Moldova	Monaco
Mongolia	Montserrat
Morocco	Mozambique
Myanmar	Nagorno-Karabakh
Namibia	Nauru
Nepal	Netherlands
New Caledonia	New Zealand

Nicaragua	Niger
Nigeria	Niue
Northern Ireland	Norway
Oman	Pakistan
Palau	Palestinian Aut.
Panama	Papau New Guinea
Paraguay	Peru
Philippines	Pitcairn Island
Poland	Portugal
Puerto Rico	Qatar
Romania	Russia
Rwanda	Saint Helena
Saint Kitts-Nevis	St. Lucia

Saint Vincent and the Grenadines

San Marino	Saudi Arabia
Senegal	Serbia
Seychelles	Sierra Leone
Singapore	Slovakia
Slovenia	Soloman Islands
Somalia	South Africa
South Georgia	Spain

South Sandwich Islands

Sri Lanka

Sudan

Suriname

Swaziland

Sweden

Switzerland

Syria

Taiwan

Tajikistan

Tanzania

Thailand

Tibet

Togo

Tonga

Trinidad & Tobago

Tunisia

Turkey

Turkmenistan

Turks & Caicos Islands

Tuvalu

Uganda

The United Arab Emirates

Ukraine

United States of America

Uruguay

Uzbekistan

Vanuatu

Vatican City State

Venezuela

Vietnam

British Virgin Islands

Western Sahara

Western Samoa

Yemen

Yugoslavia

Zaire

Zambia

Zimbabwe

Protection and Deliverance of a City

Father, I pray for the Church of the Lord Jesus Christ. Your Holy Spirit has come to us, we have received Your power and we are Your witness in _____ and in every part of the world. I come boldly to Your throne and receive Your mercy and grace to help the citizens of the city of _____.

I thank You that when You send a command to the earth, Your Word runs swiftly and the ministry of Your Word grows by leaps and bounds.

I pray for this city where you have sent us and where good things happen. We, Your people, will not let the evildoers of this city fool us; we pay no attention to their dreams. Confuse them, Lord, and frustrate their plans so that we have no violence or conflict in the city.

Open the eyes of those that follow the world's ways so that they may turn from darkness. Take them out of Satan's power and turn them towards You. Forgive them because they do not know what they are doing. The god of this world has covered their minds so that they cannot see the light of Your good news. When they repent and turn from their evil ways, You will make them clean and pure and open their eyes to Your wonderful power, for our struggle is not against flesh and blood, but against the powers of darkness and the spiritual forces of evil in the heavenly realm.

Father, I commit to make it my daily task to pray for the city of _____ so that it may be freed from the grip of the wicked. Reveal who Jesus is to the people of this city so they will know that You love them as much as You love Jesus. Your Word says You have plans for us, to take care of us and not abandon us and You give us hope for the future! Our good deeds will be known and people will bless our city and build it up. In Jesus' name I pray. Amen!

Scripture References

Acts 1:8 NCV	Luke 23:34 NIV
Hebrews 4:16 NLT	2 Corinthians 4:4 WE
Psalm 147:15 NIV	Ephesians 6:12 NIV
Acts 12:24 MSG	Psalm 101:8 NLT
Jeremiah 29:7,8 NCV	John 16:8 WE
Psalm 55:9 NLT	Jeremiah 29:11 MSG
Acts 26:18 WE	Proverbs 11:11 NCV
Ephesians 2:2 NCV	

Protection from Terrorism

Father, I come to pray about the terrorism here in our nation. With a thankful heart I offer up my prayers and request to You. I know that You are always at work for the good of everyone who loves You.

You have given me power to defeat the power of my enemy, and nothing can harm me – including attacks of terrorism. I use everything You have given me so that I can fight against the tricks of the devil.

Father, I take authority over the spirit at work in those who refuse to obey You, for our fight is not against people on this earth but against the spiritual powers of darkness.

Your Word says that You have given us the keys to the kingdom of heaven, and whatever we bind on earth will be bound in heaven. Therefore, I take authority over every attack of terrorism and bind them here on this earth so that no harm shall come near us. When we call for Your help, our enemies will be defeated because we know that You are on our side. If You are for us then who can be against us?

Thank You that You did not make us timid, but have given us power, love, and self-discipline. We sit in Your presence for You are our refuge and we are safe in You. You rescue us from the hidden traps and You shield us from deadly hazards. Your outstretched arms protect us and under them we are perfectly safe. We fear nothing, even though those around us may succumb. No harm will graze us; we stand untouched and watch it from a distance. Your angels guard us wherever we go, and if we stumble they will catch us and keep us from falling as we walk unharmed. We have nothing to fear!

Holy Spirit, I bind love and faithfulness around my neck and write them on the tablet of my heart. I honor You with thanksgiving and I keep to Your path as You reveal the salvation of God. Amen.

Scripture References

Romans 8:28	Philippians 4:5,6 MSG
Romans 8:31 NLT	Luke 10:19 WE
2 Timothy 1:7 NIV	Ephesians 6:10 WE
Psalm 91:5,6 MSG	Ephesians 2:2 NLT
Isaiah 54:14 NCV	Ephesians 6:12 NCV
Proverbs 3:3 NIV	Matthew 16:19 NIV
Psalm 50:23 NLT	Psalm 56:9 NCV

The People of Our Land

Father, I thank You for hearing my prayer. You appointed me to stand watch for the people of _____, and with the help of the Holy Spirit I will stay strong, watch, and pray!

The earth and everything on it, including its people, belong to You. Lord God, You will save us, You will bless and reward those who worship and serve You, the God of Jacob.

Lord God of heaven, You are great and fearsome, and You faithfully keep Your promises to everyone who loves You and obeys Your commands. I am Your servant, so please have mercy on me and answer the prayer that I make day and night for the people of _____ who serve You. Forgive us when we have sinned against You by choosing to disobey Your ways of truth and righteousness. You said that no matter how far away we are, if we will turn to You and start seeking Your righteousness, Your way of doing and being right, You will bring us back to the place You have chosen. Thank You for rescuing Your people by Your great strength and mighty power.

I humble myself before You. Give me a gentle and quiet spirit and make me content with who I am so that I may inherit the earth as it is promised in Your Word.

Thank You for Your forgiveness of all my sins; wash me so that I may be whiter than snow. Thank You for taking away the guilt and shame of sin and cleansing me from all unrighteousness (sin and disobedience). I petition, pray, intercede, and give thanks to You on behalf of all men and women.

I believe in You and rivers of life-giving water flow out of my heart for the healing of all the nations.

In the name of Jesus, amen.

Scripture References

Ezekiel 3:17

Nehemiah 1:5-10

Luke 21:11,25,26 WE

Matthew 16:3 NLT

Matthew 26:41 NIV

James 4:10 NCV

1 Peter 3:4 NLT

Matthew 5:5 MSG

Psalm 139:23 MSG

Psalm 24 CEV

Matthew 6:33 AMP

Psalm 51:7 NLT

Isaiah 6:6,7 NCV

James 5:16 NIV

1 Timothy 2:1 NIV

John 7:38 WE

Revelation 22:1,2 NCV

Salvation of the Lost

Father, I come to You today on behalf of all the lost men, women, and children of this world because You said in Your Word that we must talk to God for all people (1 Tim. 2:1,2). I intercede on their behalf and ask You to turn their hearts toward what is right so that they be pleasing to You and live a quiet, peaceful life.

In the name of Jesus, I command the veil that has blinded their eyes to be removed. Father, shine the light of the gospel that reveals Christ's glory, that they will know that Jesus is the Christ, the Son of the living God!

Send people across the paths of the lost so that they may hear about You and understand; bring them to repentance by Your kindness and love. Sober them up, Lord, and enable them to escape the devil's traps, having a change of heart and turning towards You. Amen.

<u>Scripture References</u>

2 Corinthians 4:4 CEB	Matthew 16:16 CEB
1 Timothy 2:1,2 WE	Romans 2:4 NIV
2 Corinthians 10:3-5 NIV	Romans 15:21 NCV
Matthew 9:38 NLT	2 Timothy 2:26 MSG

School Systems and Children

Father, I bring before You the _____ school system(s) and all the men and women in positions of authority within the school system(s).

Give them godly wisdom in every decision they face, Lord, and make knowledge pleasant to them. Discretion will watch over them and understanding will keep them and deliver them from men and women who speak perverse things. Bring men and women of honesty and integrity to our educational system and remove the dishonest people for good.

I bring before You our children that they believe in You, Lord Jesus, and are saved. Thank You for redeeming us from the curse of the law by becoming the curse for us. Thank You that our sons and daughters are not taken captive by others. Help us to direct them to the right path so that when they are older, they will not leave it. Our children do everything readily and cheerfully with no fighting or second-guessing. They go out into the world as a breath of fresh air and give people a glimpse of You, Lord. Give them knowledge and skill in all learning and wisdom and favor with everyone they come in contact with.

Lord, in the name of Jesus, I loose wrong, ungodly thoughts from the minds of the men, women, and children of the _____ school system(s), and ask You to cleanse them from everything that would defile and distract them. I loose evil desires such as sexual immorality, foolish talk, bullying, fighting, and jealousy from their minds and bind them to honesty and truth. Mold them into containers You can use to present Your gifts. Father, help them to live in the light of You, trust You, and be thankful to You with a pure heart.

Father, I pray for these children who are precious in Your sight. All our children shall be taught of the Lord; and great shall be the peace of our children. Lord, I pray for the children to be filled with peace, wisdom, knowledge, and hearts that seek Your face. I ask You to place a hedge of protection around Your precious ones. Train them to turn a deaf ear to the lie of evolution. Send godly educators to our schools to watch over them in prayer.

Touch the heart of this generation and raise up a new generation that would seek Your face, oh God of Jacob. Heavenly Father, these things I ask in Your name. I thank You that Your Word never returns back void, and You and You alone are able to do exceeding abundantly, far above all I could ask or think through the working of Your mighty power.

Thank You for hearing my prayer today, Father. In Jesus' name, amen.

Scripture References

Psalm 119:130 NCV	2 Timothy 2:21 MSG
Jeremiah 1:12 MSG	2 Corinthians 7:1 MSG
Proverbs 2:10-12 AMP	1 Corinthians 6:18 ESV
Proverbs 2:21,22 MSG	Romans 13:13 WE
Acts 16:31 NLT	Ephesians 5:4 NLT
Galatians 3:13 NIV	2 Timothy 2:22 NCV
Deuteronomy 28:32,41 NCV	Matthew 18:18 NCV
Proverbs 22:6 NLT	2 Timothy 2:26 NIV
Philippians 2:15,16 MSG	Hebrews 1:14 ESV
Daniel 1:17 ASV	Colossians 2:3 AMP
Daniel 1:9 AMP	Isaiah 29:23,24 NASB
1 John 2:16,17 NIV	

PART III:

GROUP PRAYERS: SPECIAL NEEDS OF OTHERS

Those Involved in Abortion

Introduction

This prayer has a twofold application: (1) for a people – a nation - who have permitted the legalization of abortion on demand; (2) for both the man and woman involved in the decision-making process. During moments of intercession for women and men who are dealing with past mistakes, we have identified with them in their pain. God's Word is the medicine that heals and leads to the salvation of souls.

Prayer

Father, when I think about the decision I made I am depressed, then I remember something that fills me with hope. Lord, Your kindness never fails! If You had not been merciful, I would have been destroyed. Lord, I can always trust You to show me mercy each morning. Deep in my heart I say, "The Lord is my inheritance; I will hope in Him."

I ask You to forgive me and my nation for disregarding the sanctity of life that You established. I am deeply sorry for the sin of abortion that has become an accepted and legal practice in our land. Forgive me and this nation for sacrificing our unborn children on the altar of selfish-

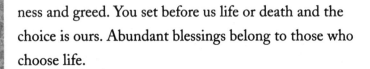

ness and greed. You set before us life or death and the choice is ours. Abundant blessings belong to those who choose life.

Lord, You knew these children before they were even formed, and You chose them to be Your very own before the foundation of the world. I realize that each person is fearfully and wonderfully made by You and You plan their days...their destinies.

Your Word says that if I admit my sin, You will forgive me and cleanse me of all wrongdoing. Therefore, Father, I admit to You my sin and the national sin that has robbed us of more children than I can count. Thank You for Your faithfulness and forgiveness.

Now, I desire to turn and be forgiven, comforted, and encouraged to keep me from being overwhelmed with deep sorrow.

I look to Jesus, who is my Savior and comforter, and welcome His peace. I cannot bring my child back again; I shall go to where this precious one is living in Your eternal presence.

We look forward to the future with hope and await the day when Jesus Christ, our God and Savior, will be revealed.

In His name we pray, amen.

Scripture References

Lamentations 3:19-24 CEV

Ephesians 1:4

Psalm 139:14-16 NIV

Psalm 119:92,93 MSG

Psalm 38:17,18 NLT

2 Corinthians 2:7 AMP

Psalm 139:2-5 NCV

2 Samuel 12:23 ESV

1 John 1:9 MSG

Titus 2:13 NLT

I. An AIDS Patient

Prayer for the Child of God

Father, You sent Your Word to set people free of whatever holds them down and to heal them. So, it is by Your Word that I bind up _____'s heartaches and ask You to heal his/her emotional and physical pain.

Help us with our doubts, Lord. Give _____ a spirit of wisdom and revelation so that he/she can know You better.

As _____ grows in grace, undeserved favor, and the knowledge and understanding of who You are, give him/her faith to receive all Your spiritual blessings. Give _____ Your peace, which is different than worldly peace.

Thank You for sending Your Son who gave His life for us so that we could be born again._____
_____has received You as his/her Lord and Savior and loves You and loves others as he/she loves himself/herself. Nothing can separate him/her from Your love and he/she is completely victorious through Your love for him/her; You always lead Your children to victory!

Father, _____ puts his/her trust in You and depends on You to take care of him/her. He/she is not anxious for anything. He/she enjoys serving You and You give him/her the desires of his/her heart. You are all the while at work in _____ energizing and creating within him/her the power and will to do Your good pleasure.

You did not give _____ a timid spirit, but a spirit of power and love and discipline. Comfort _____ so that he/she is not afraid. Give him/her a crown of beauty for ashes, and take away his/her mourning and despair so that You may be glorified.

According to Your Word, You were wounded for our transgressions and bruised for our guilt and iniquities. You desire that Your children prosper and be in health even as their souls prosper. You already paid the price for our health, peace, and well-being with the stripes You bore on Your back, so I thank You that _____ has already been healed and made whole.

Father, I pray that _____ stays alert and has a confident expectation of the blessings You still have in store for them. Help him/her not to feel disappointed or shortchanged. In Jesus name I pray. Amen.

Scripture References

Luke 4:18 WE

Psalm 107:20 NLT

Mark 9:24 MSG

Ephesians 1:17 NIV

2 Peter 3:18 AMP

Ephesians 1:3 NCV

John 14:27 NIV

John 3:3 WE

John 13:34 NLT

Romans 8:35-37 NCV

2 Corinthians 2:14 NASB

Psalm 37:3-5; 7-8 NCV

2 Timothy 1:7 NASB

Isaiah 54:4 NIV

Isaiah 61:3 NLT

Isaiah 53:5 AMP

Romans 5:4,5 MSG

II. An AIDS Patient

Prayer for One Who Does Not Know Jesus as Lord

Father, You have called us to stand in the
gap for others, therefore, I stand in the gap for
_____ so that he/she may be saved.
You, Lamb of God, took away _____'s sins.

Thank You for sending the Holy Spirit who goes
forth to convict _____ of their sin, righteousness, and judgment. Your patience and kindness leads him/her away from darkness. You free
_____ from the power of sin and bring
him/her into Your kingdom. Send people across
_____'s path to share Your Gospel in a way
that he/she will understand and make him/her come to
his/her senses so that he/she can escape from the traps of
the devil. Reveal to him/her that Jesus is the Christ, the
Son of the Living God.

As _____ grows in the grace and the
knowledge of the Lord Jesus Christ, help him/her
receive every spiritual blessing from You. Father, I thank
You that You give him/her peace of mind and heart; a
peace that cannot be taken away so he/she will not be
troubled or afraid.

Father, help _____ know that nothing can separate him/her from You and through You, he/she will have victory over every trial that comes his/her way. Use him/her to spread the Gospel of Jesus Christ.

Give _____ patience as he/she rests and waits on You. Keep him/her from anger, as it will only lead to harm.

Father, You sent Your Word to heal _____ and bring him/her from the brink of death. Heal his/her emotional and physical pains. Give him/her discernment and a personal knowledge of You so he/she can focus on exactly what You are calling him/her to do.

You were wounded for the wrong _____ did and took the punishment, making him/her healed and well again. I thank You that _____ has hope – a hope that does not disappoint, because Your love has been poured out within his/her heart through the Holy Spirit.

In the name of Jesus, amen.

Scripture References

Ezekiel 22:30 NIV

John 1:29 NCV

John 16:8-12 NASB

Romans 2:4 WE

Colossians 1:13 NCV

Matthew 9:38 WE

2 Timothy 2:26 NIV

2 Peter 3:18 NLT

Ephesians 1:3 NASB

John 14:27 NLT

Romans 8:35-37 AMP

2 Corinthians 2:14 NIV

Psalm 37:7,8 NLT

Luke 4:18 NASB

Psalm 107:20 MSG

Ephesians 1:17 MSG

Isaiah 53:5 NCV

Romans 5:5 NASB

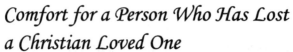

Comfort for a Person Who Has Lost a Christian Loved One

Father, I thank You that You are a High Priest who is able to understand and sympathize with _____ over the loss of his/her loved one.

I thank You that _____ does not sorrow like the rest of the world, as one with no hope, because he/she believes that You died and rose again and that those we have lost are merely sleeping; You will bring them back with You.

Your Word says, "Blessed are those who mourn, for they shall be comforted" (Matt. 5:4), so I ask You to surround _____ with Your good hope and eternal encouragement through grace.

I give You praise, Father of mercy! You are right there with _____during the hard times and You will bring him/her alongside someone else who is going through hard times so that he/she can comfort others just as God was there for him/her.

I thank You for giving _____ a crown of beauty for ashes; joyous blessing instead of mourning; festive praise instead of despair that he/she will be like a great oak tree that the Lord has planted for His own glory. Amen.

Scripture References

Hebrews 4:15,16 NCV

1 Thessalonians 4:13,14 NIV

Matthew 5:4 NKJV

2 Thessalonians 2:16 NIV

2 Corinthians 1:3,4 MSG

Isaiah 61:3 NLT

Improving Communication

Introduction

One of my children and I were having difficulty communicating, and this is the prayer the Lord gave me. As I prayed these words for her, the Holy Spirit brought transformation to my life and hers!

Prayer

Father, _____ is taught of the Lord and obedient to Your will, therefore, great shall be his/her peace. I thank You that _____ was created to be like You in true righteousness and holiness.

He/She speaks the truth in love, becoming more like Christ every day. Wickedness is an abomination to his/her lips and everything that comes from his/her mouth is full of righteousness – there is nothing crooked or perverted in them.

Incline his/her heart to Your testimonies and not towards selfish gain. I thank You that _____ does not love the world's ways (wanting his/her own way; wanting everything for himself/herself; wanting to feel important) but loves the ways of God.

_____ treasures Your wisdom and holds on to it – and it will bring him/her honor. _____ pays attention to Your words - listens closely to what You say – and never forgets Your words because they are the key to life and bring health to the whole body. _____ guards his/her thoughts and does not let his/her thoughts run his/her life.

_____ lives in happiness with others. He/she has a spirit of humility and does not think of himself/herself as being better than others but puts the interests of others above his/her own – just as Jesus does.

Thank You, Father. In Jesus' name, amen.

Scripture References

Isaiah 54:13 ESV

Ephesians 4:23,24 NIV

Ephesians 4:15 NLT

Proverbs 8:6-8 NASB

Psalm 119:36

1 John 2:15,16,21 MSG

Proverbs 4:8,20-23 NCV

Philippians 2:2-5 WE

Deliverance from Satan and His Demonic Forces

Introduction

If the person for whom you are interceding has not confessed Jesus as Savior and Lord, pray specifically for his/her salvation if you have not already done so. Stand and thank the Father that it is done in the name of Jesus. Then pray the following prayer.

Prayer

Father, I come boldly to You, trusting in You because You are so good to us and help us when we need it. Therefore, I stand in the gap on behalf of _____, knowing that the Holy Spirit prays for him/her with groanings that cannot be expressed in words. Free him/her from the devil's chains! Help him/her to take up the shield of faith to extinguish anything the devil throws at him/her.

Your Word says whatever I tie on the earth will be tied in heaven. What I set free on earth will be set free in heaven. You say for me to use Your name to cast out demons.

In the name of Jesus, I tie _____'s spirit, soul, and body to Your will and purpose for his/her life.

I tie his/her thoughts, will, and emotions to the will of God, so that his/her thoughts, feelings, and purposes line up with Your heart.

I loose every wrong and ungodly pattern of thinking, attitude, idea, desire, belief, habit and behavior from him/her and I smash every stronghold associated with these things. I loose any unforgiveness, fear, and distrust from him/her, in Jesus' name.

Father, I know _____'s struggle is not against humans, but against the dark spiritual forces of evil. I thank You that You disarmed the powers that were aimed at him/her and made a public example of them, triumphing over them at the Cross. Thank You that the devil has been defeated and no longer has an advantage over _____.

Father, send your angels out to help and assist _____ so that he/she will be saved.

Father, I lay hold of _____'s salvation, proclaiming life to him/her. I call that which does not exist into being; fixing my eyes on what is unseen. Satan shall not have an advantage over _____ because I am not ignorant of his schemes. I stand in the gap on _____'s behalf and resist the devil and he has to run far from _____. Satan has no

place in _____ because we have won the
fight against him by the blood of the Lamb. Because I'm
standing in the gap for _____, no one
can put a hand on him/her; he/she is protected from
every assault of the enemy. Thank You for giving Yourself for _____'s sins to free him/her from
the evil world and for transferring him/her to the kingdom of Your beloved Son.

Father, I ask You to fill the unoccupied places within
_____ with Your Word, love, peace,
wisdom, righteousness and knowledge of You, in the
name of Jesus.

I thank You that _____ is no longer a
slave to anything. Help him/her come to his/her senses
so that he/she may escape from the snare of the devil.
Thank You for coming to the earth with the purpose of
destroying the devil's activities. Thank You for setting
_____'s life right, putting it together,
and completing it with joy. Praise the Lord! Amen.

Note: This prayer may be prayed as many times as
necessary. It takes time to realize the faith that leads
you into a position of praise and thanksgiving. Stand
firm, fixed, unmovable, and steadfast, remembering that
greater is He that is in you than he that is in the world.

Scripture References

Hebrews 4:16 WE

Ezekiel 22:30 AMP

Romans 8:26 NLT

Isaiah 58:6 NCV

Ephesians 6:16 NIV

Matthew 18:18 WE

Mark 16:17 NCV

Ephesians 6:12 NIV

Colossians 2:15 AMP

Matthew 12:29 MSG

Hebrews 1:14 WE

Romans 4:17 NASB

2 Corinthians 4:18 NIV

2 Corinthians 2:11 NASB

James 4:7 NIV

Ephesians 4:27 NLT

Revelation 12:11 WE

Luke 10:19 MSG

Galatians 1:4 NCV

Colossians 1:13 NASB

Matthew 12:43-45 AMP

1 Corinthians 6:12 NLT

2 Timothy 2:26 NKJV

1 John 3:8 Phillips

Romans 14:17 MSG

Deliverance from Cults

In the name of Jesus, we come before You in prayer for _____ (those, and families of those, involved in cults). We believe that Your Word runs swiftly throughout the earth and cannot be chained.

Father, thank You for reaching all those from the sky to the sea; for rescuing them from the grip of those who lie and knife them in the back. Silence those who teach what they should not teach, bringing confusion to families for the sake of their own gain. Open _____'s eyes so he/she sees that these teachings are foolish.

Lord, execute justice for the oppressed. Set the prisoners free, open the eyes of the blind, and lift up those who are bowed down. Heal the brokenhearted and bandage their wounds; bring the wicked down into the dust. Turn the hearts of the fathers towards their children, Lord, and bring back those who do not obey so that they will want to do what is right.

Father, we do not weep any more because we know that _____ will return to You and to their own land. We have nothing to fear and do not worry because You will bring our children out of exile – our sons and daughters from faraway places - bring them home

safe and secure. We shall see _____
walking in the ways of piety and virtue, revering Your
name, Father. Those who err in mind will know the
truth and those who criticize will accept instruction. You
said in Your Word "I will contend with those who contend with you, and your children I will save" (Isa. 49:25
NIV), therefore, You give safety to _____.

Be a shield round about _____ and send Your
messengers to protect him/her from those who are lovers
of self, lovers of money, proud, arrogant, contemptuous
boasters, abusive, disobedient, ungrateful, unholy, profane,
loose in morals and conduct, and haters of good. Turn
him/her away from these people so they are not able
to worm their way back into homes and captivate
_____ . I loose lies, various evil desires and se-
ductive impulses from _____'s mind, and You will
make their ungodly ways obvious to everyone.

Send Your angels out to break down the evil forces
that come against _____. Give him/her the
wisdom to receive the salvation that comes by trusting in Christ Jesus. Bring him/her home safely into the
kingdom of heaven. Glory to You, Father, for delivering
_____, for whom we intercede, out of captivity
through the cleanness of Your hands. Amen.

Note: Pray this prayer until faith arises in you. Then you will know that God will perform His Word in the life of the one for whom you are interceding. The Holy Spirit is your Helper. When you perceive the intercession is completed, surround the individual with songs and shouts of deliverance in your prayer closet.

Scripture References

Psalm 147:15 NIV

2 Timothy 2:9 NLT

Psalm 144:7,8 MSG

Titus 1:11 NASB

2 Timothy 3:9 NCV

Psalm 146:7,8 AMP

Psalm 147:3-6 NLT

Luke 1:17 WE

Jeremiah 31:16,17 NLT

Jeremiah 46:27 MSG

Isaiah 43:5,6 NCV

Isaiah 29:23,24 NASB

Isaiah 49:25 NIV

Matthew 18:18 NASB

2 Timothy 3:2-9 AMP

Hebrews 1:14 MSG

2 Timothy 3:15 NLT

2 Timothy 4:18 WE

Job 22:30 NIV

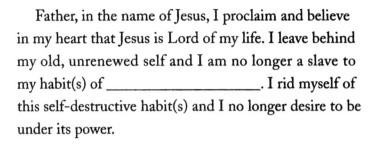

Deliverance from Habits

Father, in the name of Jesus, I proclaim and believe
in my heart that Jesus is Lord of my life. I leave behind
my old, unrenewed self and I am no longer a slave to
my habit(s) of _____. I rid myself of
this self-destructive habit(s) and I no longer desire to be
under its power.

No test or temptation that comes my way is beyond
what I can handle because You will never let me down
or allow me to be pushed past my limit. You are there to
help me through it.

Therefore, I put on the armor of God so I can resist
temptation and stand firmly in place. I have a belt of
truth around my loins; a breastplate of integrity and right
standing with God; my feet are shod with peace and are
stable in preparation to face the enemy; I have a shield
of faith to quench all the flaming missiles of the devil, a
helmet of salvation, and the sword of the Spirit, which is
the Word of God.

Clothed in Your armor, I discipline my body and
subdue it. With every temptation, I choose the way
of escape that You provide. Victory is mine because I
belong to You, Lord, and You are stronger than any spirit
that is in the world.

Thank you, Lord, that I am a new creation. The old
has gone, and the new is here!

Scripture References

Romans 10:9,10 WE

Ephesians 4:21,22 NCV

1 Corinthians 6:12 MSG

1 Corinthians 3:9 NIV

James 1:21 NLT

1 Corinthians 10:13 MSG

Ephesians 6:13-17 AMP

1 John 4:4 WE

2 Corinthians 5:17 NIV

Deliverance from Corrupt Companions

Introduction

This is a prayer of Intercession that I wrote when our
son was a teenager. Even though he made unwise choices
and traveled the road of disobedience for a season, David
did not escape the Spirit of God. "Train a child in the
way he should go, and when he is old he will not turn
from it" (Proverbs 22:6 NIV).

Prayer

Father, in the name of Jesus, I ask You to open the
eyes of _____'s understanding, so that he/
she is not misled by bad company. Help him/her to make
a clean break with everything that defiles and distracts
him/her. Make him/her holy and useful to the Master,
ready to do any good work.

Lord, You know _____. You are thoroughly
familiar with all his/her ways…You surround him/her—
front and back, and Your hand is on him/her. There is no
place he/she can go to get away from Your Spirit. Thank
You for the angels who protect _____ wherever he/she goes.

Give _____ the wisdom and the courage to
shun wild parties and drunkenness, sexual promiscuity

and immoral living. In the name of Jesus I loose malice, deceit, hypocrisy, envy and slander from him…spirit, soul and body. Give him/her a willing heart so that he/she might be loyal to the government and its officers, obedient and always ready to do what is good. Send wise companions to _____, so he/she may become wise.

Thank You, Lord, that _____'s sins have been forgiven and he/she has overcome the evil one, because the Word of God lives in him/her. His/Her eyes have been opened to the truth and he/she abides in You and has been set free from the law of sin and death. Thank You for watching over Your Word and carrying out all your plans, in Jesus' name! Amen.

Scripture References

1 Corinthians 15:33,34 NIV	Proverbs 28:7 AMP
1 Thessalonians 5:22 AMP	2 Timothy 2:21 NCV
2 Corinthians 7:1 MSG	1 John 2:12-16 NIV
Romans 13:13 NLT	1 John 2:21,24 NCV
1 Peter 2:1 NASB	1 John 3:9 NASB
Romans 13:1,2 NIV	Romans 8:2 NASB
Titus 3:1 NLT	Jeremiah 1:12 NLT
Proverbs 13:20 MSG	Proverbs 91 CEB

Deliverance from Mental Disorder

Father, Your Word says to call on You for help when we're in trouble and You will help us. So, I come to You with confidence, that I may find mercy and grace to help _____ in this time of need.

I commit to pray on the behalf of _____, standing in the gap before You for him/her. You defeated the devil for _____ and we take back everything Satan has stolen from him/her.

You brought _____ out from the pit and corruption of _____ (name disorder: schizophrenia, paranoia, manic depression, etc.). Father, You did not give _____ a timid spirit, but gave him/her a spirit of power, love, and self-discipline.

In the name of Jesus, I stand in the gap for _____ until he/she comes to his/her senses and escapes from the trap of the devil, who has taken him/her captive to do his will. I free him/her from the wrong things he/she has done.

Father, You deliver and draw _____ to You, out of the control of the kingdom of darkness and have transferred him/her into the kingdom of Your Son.

Because _____ belongs to You, he/she has been set free from the power of sin. He/She is no longer double-minded or unstable about everything he/she thinks, feels, and decides. He/She turns from all moral filth and humbly accepts Your Word in his/her heart.

Lord, bless _____ with loving kindness and give him/her peace. You gave Your life to pay for all the wrong things _____ has done and have set him/her free. I give You glory for ever and ever. Amen.

Scripture References

Hebrews 4:16 NASB	Ephesians 6:12 NCV
Psalm 50:15 MSG	Colossians 1:13 AMP
Psalm 56:13 NLT	Romans 8:2 NLT
Psalm 103:4 NCV	James 1:8,21 NIV
2 Timothy 1:7 NIV	Galatians 1:3-5 WE
John 20:23 WE	Ezekiel 22:30 MSG
2 Timothy 2:26 NIV	Matthew 12:29 NASB

Employment

Father, _____ needs employment; a job where Your abundant supply is released to his/her good and benefit.

Father, I believe and confess Your Word over _____, knowing that every word You give comes true. Your words do not return to You empty, but succeed in doing what You sent them to do. Father, You are his/her source of all comfort and encouragement and he/she is strong and courageous, standing firm in the faith.

_____'s desire is to owe no man anything except love. Therefore, he/she is strong and does not let his/her hands be lazy because he/she knows that payday is coming. His/her pay is not given as a gift, but as something earned. _____ makes it his/her goal to live a quiet life, working with his/her hands so that he/she will not have to depend on others; You, Lord, supply all his/her needs.

He/She works quietly and earns his/her own food and other necessities and does not tire of doing good. _____ maintains good works – honest labor and honorable employment – so that he/she may be fruitful.

Father, because _____ has obeyed Your Word, You have opened a door for him/her that no one can shut.

_____ is not afraid or discouraged because he/she knows You are God, and You will always be with him/her. You give him/her strength and hold him/her in Your victorious right hand. In the name of Jesus, I loose worry and fretting from his/her mind. He/She brings his/her concerns to You and You give him/her peace and wholeness, displacing the worry at the center of his/her life. _____ guards his/her mouth and tongue, keeping himself/herself out of trouble.

_____ prizes wisdom and acknowledges You and You make his/her paths straight and promote him/her. Therefore, he/she increases in wisdom and in favor with You and with man. In Jesus' name, amen.

Scripture References

Jeremiah 1:12 MSG

Isaiah 55:11 NCV

2 Corinthians 1:3 NLT

1 Corinthians 16:13 NIV

Romans 13:8 NASB

2 Chronicles 15:7 MSG

Romans 4:4 NCV

1 Thessalonians 4:11,12 NLT

2 Thessalonians 3:12,13 NCV

Luke 2:52 NIV

Titus 3:14 ASV

Revelation 3:8 WE

Isaiah 41:10 NLT

John 16:33 WE

Philippians 4:6,7 MSG

Philippians 4:12,13 NASB

Proverbs 21:23 NIV

Proverbs 3:6 NASB

Proverbs 4:8 AMP

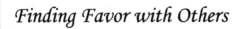

Finding Favor with Others

Father, in the name of Jesus, You smile on_____
_____ and are gracious and kind to him/her. He/
she is the head and not the tail, above and not underneath.

Thank You for favor for _____ who seeks
first Your kingdom and finds delight in good. Grace
(favor) is with _____ who loves the Lord
Jesus with an undying love. He/She gives favor, honor,
and love to others and You pour out on him/her a spirit
of favor until his/her cup runs over. Crown him/her with
glory and honor because he/she is Your masterpiece,
which has been created new in Christ Jesus. He/she is
strong, wise, and blessed by You.

Give _____ knowledge and skill in
all learning and wisdom. Cause him/her to find favor,
compassion and loving-kindness with _____
(names). _____ finds favor in the sight of all
who look upon him/her this day, in the name of Jesus.

I pray that _____ knows the love of Christ
and is filled up with the fullness of God. You are doing far
more beyond all that _____ asks or thinks,
because Your mighty power is at work in him/her.

Thank You, Father, that _____ is well-
favored by You and by man, in Jesus' name! Amen.

<u>Scripture References</u>

Numbers 6:25 NLT

Psalm 8:5 NCV

Deuteronomy 28:13 NASB

Ephesians 2:10 NLT

Matthew 6:33 NCV

Luke 2:40 WE

Proverbs 11:27 MSG

Daniel 1:17 AMP

Ephesians 6:24 NIV

Daniel 1:9 AMP

Luke 6:38 WE

Esther 2:15,17 NLT

Zechariah 12:10 NIV

Ephesians 3:19,20 NASB

Healing of the Handicapped

Introduction

Over the years, I have found it necessary to seek the face of God on behalf of a baby or child that I'm praying for. In a certain family situation that would require a supernatural act of God (a miracle), I had prayed all that I knew to pray. One morning during my quiet time, I realized that I didn't know how to pray, and that more than a "blanket" prayer was needed. I asked the Holy Spirit to give me a scripture specifically for this child, and He did. With the help of the Holy Spirit, you do all that you know to do, and having done all to stand, stand giving glory to the Father.

Prayer

Father, thank You for _____who is a gift from You. I know that nothing is impossible for You, and all things are possible to those who believe. I believe; Lord help my unbelief. I purpose not to be moved by what I see, but I will keep my eyes on Jesus who is the perfecter of my faith.

I'm thankful that _____ is an open book to You. You formed him/her in his mother's womb, and he/she is marvelously made...body and soul, marvelously made!

I thank You, High God-You're breathtaking! I worship
You in adoration-what a creation! You know _____
inside and out, you know every bone in his/her body;
You know exactly how he/she was made, bit by bit, how
he/she was sculpted from nothing into something. Like
an open book, You watched _____ grow from conception to birth; all the stages of his/her life were spread out
before You. The days of his/her life all prepared before
he/she even lived one day. Father, I come asking You for
a miracle in _____'s body according to Your will
and for Your glory.

Also, I ask You to raise up medical researchers who
will seek You for answers in this area. You will never
leave our family without support, and I ask You to send
helpers—doctors, nurses, volunteers, hospital orderlies
and attendants—who are called and appointed by You.
In the name of Jesus, I bind the minds of those who are
helping us to the wisdom of God.

Where there are dormant brain cells, organs, glands
(sweat, thyroid, etc), I command them to be activated in
the name of Jesus. Where there are damaged brain cells,
organs, glands I ask You for a creative miracle in the
Name that is above all names. As I and my family attend
to my child, we will speak words of life and wholeness to
his/her spirit, soul and body.

Father, You are my source of all comfort and You are the Strength of my life. You will perfect that which concerns me. To God be the glory; great things You have done!

Father, I set my prayer before You like incense. Thank You for hearing my prayer. Praise the Lord! Amen.

Scripture References

Psalm 139:13-16 MSG

Mark 16:17 MSG

Jeremiah 1:12 NIV

1 Peter 2:24 NLT

Psalm 146:8 AMP

2 Corinthians 4:4 NLT

Mark 7:35 NCV

Psalm 103:20 AMP

Galatians 3:13 MSG

Luke 1:37 ESV

Ephesians 1:17,18 NIV

Ephesians 2:6 ESV

Jeremiah 32:27 NIV

1 Thessalonians 5:23 NIV

Proverbs 2:21,22 MSG

Psalm 141:2 NIV

Romans 3:4 NCV

Mark 11:23,24 AMP

Psalm 42:11 NASB

Acts 3:16 NCV

Matthew 8:17 NIV

Nehemiah 8:10 ASV

John 10:10 WE

Proverbs 20:12 NCV

Matthew 9:37,38 AMP

Romans 8:2 NLT

Psalm 119:89 AMP

2 Corinthians 1:3 NLT

Matthew 18:18 NASB

Mark 9:23 NASB

Psalm 127:3 NLT

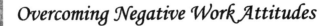

Overcoming Negative Work Attitudes

Thank You, Father, You see the struggle I am having with my employers and fellow-employees. I desire to put off the negative attitudes and put on positive attitudes. I bind mercy, love, discernment and kindness to my mind, and loose all judgments and bad feelings towards others from my mind. I ask You, Holy Spirit, to remind me of godly instruction and my heart will store the commands of my Father. Your words that I've hidden in my heart will enable me to live a long time and provide me with well-being. Thank You for creating in me loyalty and faithfulness. I tie them on my neck and write them deep within my heart. Then I will find favor and approval in Your eyes and in the eyes of my employers and fellow-employees.

God, You are the one who enables me both to want and to actually live out Your good purposes at my place of employment. I do everything without grumbling and arguing so that I may be blameless and pure, Your innocent child.

I hear Your Word and do Your Word, not working to make myself look good or flattering people at my work-place, but I act like a slave of Christ, carrying out Your will from my heart. I serve my employer enthusiastically, as though I am serving the Lord, and I know that You will reward every person who does what is right.

I honor You, my Lord, and my work is a sincere expression of my devotion to You, in the name of Jesus. Amen.

Scripture References

Proverbs 3:1-4 CEB

Jeremiah 1:12 MSG

Colossians 3:22-24 NLT

Ephesians 6:5-8 CEB

Philippians 2:14,15 NCV

Hedge of Protection

Father, in the name of Jesus, I pray a hedge of protection around _____. Be a wall of fire around him/her, Lord, and set Your angels around him/her as a circle of protection.

I thank You that _____ lives in the shelter of the Most High and finds rest in the shadow of the Almighty, for You are his/her refuge and place of safety. _____ puts his/her trust in You. You cover him/her with Your feathers, and he/she hides under Your wings. Your truth is his/her shield and protection; he/she does not fear any danger at night or an arrow during the day.

You, Lord, are _____'s refuge and no harm will overtake him/her; no disaster will come near him/her. You guard him/her in everything he/she does.

Because _____ loves You and has made You Lord of his/her life, when he/she calls to You, You will answer him/her. You will protect him/her and will be with him/her during troubled times. You give _____ a long, full life and show him/her Your salvation. Amen.

Scripture References

Ezekiel 22:30 NLT	Psalm 91:4,5 NCV
Zechariah 2:5 NIV	Psalm 91:8-11 NIV
Psalm 34:7 MSG	Psalm 91:14-16 NCV
Psalm 91:1,2 NLT	Luke 21:18 WE

Prison Inmates

Introduction

The following prayers were written in response to letters from prisoners requesting prayers to be used by them in special circumstances.

I. Prayer for an Inmate's Protection and Future

Father, I purpose in my heart to be kind to others, tenderhearted, forgiving others, just as You forgave me of my sins through Christ.

I am a child of God, whom You love, and it is my desire to be just like You. Therefore, I choose to live a life of love.

Father, You are my place of safety and protection. You are my God and I trust You. You cover me with Your feathers and under Your wings I hide. Your truth is my shield and protection.

Because You are my Lord, no harm will overtake me and no disaster will come near me. You command Your angels to guard me in all my ways.

When I call on You, You answer me and You are with me in trouble. You satisfy me with long life and show me Your salvation.

In Jesus' name. Amen.

Scripture References

Ephesians 4:32 NLT

Ephesians 5:1,2 NCV

Psalm 91:1,2,4 NCV

Psalm 91:9-11 NIV

Psalm 91:15,16 NIV

II. Prayer for an Incarcerated Parent and His/Her Children

Lord, hear my voice – be merciful to me and answer me. I seek Your face, so don't hide from me now. You have been my helper.

Thank You for sending people across my path to tell me about You and Your love for me.

You said to let the little children come unto You, and You see my children who feel abandoned and alone. I repent for neglecting them, hurting them by my actions. Even though I walked away from them, Father, I ask You to take them in. Replace their sorrow with gladness. Send wise counselors to help them.

Father, I have sinned against You, my children, and myself. Your Word says to confess my sins and You will forgive me. I repent and ask You to cleanse me from all the wrongs I have done. Thank You for forgiving me. I pray that my children will forgive me as well, so that we can be a family again. I cast the care of my children on You.

Teach me Your ways, Lord, so I can live according to the truth. I thank You that Your hand is on me and

You will promote me at the right time. I delight in You and You give me the desires of my heart. Give me the patience I need to run the race that is set before me.

In Jesus' name, I pray. Amen.

Scripture References

Psalm 27:7-10 NIV	Isaiah 61:3 NCV
Matthew 9:38 NLT	Psalm 37:4 AMP
1 John 1:9 NCV	Psalm 86:11 NLT
1 Peter 5:7 MSG	Hebrews 12:1 AMP
Psalm 138:8 NIV	

III. Personal Prayer for His/Her Family and Caregivers

Father, I have sinned against You, my family, and myself. I repent of these sins and ask You to forgive me.

Your Word says that if I freely admit that I have sinned and confess my sins, You will forgive me and cleanse me from all unrighteousness. Thank You for forgiving me. I pray that my children will be willing to forgive me as well so we can be a family again.

I thank You for those who have taken responsibility for my children while I am away. I thank You that he/she is in Christ Jesus, and lives a life worthy of You and pleases You. His/Her mouth shall speak of wisdom; and the meditation of his/her heart shall be understanding. I pray that you give him/her strength, a wise mind, and a spirit attuned to Your will so that he/she can rear the children You gave to me. I repent for failing to assume my responsibilities as a parent and ask You to reward the one who is taking care of them.

Lord Jesus, I thank You that I am put right with God and have been made holy and set free from sin.

There is violence here in prison, but I look to You. Hide me in the shelter of Your presence and keep me safe in Your dwelling from accusing tongues.

In the name of Jesus I pray, amen.

Scripture References

1 John 1:9 AMP

Psalm 49:3 NIV

1 Corinthians 1:30 NCV

Colossians 1:9,10 MSG

Colossians 3:23,24 NLT

Psalm 31:20 NIV

Renew Fellowship

Father, You are alert and active and watch over Your Word to perform it. I believe that _____ is taught by You and obedient to Your will. Great is his/her peace. He/She remains faithful to the things he/she has been taught because he/she knows they are true.

_____ continues to hold to the things he/she has learned. Father, You will heal _____, guide _____ and comfort _____.

You give him/her eternal life and You deliver _____ _____from the evil one. No one can steal him/her out of Your hand.

I pray that _____ will come to his/her senses and escape from the devil's trap that has held him/her captive and that _____ would judge himself/herself.

_____ has become a fellow heir with Christ and shares in all He has for him/her. He/She does not throw away his/her confidence, because it will be richly rewarded.

I thank You for giving _____ a spirit of wisdom and a revelation knowledge of You. Thank You that he/she enjoys fellowship with You and with other believers.

In Jesus' name, amen.

Scripture References

Jeremiah 1:12 AMP

2 Timothy 2:26 NLT

1 Corinthians 11:31 NASB

John 6:45 NCV

Isaiah 54:13 NIV

Matthew 18:18 AMP

2 Timothy 3:14,15 NLT

Hebrews 3:14 NCV

Isaiah 57:18 NCV

Hebrews 10:35 NIV

John 10:28, 29 MSG

Ephesians 1:17 NASB

1 John 5:16 NIV

1 John 1:3 MSG

Spirit-Controlled Life

Father, I pray for all Christians everywhere. Help us receive instruction from our pastors and teachers so that we will be equipped for the work You would have us to do.

We have been set free from the law of sin and death through Christ Jesus, and purpose to live by the Spirit and not according to the flesh, because we are Your children. We do not let evil conquer us, but conquer evil by doing good. We are more than conquerors because of Your love for us. We clothe ourselves with the Lord Jesus and forget about satisfying our sinful, selfish desires.

We are doers of the Word and are not merely listeners. We are pure, peace loving, gentle at all times, willing to yield to others, full of mercy, good deeds, and sincerity. We keep ourselves free from the love of money and are satisfied with the things we have.

We are strong in the Lord and in the strength of His might. We submit ourselves to you, Lord. We resist the devil and he will flee from us. We come near to You and we do not fear because You promised never to leave us or abandon us.

Thank You, Father, for making us complete in Christ Jesus. You rule over all. In Jesus' name, amen.

Scripture References

James 3:17 NLT

Romans 12:21 NLT

Romans 13:12,14 NCV

James 1:22 AMP

Romans 8:2,4,9,14,31,37 NIV

Hebrews 13:5 NCV

Ephesians 6:10 NASB

James 4:7,8 NIV

Colossians 2:10 NASB

To Receive Jesus as Savior and Lord

Father, it is written in Your Word that if I declare with my mouth, "Jesus is Lord" and if I believe in my heart that You raised Him from the dead, then I will be saved. So, I declare with my mouth that Jesus is my Lord. I make Him Lord of my life right now. I believe in my heart that You raised Jesus from the dead. I am putting my past life behind me and I close the door to Satan and any of his devices.

I thank You for forgiving me of all my sin. Jesus is my Lord and I am a new person. The old things have passed away and now all things have become new in Jesus' name. Amen.

Scripture Reference

John 3:16	John 14:6
John 6:37	Romans 10:9,10 NLT
John 10:10b	Romans 10:13
Romans 3:23	Ephesians 2:1-10 NCV
2 Corinthians 5:19	2 Corinthians 5:17
John 16:8,9	John 1:12
Romans 5:8	2 Corinthians 5:21

To Receive the Infilling of the Holy Spirit

Father, I am Your child because I believe in my heart that Jesus has been raised from the dead and I have declared with my mouth that He is my Lord.

Jesus said that the Heavenly Father is ready to give the Holy Spirit to anyone who asks. I ask You now in the name of Jesus to fill me with the Holy Spirit. I step into the fullness and power that I desire in the name of Jesus.

Scripture Reference

John 14:16,17	Acts 10:44-46
Luke 11:13 NLT	Acts 19:2,5,6
Acts 1:8a	1 Corinthians 14:2-15
Acts 2:4	1 Corinthians 14:18,27
Acts 2:32,33,39	Ephesians 6:18
Acts 8:12-17	Jude 1:20

About the Author

Germaine Griffin Copeland, founder and president of Word Ministries, Inc., is the author of the *Prayers That Avail Much®* books, *A Global Call to Prayer* and other publications. Her writings provide scriptural prayer instructions that will help you pray more effectively.

Word Ministries, Inc. is a prayer and teaching ministry whose vision is to unite followers of Jesus for the purpose of praying *Prayers That Avail Much®*. Through her writings and multiple prayers, they are equipping believers to be more effective intercessors and fruitful workers in God's Vineyard. Germaine is training other prayer leaders in the First Fruit Prayer Groups that meet during the first week of each month with a common agenda. As more prayer groups are added, the company of intercessors is marching across the land, even to other countries.

On the website, www.prayers.org, you can sign up to be a member of the Global Company of Intercessors and receive bi-monthly prayer assignments. You may also subscribe to the Daily Prayers. We are praying for the nations, for God's will to be done on every continent.

Germaine is the daughter of the late Reverend A. H. "Buck" and Donnis Brock Griffin. She and her husband, Everette, have four children, eleven grandchildren and their prayer assignments increase as great-grandchildren are born into the family. Germaine and Everette reside in Greensboro, Georgia, on beautiful Lake Oconee.

Mission Statement

Word Ministries, Inc.

Equipping the body of Christ to be effectual Intercessors and fruitful Workers in the Vineyard.

You may contact Word Ministries by writing:

Word Ministries, Inc.

P.O. Box 289

Good Hope, Georgia 30641

-or calling-

770.267.7603

www.prayers.org

Please include your testimonies and praise reports when you write.

Other Books by Germaine Copeland

A Call to Prayer

Prayers That Avail Much
Commemorative Gift Edition

Prayers That Avail Much
Commemorative Leather Edition

Prayers That Avail Much for the Workplace

Prayers That Avail Much Volume 1

Prayers That Avail Much Volume 1
Mass Market Edition

Prayers That Avail Much Volume 2

Prayers That Avail Much Volume 3

Prayers That Avail Much for Men — pocket edition

Prayers That Avail Much for Women — pocket edition

Prayers That Avail Much for Mothers — paperback

Prayers That Avail Much for Moms — pocket edition

Prayers That Avail Much for Teens
Mass Market Edition

Prayers That Avail for the College Years

Prayers That Avail Much for Graduates

Oraciones Con Poder — Prayers That Avail Much
(Spanish Edition)

JUST ONE DAY OF FAVOR CAN CHANGE YOUR LIFE...

"Dr. Dave Martin is an incredibly anointed life coach. The nuggets shared in his book, The Force of Favor, have greatly impacted our church. As you read this book, expect God's favor to increase in your life!"

Jentezen Franklin, Acclaimed Author of "Fasting"
Pastor–Free Chapel, Gainesville, GA & Free Chapel, Irvine, CA

THE FORCE OF FAVOR

In the pages of this powerful book, you will discover strategic keys to unlock incredible, God-given favor in your life. You may need favor on your job, with your spouse, with your child, in your finances or in your health. God's desire is for us to increase favor in every area of our lives.

This book will teach you the source of favor and seven ways to increase favor in your personal journey.

The Force of Favor
by Dr. Dave Martin

$14.99 224 Pages
ISBN: 978-1-60683-353-7

Other Books by
Dr. Dave Martin

**The 12 Traits
of the Greats**
$19.99 Hardback
ISBN: 978-1-60683-313-1

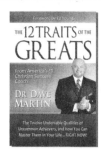

Available at bookstores nationwide and online at
www.HarrisonHouse.com or call (800) 888-4126

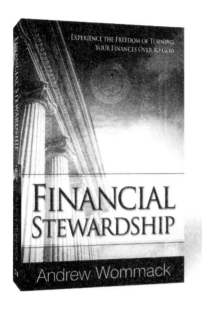

The Harrison House Vision

Proclaiming the truth and the power

Of the Gospel of Jesus Christ

With excellence;

Challenging Christians to

Live victoriously,

Grow spiritually,

Know God intimately.